Culture, Suicide, and the Human Condition

Culture, Suicide, and the Human Condition

Edited by

Marja-Liisa Honkasalo and Miira Tuominen

berghahn
NEW YORK • OXFORD
www.berghahnbooks.com

First published in 2014 by

Berghahn Books
www.berghahnbooks.com

Library of Congress Cataloging-in-Publication Data

Culture, suicide, and the human condition / edited by Marja-Liisa Honkasalo and Miira Tuominen.
pages cm
Includes bibliographical references and index.
ISBN 978-1-78238-234-8 (hardback) – ISBN 978-1-78238-235-5 (ebook)
1. Suicide–Social aspects. 2. Suicide—Philosophy. I. Honkasalo, Marja-Liisa. II. Tuominen, Miira.
HV6545.C786 2014
362.28–dc23 2013022200

British Library Cataloguing in Publication Data

A catalogue record for this book is available from the British Library

Printed on acid-free paper

ISBN: 978-1-78238-234-8 hardback
ISBN: 978-1-78238-235-5 ebook

Contents

Illustrations

FIGURES

TABLES

Acknowledgments

The core of this collection is the conviction that, despite the dominant psychiatric paradigm that takes suicides as rather straightforward symptoms of depression, the way in which the suicides themselves grasp their own action has a central role in how we should understand it. As such, the topic of the collection is not simply how to explain suicide on some level of generality. Rather, it addresses the question of how the suicides themselves and their communities *make sense* of this puzzling and shocking phenomenon. A crucial early step in the development of this collection was when Marja-Liisa Honkasalo gained access to the suicide notes in a Finnish population-based suicide prevention project. What did these people themselves write about their decision? Further, given that it is plausible to suppose that the self-understanding of suicides varies from one culture to another, it immediately became evident that in order to understand suicide more broadly, various divergent cultural contexts needed to be studied. In this respect, particularly illuminating are those cultures that have high suicide rates but are situated within a community of a low suicide rate. What is it in this particular community that triggers the frequent occurrence of suicide? What kind of cultural and social factors distinguish these communities from the wider culture? Even in those areas it is clear that not everyone commits suicide. Thus we are led to the conundrum of suicide: its statistical stability combined with individual unpredictability.

In order to understand these questions, a dedicated meeting was organized at the Helsinki Collegium for Advanced Study, where the contributing authors were able to coordinate and refine the chapters. We thank The Finnish Cultural Foundation and Academy of Finland for supporting the event economically. We would also like to extend our warm thanks to Mette Sundblad who kindly and efficiently assisted us in bringing about this event. We are most grateful to all the participants for taking part in the discussions and letting us publish their contributions in this collection as well as for their great patience in the editing process. We would also like to extend our gratitude to Professor Jouko Lönnqvist for the suicide notes of Finnish men.

The editing process would have been much slower and much less efficient were it not for our research assistants, Aino Lahdenranta and Varpu Alasuutari, who have been of invaluable assistance and performed their tasks swiftly and gracefully. We editors owe our deepest thanks to Aino and Varpu. When it comes to the contributions of the collection, special thanks to Professor Arthur Kleinman, who wrote the Afterword with awe-inspiring speed and profundity.

Finally, we would like to thank the staff of our publisher, Berghahn Books, for pleasant and efficient co-operation: Ann Przyzycki DeVita, Adam Capitanio, Elizabeth Berg, and our masterly copy editor Jaime Taber, who read the whole manuscript and suggested many helpful improvements.

Marja-Liisa Honkasalo and Miira Tuominen
Helsinki, August 2013

Introduction

Varieties of Suicide

Inquiring into the Complexity of Human Experience

Marja-Liisa Honkasalo and Miira Tuominen

In whatever direction you may turn your eyes, there lies the means to end your woes. See that precipice? Down that is the way to liberty. See you that sea, that well? There sits liberty—at the bottom. See you that tree, stunted, blighted, and barren? Yet from its branches hangs liberty. . . . Do you ask what is the highway to liberty? Any vein in your body.

—Seneca, *De Ira* 3.15,14

Instead of seeing in them [suicides] only separate occasions, unrelated and to be separately studied, the suicides committed in a given society during a given period of time are taken as a whole, it appears that this total is not simply a sum of units, a collective total but itself a new fact *sui generis* with its own unity, individuality and subsequently own nature—a nature furthermore, dominantly social.

—Durkheim, *Suicide: A Study in Sociology*

Grandpa leaves the motorbike to you. Drive carefully. Take the school seriously and be a good man.

—A suicide note by a Finnish man

But do you believe that there are lives which do not have any meaning? Like mine. This is why I have decided to end it . . . I leave a letter behind where I confirm in full power of my body and soul my last will and that you don't have anything to do with my death. Only my own feelings toward myself are important.

—A suicide note by a Finnish man

GENERAL CONSIDERATIONS

Global Statistics

The World Health Organization (WHO 2012) just reported that nearly a million people across the world commit suicide every year,[1] and approximately ten million attempt to do so. On a global scale, about 2 percent of an estimated total of 90 million deaths can be classified as intentional and self-inflicted. What is more, a slight but troubling worldwide tendency points toward an increase in the incidence of suicide. In particular, this tendency is found among women in general, in the middle-aged population, and among the elderly, meaning men and women over 75 years old. In the 15–44 age group, suicide is among the three leading causes of death (WHO 2004). In general, men commit suicide more often than women, except in rural areas in some Asian countries, where the reverse holds true. Suicide rates are high among Asian women, especially in populous countries like China and Sri Lanka.[2] In general, international suicide statistics are remarkably steady with regard to both gender and age dependency, as well as differences between urban and rural areas. In addition, there are noteworthy but little discussed statistical difference among religions. The suicide rate among the Muslim population is extremely low, whereas Lutheran populations have very high rates. The suicide rate among men is also extremely high in former Soviet countries—Lithuania had the world's highest suicide rate in 2011—which are difficult to classify according to religion (see table 0.1).

Current sociological research has shown that in Europe and North America, a low socioeconomic position is a considerable risk factor for suicide that applies to both men and women (Lorant et al. 2005).[3] The unemployed constitute a special risk group. This new research trend suggests that suicide should also be studied as a social phenomenon in the larger context of poverty and inequality. These results strengthen the Durkheimian tenet that suicide is subject to the same social forces and regularities that exist in all human action. This, in turn, indicates that suicide should not be treated as a separate category of pathological behavior but rather understood within a larger network of cultural, social, and economical factors, like any other form of human action.

Problematic Demarcation of the Phenomenon

According to the WHO, a suicide is "an act with fatal outcome, which was deliberately initiated and performed by the deceased, in the knowledge or expectation of its fatal outcome, and through which the deceased aimed at realizing changes he/she desired."[4] This definition contains several important statements. First, it determines a suicide as an act that results from a *deliberate decision* and thus presupposes an agent who knowingly and deliberately decides to carry out the fatal action that he or she knows, or at least expects, will end his or her life. Second, the definition also assumes that the agent has a very specific aim in committing suicide: the agent is held to be implementing certain changes specifically desired by him or her.

Table 0.1. Highest and Lowest Suicide Rates According to the World Health Organization

15 Highest Suicide Rates (WHO)

Men

Country (year)	*Suicides/100.000 deaths*
Lithuania (09)	61.3
Russian Federation (06)	53.9
Belarus (07)	48.7
Sri Lanka (91)	44.6
Hungary (09)	40.0
Latvia (09)	40.0
Republic of Korea (09)	39.9
Guyana (06)	39.0
Ukraine (09)	37.8
Japan (09)	36.2
Slovenia (09)	34.6
Estonia (08)	30.6
Republic of Moldova (08)	30.1
Finland (09)	29.0
Belgium (05)	28.8

Women

Country (year)	*Suicides/100.000 deaths*
Republic of Korea (09)	22.1
Sri Lanka (91)	16.8
China, selected rural areas (99)	14.8
Japan (09)	13.2
Guyana (06)	13.4
Switzerland (07)	11.4

(continued)

Table 0.1. *(continued)*

China, Hong Kong SAR (09)	10.7
Hungary (09)	10.6
Lithuania (09)	10.4
Belgium (05)	10.3
Finland (09)	10.0
Serbia (09)	10.0
Russian Federation (06)	9.5
Slovenia (09)	9.4
Kazakhstan (08)	9.4

10 Lowest Suicide Rates

Men

Country (Year)	*Suicides/100.000 deaths*
Sao Tome &Principe (87)	0.0
Egypt (09)	0.1
Jordan (08)	0.2
Syrian Arab Republic (85)	0.2
Jamaica (90)	0.3
Iran (91)	0.3
South Africa (07)	1.4
Peru (07)	1.9
Kuwait (09)	1.9

Women

Country (Year)	*Suicides/100.000 deaths*
Egypt (09)	0.0
Jordan (08)	0.0
Syrian Arab Republic (85)	0.0
Jamaica (90)	0.0
Maldives (05)	0.0
Iran (91)	0.1
South Africa (07)	0.4
Peru (07)	1.0
Kuwait (09)	1.7
Sao Tome &Principe (87)	1.8

NB. The figure is 0.0 *for both genders* in Antigua & Barbuda (95), Grenada (08), Haiti (03), Honduras (78), Saint Kitt and Nevis (95). These countries are not included in the list.

Despite the relative clarity of the definitions, it is well known that suicide is a difficult phenomenon to determine precisely—as of course most phenomena are. Inherent in it is the additional difficulty that the agents cannot be interviewed and questioned about their desires and motivations and how they themselves understand their decision and the changes they supposedly wished to implement when taking fatal action on themselves. Further, an engaging study by Susan Rose Blauner (2002), who herself survived three suicide attempts, argues that it is not really death that a suicide is after but rather—for her, as for so many other people who commit suicide—the cessation of emotional pain. She herself realized this during her first attempt, when the medicine started to take effect. She became terrified upon seeing that she was tied to a hospital bed and could not help herself (7).[5] This raises the difficult question of to what extent an act is deliberate if, while putting her decision into action, the agent realizes she was crucially mistaken about wanting to instigate the fatal outcome her action was about to lead to.

Meanwhile, well-known borderline cases of self-inflicted deaths challenge the definition of suicide.[6] One long-lasting debate concerns self-inflicted deaths of sacrifice. The early Christian martyrs were accused of being mere suicides, since with their Christian teachings they were held to have been provoking Roman officials to put them to death (church father Clemens of Alexandria, *Stromata* 4.4.17.1–3; see also chapter 3 below). Even though we need not suppose that Clemens was right, sacrifices constitute a well-known borderline case vis-à-vis definitions of suicide. Cases in which the agent sacrifices himself for the nation are well known from the war situation. Durkheim classifies sacrifice as a special altruistic type of suicide, characterized by tight integration into one's social group or nation. Sacrifices also occur in everyday situations and to benefit others by, for example, receiving money from death insurance, a common motive in the US during the Great Depression in the 1930s, when many people in financial crisis committed suicide to rescue the family's economy and honor. Suicide was subsequently excluded from coverage under most life insurance policies (for the clause, see, e.g., Schuman 1992–93). Such suicides would be included in the cases the WHO definition covers, but as self-killings, they clearly differ from suicidal deaths that do not involve the element of sacrifice. Another problematic class of cases includes self-inflicted deaths with an element of coercion. Perhaps the WHO definition, according to which the decision needs to be deliberate, can be taken to rule such cases out. However, as chapter 3 shows, cases like Socrates' death, combining coercion with free, deliberate decision, constitute demarcation problems in this respect.

In addition to definition problems, numerous types of deaths make it difficult to determine whether they were suicides or not—some traffic accidents, for example, belong to this category. And in some alcohol-related deaths, one suspects a strong suicidal element even though it is debatable whether the fatal action was deliberately chosen precisely *because* it was fatal or *despite* being fatal. In the former case, the death would be a suicide, according to the WHO definition; in the latter, perhaps not. In any event, this raises the question of how to determine which category a given case belongs in.

A final problem related to the definition of suicide is the category of "extended suicide." In such a case, in addition to killing him or herself, the agent deliberately kills several other people at the same time. Even though such deaths unquestionably involve a suicide (the death of the agent by his or her own hand), the actions also amount to several capital crimes at the same time. We are convinced that it is morally problematic to apply the notion of extended suicide to such cases: the supposition that a suicide covers the deaths of other people is simply untenable. Rather, the phenomenon should be described as murder/homicide cum suicide. It is crucial to distinguish between these deaths, since arguments about the justifiability of suicide obviously do not apply to murder and homicide. Therefore, on no account should the notion of suicide be extended to the deaths of other people.

Despite these ambiguities, the WHO definition has ethically important, far-reaching implications. As indicated, it requires that the agent is capable of making decisions for which he or she is responsible. The definition also seems to entail that the person who commits suicide is a rational agent, who evaluates certain courses of action in terms of whether they lead to the desired outcome.

Our Approach: Suicide as Human Action

In this anthology, we shall discuss suicide as a form of human action. We argue that it should not be isolated as a separate realm of pathological behavior. Rather than offering culturally or socially deterministic explanations or reductive explanations in terms of neurobiochemistry or psychopathology, we treat suicide as a form of action deeply related to various cultural ways of conceiving the world and the human position in it. Our goal is by no means to deny the existence of social, cultural, or psychopathological risk factors; rather, we point to the explanatory gap between such factors and the individual occurrence of suicide. Belonging to a certain risk group, suffering from a particular mental ailment, or living within a certain culture does not exhaustively determine whether or not an individual commits suicide. The factors only produce the result of suicide when combined with the individual's deliberate decision, as is the case with any other form of human action on the individual level. It escapes exhaustive explanation.

The main argument arising from the vast array of literature in the humanities and social sciences (Minois 1999) and the contributions to this volume is that suicide is and has been a profound human phenomenon throughout significant periods of human history. As such, it touches upon such fundamental issues as the human self; one's conception of the world; life and death; relation to others; morality, and the good life; sacrifice and responsibility; and disease, to name but a few. More specifically, how should we understand the agent of suicide? Is there a way of combining the viewpoints of various research traditions? Some studies see the suicide as a sufferer of a mental illness such as depression, or a victim of political propaganda, rather than a reflective person who is responsible for his or her own actions and perhaps has profound reasons for making such a decision. Which ways of defining loyalty tie the element of sacrifice to accounts of suicide? How does it affect our analysis, if we suppose that the person who commits suicide sacrifices him- or herself for society, or for the honor of his or her community? Moreover, if we consider suicide a violent act, is the suicide a victim or a perpetrator of violence, a sacrificer or the sacrificial victim? Does the suicide perform an act of violence toward him- or herself, his or her family or relatives, God or the gods, or perhaps society?

From the theoretical viewpoint, suicide raises questions about the interrelation between cultural and social structures and the individual's sphere of action. To what extent do cultural factors determine the decisions of an individual? From a methodological point of view, studying suicide uncovers crucial suppositions and practices within cultures, be it one's own or another. Scrutinizing the history of one's own culture also sheds light on aspects that may at first glance seem self-evident or unquestionable. Synchronic and diachronic research on suicide raises crucial questions about liberty, moral agency, violence responsibility, and sacrifice, and brings to light fundamental ideas concerning how the individual is related to other people within a community or society. As for violence, we shall consider it both a structural phenomenon and one pertaining to interpersonal relations. At the same time, we shall question any clear line of demarcation between these two domains—that is, we do not take for granted a sharp distinction between the public and private domains.

In addition to considering suicide as a social fact and a cultural phenomenon in this anthology, we claim that a cluster of other thematic elements are necessary for understanding suicide: (1) moral decisions; (2) moral and political judgments; (3) moral emotions such as shame, guilt, or pain; and

(4) mental disturbances seen from the viewpoint of the agent's thoughts, not simply as physiological or chemical processes. Our point is not simply that this cluster of analytical tools selects from a wider spectrum of suicides a certain subtype, one in which the person is a moral agent. Rather, our claim is that the phenomenon cannot be fully understood without taking into account the agent's perspective in its cultural and social context. By approaching suicide as part of a larger network of human and cultural practices, we gain a richer, more profound understanding of the meaning and grounds for the chosen course of action than we acquire by simply considering it a form of psychopathology. Therefore our approach highlights the elements of freedom and fragility, moral emotions and narrative necessity, and contingency and unexpectedness in the various cultural contexts discussed in the collection. In sum, the concepts and analytical tools needed to account for human practices more generally are necessary for understanding suicide as well.

EXPLAINING SUICIDE: EXISTING RESEARCH

Disciplinary Approaches, Research Perspectives

Current research approaches the problem of suicide from three main viewpoints. The foremost perspective discusses suicide as a *medical and psychiatric problem*. In the current protocols of the WHO, suicide is delineated as both a psychiatric and a major public health problem. Consequently, the current trend in the field of suicide research is to attempt to define suicide in psychiatric terms. Improving diagnostics of depression in Western countries have furthered the attempt to establish a link between depression and suicide, or even to suggest that they belong to the same category of psychiatric phenomena and hence can be addressed as such in suicide prevention programs, the former being a risk factor of the latter. This has caused a tremendous increase in the prescription and use of anti-depressive medication. Its use has been most pronounced in Western countries and, it has often been claimed, explains national decreases in suicide mortality. However, the causal relationship is controversial: in Finland, for example, although the decrease in suicide has been most marked among men, it is women who are the main users of anti-depressive psychopharmaceuticals (Klaukka et al. 2005).[7]

Second, sociological research since Durkheim points to the importance of macro-social forces, identifying suicide as a *social phenomenon*. This line of research is prominent in contemporary cross-cultural studies that have discovered "suicide belts" such as the Finno-Baltic area, Northern Russia, and China. Moreover, the impacts of war, revolution, and political change are conspicuously present in suicide statistics (Wasserman and Värnik 1998; Värnik et al. 2005). Currently, as indicated above, sociological research on social inequity suggests that suicide mortality depends on socioeconomic factors such as education level and social class.

Thirdly, the distribution of suicides is often strikingly uneven across local settings, which would seem to indicate that local social and cultural dynamics are crucial in the incidence of suicide (see chapters 1 and 2 below; Desjarlais et al. 1995). Anthropological studies show that suicide can hardly be understood without grasping the local dynamics and local meanings assigned to the act. From this perspective, suicide is a *human act embedded in a cultural context.* The persistence of regional and gender trends and the changing patterns in relation to larger societal changes further stress the significance of cultural and societal factors.

These three disciplinary domains mainly explain suicide from two perspectives: external and internal. From the external perspective, suicide is a result of social structural forces: destruction, dissolution, or disruption of social structures and/or social bonds. Durkheim's explanation of suicide is based on a tension between the social forces he calls regulation and integration. Meanwhile, a representative of the internal approach, the psychoanalytical perspective–introduced by Durkheim's contemporary Freud and focused on the suicide him- or herself–has been dominant. Instead of following the Durkheimian research trend, we shall employ the agent's internal perspective in a cultural context. In the following, we shall briefly consider earlier research traditions and the problems related to the explanation of suicide.

Suicide as a Product of Social Forces and Culture

Researchers in the social sciences have applied two main, diverging approaches to suicide. In the Durkheimian heritage just discussed, they consider suicide as a social fact dependent on social forces, notably the degrees of imbalance between social integration and moral regulation. Thus, suicide as a phenomenon is not explainable without reference to social forces and social structure, whereas the agent's internal perspective is not yet present in the analysis. Change and persistence in macro-level social dynamics are connected with suicide mortality. This tradition has current applications within some epidemiological suicide studies. As mentioned, studies on social inequality and health differentials point to consistent correlations between socioeconomic position and mortality. Economic, educational, and employment status have all been shown to be strongly associated with suicide mortality.

The anthropological ways of explaining suicide depart from this model in that they start with the acting person in his or her culture and highlight the social relationships through which people create meaning in their own lives. Baechler (1999) summarizes some crucial features in his definition of suicide as a plural, as *suicides*. According to him, suicide denotes all behavior that seeks and finds a solution to an existential problem by making an attempt on the life of the subject. In the struggle of life, people use social strategies that are embedded in cultural contexts but also have individual underpinnings. Suicides are thus coeval with the human condition. Anthropologists, whose studies attempt to disclose people's own understanding of what lies behind the attempts to take their own lives, offer explanations differing from those of sociologists, which combine the agent's perspective with external approaches. The anthropological approach also concerns multiple cultural interactions within one and the same ethnographic study and thus presents a methodological opposite to large-scale inquiry about social forces.

Early cross-cultural studies in anthropology attempted to explain suicide on the basis of cultural features, such as the depressiveness or aggressiveness of a culture or an ethnic personality pattern (Devereux 1961). On the other hand, anthropologists have also emphasized cultural emotions such as shame, anger, or loyalty as explanatory factors (Firth 1961). Some studies point to life crises, ambiguity in social roles, or institutional exclusion or abandonment. Culture-bound dynamics may explain why certain crises may have caused specific actors to become suicide casualties. Learning and imitation account for the stability of suicide over a period of time.[8] Recent cross-cultural studies carried out in countries with high incidences of suicide have emphasized that structural violence and social relationships embedded in violent contexts are a key factor in suicidal acts (Staples and Widger 2012; Kral 2012).

Suicide as Resulting from Intra-Psychic Forces

Psychiatric explanations of suicide have been influential for over a hundred years and currently constitute the prevailing scholarly approach to suicide. Although not all psychiatric theories and therapies are explicitly Freudian, psychiatric theories have their roots in Freud and psychoanalysis. The preventive and therapeutic approaches to suicide in Western world (especially Europe, North America, and Australia) are all, more or less, based on psychiatric theories. From the point of view of research on culture and philosophy, psychoanalysis has exercised a powerful capacity to turn social, moral, and cultural problematics into the dynamics of one's inner life and, equally importantly, to pathologize suicide. Ever since the early theories of psychoanalysis, notably those on the destructiveness of the ego and aggression directed toward oneself, psychoanalysis and psychoanalytically based theories have grounded explanations based on internal factors.

Freud (1917) writes in "Mourning and Melancholy":

> If one listens patiently to the melancholic's many and various self-accusations, one cannot in the end avoid the impression that often the most violent of them are hardly at all applicable to the patient himself but that with significant modifications they do fit someone else, someone whom the patient loves or has loved or should love. Every time one examines this fact this conjecture is confirmed.
>
> . . .
>
> So we find the key to the clinical picture: we perceive that the self-reproaches are reproaches against a loved object which have been shifted away from it on to the patient's own ego.

According to Freud, violence in the context of suicide is a personality trait—as opposed to being social or cultural—one's aggression turned inwards upon oneself. This means that instead of formulating the phenomenon in terms of structural violence, the discussion uses the notion of aggression as a personal characteristic. In *Mourning and Melancholy*, Freud stated that aggressive and murderous wishes toward others, especially the primary object, are redirected back to oneself. According to this idea, one can kill oneself only upon having wanted to kill another person. Hence the model is not genuinely intersubjective, because aggression represents the ego's original reaction to objects of the external world that are understood as the subject's representations (Freud 1917: 252). Freud also emphasizes the paradox of suicide—the ambiguity of love and hate. While connecting suicide to melancholy, he explains suicide by pointing to the narcissist identification with the lost, ambivalently loved and hated object, which overwhelms the melancholic or suicidal person (Freud 1915). The Freudian approach to understanding suicide includes the concepts of aggressive drive, internalization of aggression, detachment of oneself, and a behavior called acting out. The latter symbolizes a childhood trauma, which the person tries to relieve by reenacting the trauma in the present life situation. Thus suicide is also linked to the original trauma. Freud developed his concept of aggressiveness later in "Beyond the Pleasure Principle" (1920), where he actually presented the notion of a separate aggressive drive that he linked to death and destructive instincts.

Freud's idea has become the canon of the psychoanalytic understanding of suicide. In this framework, suicide is conceived as a result of profoundly intrapsychic forces and processes in all their ambivalence.[9] Menninger (1937) later developed the idea of ambiguity in three intrapsychic dimensions: the wish to kill, which entails aggressiveness of the ego and hatred; the wish to be killed, which is the masochistic component of the dynamics; and the wish to die (Freud 1920). From another psychodynamic viewpoint, Fenichel (1990: 294) has emphasized the role of an overtly harsh superego. Suicide, in his view, is about the wish to kill the other (mainly the objects of childhood love represented in the superego). In this way, "at the root of suicide you find the re-emergence of . . . the original annihilation of the deserted hungry baby" (Fenichel 1990: 400).

In later theories, relationality and relationships with others (still mainly in the heterosexual family setting) began to play a prominent role. Notably, object-relation theories (Klein 1957) and theories of narcissism developed an analysis centered on destructiveness and aggression in relation to the other, mainly the Freudian primary object. Thoughts of identification with the destructive relation or object are central, and according to these theories, the only way to destroy the ambiguously loved/hated object is to destroy oneself. In later developments, the role of the family and the social interaction within it and with important people in one's environment become significant in the explanations. Psychoanalytically based theories do not see the subject or the ego as profoundly embedded in society or culture but focus instead on the inner dynamics of the subject. They analyze suicide similarly. One should not underestimate the role of psychodynamic thinking in the "psychopolitics"[10] that backgrounds a vast array of Western subjectivity theories and also reaches into various other social domains, notably health and social politics and policy.

It is important to note that psychoanalysis and many psychiatric therapeutic approaches to the human subject and suicide focus on the inner life and/or the mind of the subject by considering that subject's thoughts, representations, traumas, and emotions. This means that such approaches are internal, in the sense that they concentrate on the contents of the mind of the person. By contrast, several current suicide prevention programs (e.g., in Finland; see Sosiaali- ja terveyshallitus 1992 and WHO 2012) base their major prevention practice on serotonin-antagonist and reuptake inhibitor medication, thereby reducing the inner life of the subject to brain chemistry. Such approaches to suicide resemble the psychoanalytical theories in the sense that they focus on the subject without considering him or her in the wider network of society and culture. However, they differ drastically from therapies focused on the contents of the subject's thoughts and emotions. Our approach, in contrast, underlines the vital importance of regarding the subject as a moral agent who is profoundly embedded in culture and society.

Suicide as an Inherited Behavior Disposition

Several studies on possible contributors to the complexity of suicidal behavior have investigated genetic factors or other hereditary bases of suicide. It has long been known that suicidal behavior runs in families, probably as a factor independent from major depression (Dwivedi 2012). However, because it is difficult to distinguish empirically between the social and genetic factors behind different behavioral patterns, most research concerns gene-environment interaction. Earlier, endogamous populations, such as Navajos or other groups living in border zones without major social exchange with other groups, were the focus of special interest.[11] Such studies have aimed mainly at searching for a general genetic background of "suicidal behavior." This type of behavior is explained either in terms of specific ways of acting or with reference to personality traits, such as aggressiveness or impulse-aggressive personality. The behavioral types or personality traits are determined by questionnaire or psychiatric clinical studies. The latter approach is dominant particularly in forensic psychiatry. The current research interest focuses on neuropsychobiological factors that may explain suicidal personality or aggressiveness, especially how the serotonergic pathway is related to the serotonergic system (Bondy and Buttler 2006). Although genetic factors account for some part of the variance in suicidal thoughts and behavior, specific genes that contribute to vulnerability to suicidal behavior remain unknown, despite numerous candidate genes association studies, especially relating to the serotogenic system (Zalsman et al. 2002).

Some evidence for a genetic explanation of suicide has been found in a Finnish study on violence and violent behavior more generally. Researchers pinpointed a genetic variant of a brain receptor molecule that may contribute to violently impulsive behavior when people who carry it are under the influence of alcohol. Some other studies point to hereditary factors in alcohol abuse and dependency and link these factors to findings of problems in the serotonin system. Other genetic studies point to alterations in brain chemistry, notably serotonin, and still others to genetically defined predisposition to suicidal behavior.

Violence as a Structural Phenomenon

Violence toward oneself is, and in Western history has been, at the very core of the definition of suicide. In the WHO definition of violence ("Definition and Typology of Violence" 2012), and consequently in official documents of member countries as well as in the international classification of causes of death,[12] suicidal behavior is defined as violent and suicide as a violent cause of death. WHO documents define violence broadly as "the intentional use of physical force or power, threatened or actual, against oneself, another person, or against a group or community, that either results in or has a high likelihood of resulting in injury, death, psychological harm, maldevelopment, or deprivation." The WHO also presents a typology of violence that has been applied in national policy as a useful way to understand the contexts in which violence occurs and the interrelations between types of violence. It distinguishes subtypes of self-directed, interpersonal, and collective violence, within which suicide and suicidal behavior are classified as self-directed violence.

Historically, the notion of suicide has a conceptual connection to homicide. The two words are constructed on the same root, "cide", from the Latin *occidere*, which means to kill. Classical Latin, however, does not form compounds with pronouns (in this case *suus*), and the term *suicidium*, of much later origin, dates from the seventeenth century. In English, the word's first reported occurrence is from 1643 (Sir Thomas Browne's *Religio Medici*), and *The Oxford English Dictionary* first mentioned it in 1651 (see Griffin 1986: 68). Because of the postclassical connection to homicide, suicide as a "deviant behavior" has been a topic of criminological research (Messner and Rosenfeld 1999).

In criminology, the relation between poverty and crime is a classical question. The connection has been strong throughout the history of criminology, especially with regards to homicide, although according to some recent research this is also true of suicide (see, e.g., Kivivuori and Lehti 2006, Savolainen et al. 2008). Durkheim pointed to this relationship more than a hundred years ago, and despite modernization the correlation is still observable, though more controversially, in several countries. Low levels of income and education, often connected with heavy use of alcohol[13] or drugs, are among the strongest predictors of homicide and victimization (Messner and Rosenfeld 1999)—and also of suicide (Mäki 2010). In this analysis, violence is specific to certain subcultures (see, e.g., Wolfgang and Ferracuti 1967) as a way of acting and gaining vehicles for social power. But even though the probability of crime, violence, and suicide is statistically higher among certain cultural groups, belonging to such a subculture does not irrevocably determine that an individual in these circumstances will become the victim or perpetrator of violence or commit suicide.

Beyond the general level of definitions and statistics, suicide is related to violence in more intricate ways. Suicide is classified as a violent cause of death, but one can ask whether all suicides are violent in a deeper sense of the term. For example, dying by shooting oneself in a rage seems to differ from fatally overdosing on medicine after careful deliberation. One striking application—and, we claim, a misapplication—of the notion of suicide in a context of violence is "murder-suicide" or "extended suicide," which has recently challenged the study of social violence more generally. In these cases, suicide is part of a hybrid complex of violent phenomena. We have argued above that using the notion of suicide to cover the whole complex of violence in such cases is untenable: violent acts toward other people should be understood in their own right, and a suicide occurring after them as a case of its own (Nikunen 2011; Rajan 2011).[14] In these hybrids, suicide is embedded in acts of violence conceived and expressed in moral terms, often toward the agent's family members or relatives, such as in honor killings. They tend to involve an intricate web of motives and actions, as is the case in school shootings and domestic violence. Such cases therefore should be discussed from the viewpoint of violence, rather than being automatically lumped together with other suicides.

The bulk of cross-cultural anthropological research analyzing suicide does not find social violence to be a core factor. However, recent studies on contemporary complex societies show that in several cases, the larger context of social and political violence merits inclusion in explanations and conceptualizations of suicide.[15] This viewpoint is vital for understanding hybrid cases such as suicide bombers, "extended suicides" in the context of domestic violence, and cases such as school shootings. It is also a key factor in analysis of suicide in cultures with a long history of social and political violence, the Near East being one example. How is violence acted and reenacted among individuals living in a context of high incidence of violence? The relevant connections between these domains have not been sufficiently studied, which complicates the understanding of the phenomenon.

A Cultural Skein of Narratives

What role do cultural factors play in the explanation of suicide? Are there suicidal cultures that cause some of their members to commit suicide?[16] If so, can we predict who the victims will be?[17] If culture has such a powerful role in human action, how does it communicate its effect at an individual level?

Several contributions in this collection examine the cultural ways in which suicides are presented in local suicide stories that refer to problems the deceased experienced while alive. These stories are partly a way for community members to make sense of the shocking fact that someone has taken his or her life. Further, as becomes clear particularly in chapter 2, the narratives also contain an element of liberating the community from the responsibility of having left the future suicide to a very uneasy, suppressed social or economic position with little power to determine his or her own affairs. Thus these stories do not necessarily reflect the reasons that in fact led the people to their ultimate decisions. In any case, these stories seem to take on a life of their own, offering categories by which acts of suicide can easily be classified and explained. As the Vaqueiros (cattle-raising mountain people of Western Asturias in Northern Spain) discussed below in chapter 2 might say: the person had lost the grace of life (a process or state they call *aburrimiento*) and already begun the process of dying. In another example, in a rural area in Northern Finland where the suicide rate is very high among young men especially, a police officer referred to them hanging themselves in a barn in spring as "a local custom."

Such narratives of course are, in a sense, post hoc explanations—attempts to make sense of something troubling and even shocking.[18] However, suicide prevention programs have also taken note that the way suicides are publicly presented affects the incidence of suicide. These programs specifically recommend avoiding stories that portray suicide as a solution to common problems, such as bullying at school, as news presentations with this kind of a narrative have been observed to correlate with an increase in the suicide rate in the community (see, e.g., Sosiaali- ja terveyshallitus 1992). From this point of view, the cultural narratives that aim to make sense of suicide in the community seem clustered in complex networks or skeins of stories in which some member of the community has, in a way, "solved" his or her personal problems by committing suicide. As such, the stories can, as chapter 1 shows, acquire a tragic necessity of their own and can also provide a blueprint or model of action for people encountering similar problems.

Even though the complexes of suicidal narratives appear to become self-fulfilling prophecies in some cases—writing themselves, as it were, into reality—attention devoted to these cultural mechanisms should not be taken as a claim to an exhaustive explanation of suicide. The suicidal blueprints for action clearly appeal only to some people, and they certainly do not cause suicides in a deterministic manner. By contrast, the narratives live on in the ways people make sense of their own actions and the actions of others, and in such a complex it is never obvious why some individuals are drawn to one narrative rather than another. However, as Susan Blauner's (2002) book shows, narratives also have counterforce and can, at least in individual cases, function as instruments of suicide prevention. Blauner's book–one person's suicide prevention program–contains specific instructions on how to avoid acting on suicidal thoughts and how to alleviate the emotional pain that adds force to the impulse to attempt suicide. She emphasizes that it is vital to avoid constructing romanticized scenarios and stories about the effect the suicide is supposed to have on others. Therefore, her contribution itself produces a narrative and also offers tools to disarm narratives that present suicide as a solution to emotional pain.

Combined with our approach to suicide as a decision, the emphasis on cultural narratives suggests a view that enables both improvements on a societal scale and benefits at the individual level as the agent becomes a source of narratives that counter the cultural pattern of suicide. In this way, we underline not only human fragility but also the human capacity for empowerment.

Enigmatic Suicide

Despite several controversies and methodologically varying backgrounds, researchers within the field agree that suicide's combination of statistical stability and individual unpredictability presents something of a mystery. As mentioned, identifiable social and structural risk factors have a statistical predictive force, but they do not apply to the individual. The same holds for mental disturbances: some make the person more likely to commit suicide, but no psychic disturbance alone determines the individual's decision. However, such an explanatory gap is not exclusive to suicide: crime and violence, for example, are statistically regular but similarly individually unpredictable, and indeed, a similar explanatory gap applies to human action generally.

In sum, none of the theories offered so far can fully explain why certain individuals commit suicide and others do not, except by way of the platitude that those who do seem to have decided to do so. Ideological, cultural, and social superstructures as well as biological regularities and psychological or social risk factors offer only a partial explanation. It is always the actual (moral) judgment of an individual, not a set of abstract values or external factors, that makes a person do what he or she does. To understand suicide, we need to do the impossible to the extent that it is possible: to listen to what the suicides themselves have to say about how they understand the conditions of a good life and their own role in maintaining it. In addition, we need to recognize the person's evaluations and conclusions concerning the conditions and limits of moral agency (Kleinman 2007). This is the main ethical point of this anthology.

THE CONTENT OF THE BOOK

Until recently, the field of suicide research was divided into relatively separate lines of inquiry. This collection counters this tendency by bringing together approaches from previously separate areas of suicide studies. In doing so, it becomes part of a new international movement toward a more comprehensive understanding of suicide. The collection is unique in combining contemporary discussion in several disciplines with historical and philosophical approaches to suicide. The thematic current of moral perspective runs through the anthology. Moral agency, judgment, and emotions form a triad that systematizes and unifies the varying approaches, theoretical frameworks, and disciplines as well as methodologies applied by the volume's contributors.

Therefore a seemingly narrow problem, suicide, leads to the greatest, most difficult questions pertaining to human agency: determinism and the question of freedom. Of course these massive questions cannot be tackled within the confines of this anthology. What is important for our present concerns is that despite long-lasting debates about free will, philosophers agree virtually unanimously that moral agency requires responsibility—and responsibility, in its turn, requires at least a minimal sense of freedom of decision. In brief, this collection highlights the point that suicide is largely a moral question that needs to be considered in the context of people's deliberations over decisions they make within a domain of contingent schemes, conceptions, and practices inherent to the larger fabric that constitutes the human condition.

SUICIDE: CROSS-CULTURAL PERSPECTIVES

In chapter 1, Charles Macdonald and Jean Naudin discuss the possibilities that phenomenological psychology offers the understanding of suicide. Macdonald's anthropological contribution is based on his long-term ethnographic work on the Palawi Islands in the Southern Pacific in a peaceful society with an extremely high rate of suicide amidst a population with a very low suicide rate. The authors present an idea of a "narrative analysis" or "co-entanglement of histories" stemming from the work of phenomenological psychology, which enables them to extend their scrutiny from individual pathology to a wider field of collective behavior. This leads to understanding culture through the dynamics of entangled narratives by which subjects project themselves in the world and thus define their own identities. It points to the relational nature and interdependence of individual cases, and stresses the link between the cases in the history of the community. In the sense that a particular culture forms a skein of (hi)stories–the history of all individual histories, in an ongoing and plural narrative experience–suicide becomes part of the culture of the group.

Another community with a high suicide rate amidst a populace with a much lower one is the Vaquieros population considered by María Cátedra in chapter 2. Her basic argument is that it is time for the field of suicide research to start asking different questions. Starting from meaning-centered anthropology, she maintains that it is crucial to examine cultural assumptions concerning suicide and their impact on individuals and groups in the context of life and death. The proposed method, ethnography, is highly local, with a strong focus on context. Suicide, like everything else that is complexly human, takes place in a powerful social and cultural context that includes comprehensive conceptions of the world and the otherworld. Among the Vaqueiros, Cátedra claims, suicide is the most cultural way of dying: they see the passage to the otherworld as already taking place in this life–sometimes early in life, blurring the borderline between life and death and making the transition from one to the other a long itinerary. Since suicide has different meanings for different cultures, it is erroneous to assume that "a suicide is a suicide" when making cross-cultural comparisons. Meaning cannot be separated from the context of human life and death, and moral attitudes are often relevant to the epidemiology of suicide and might differentiate and imply diverse motivations for suicide. Since meaning precedes action, individuals who commit suicide do so with reference to cultural-normative specific values and attitudes. To understand suicide, we need to know what it means for the person and for the culture.

ANCIENT AND MEDIEVAL APPROACHES

Socrates' death, an archetypal example of a philosophical way to die in Western culture, raises the question of suicide. One reason for this is its description in the dialogue *Phaedo*, in which Plato also, albeit very briefly, lets the discussants consider the justifiability of taking one's own life. As Miira Tuominen argues in chapter 3, another, even more important reason to point to this example is the need to ask whether Socrates took his own life. He clearly and firmly decided to die, and he is presented as making the decision freely and solely on the basis of what he considered good. However, in a sense he acted under coercion because he had already been sentenced to death. Lack of coercion can be taken as a reasonable requirement in defining an act as suicide. Tuominen argues that these elements constitute an impasse in Plato's discussion of the demarcation problem of whether Socrates took his own life or not. In addition, Tuominen argues that the discussion of the justifiability of taking one's own life ends inconclusively. In fact, the factor in the dialogue that ends the discussion is not the resolution of a contradiction or tension between the claims discussed in the context; rather, the argument ends when Socrates finally lets Crito convey the guard's message that Socrates should avoid heating himself up, lest the effect of the hemlock be diminished. Socrates does not obey but continues the discussion, leaving aside the question of taking one's own life to argue that philosophers need not fear death but rather should welcome it with a hopeful spirit.

Chapter 4, by Malin Grahn, concentrates on self-killing in Stoicism as well as in ancient tragedy. Grahn argues that despite their fame as a school with a positive attitude toward suicide, the Stoics should be discussed in the framework of their philosophy of the good life. The Stoics argued that the most important thing is to live well, an aim relevant to considerations of self-killing. If the possibilities of a good life have been destroyed–which, for the Stoics, is not a question of external circumstance–then self-killing is a legitimate way to liberate oneself. However, this should not be taken to suggest they generally tended to favor suicide. The dictum that one is always free to release oneself should be interpreted as underlining the role of the human agent's decision and activity, not as an exhortation to suicide. Discussing suicide in tragedy in the second section of her essay, Grahn points out that within the tragic context, suicide is predominantly a female phenomenon–and one that usually involves a strong sexual motive. This suggests that the ancient philosophical conception of suicide was sharply divided with respect to gender. However, Grahn concludes, the Stoics too extended their therapeutic arguments to tragic women such as Phaedra and Medea, so these women should also be understood as moral agents capable of moral deliberation, particularly about whether the decision to take their lives is a rational one.

In chapter 5, "Moral Philosophical Arguments against Suicide in the Middle Ages," Virpi Mäkinen switches the focus to the dawn of a controversy in another historical era. In the early Middle Ages (from the sixth century onwards), suicide became both a mortal sin and a secular crime. Those who committed suicide while accused of a crime were denied a Christian burial, a requirement for going to Heaven. In the next century, even attempted suicide became an ecclesiastical crime punishable by excommunication. The fifth commandment was the most important single textual basis of suicide commentaries, and the Augustinian "thou shalt not kill" school of anti-suicide doctrine was common among the Scholastics. Suicide was generally understood as homicide and a sin against oneself and the community; it was contrary to justice and charity, as well as to God, the creator of the human being. The discussion concludes by distinguishing between two alternative conceptions of suicide: as an act by the human agent or as a passive yielding to internal and external, uncontrolled forces.

MORALITY, POLITICS, AND VIOLENCE: SUICIDE IN CONTEMPORARY SOCIETIES

In chapter 6, Susanne Dahlgren takes up the issue of female–and social structural–violence in her essay "'She Kissed Death with a Smile': The Politics and Moralities of the Female Suicide Bomber," which focuses on Palestinian suicide bombers. She argues against presenting the female suicide bombers as merely depressed individuals or victims of propaganda, maintaining that instead their acts should be considered within the framework of political violence. The women have chosen the action with specific political purposes, motives that are often ignored in the Western media presentations of these bombers. The essay discusses the controversies women create by engaging in violence and making suicides public. Its main conclusion is that a crucial ambiguity remains: on the one hand, the suicide bombings can be classified as altruistic suicides of martyrdom; on the other, they are violent acts and crimes in a public space, and as such warrant discussion in the context of violence in the public, political domain.

Chapter 7, Marja-Liisa Honkasalo's essay "When We Stop Living, We Also Stop Dying," focuses on suicide in a notably violent country, Finland, where rates of male homicide and suicide alike have been among the highest in Europe. Focusing on letters written by men who have committed suicide, Honkasalo studies the problem of moral agency, first as delineated by macro-level determinants, and subsequently as a gendered act embedded in the subtle contexts of everyday life. In contrast to contemporary psychiatric suicide research, which categorizes suicide as a type of pathology–or as a more or less mentally disturbed act–the main focus of the essay is on the social actor as he describes himself in his suicide note. Hence the person who commits suicide is a moral agent who reflects upon and evaluates his life and death, seeing suicide as a solution to the shameful failures of life. The essay studies agency from the viewpoint of moral emotions, notably shame, an intense presence in the letters that figures as a core element in a complex of cultural narratives concerning the agent's duty to survive and cope alone in society.

The anthology concludes with an epilogue by Harvard University's Professor Arthur Kleinman.

NOTES

1. See also the report from 2005 in which the WHO estimates that by 2020, about 1.5 million people will commit suicide yearly.
2. On the high incidence of women's suicide in rural China, see notably Wu Fei 2010; Wasserman and Wasserman 2009, esp. part 1, "Suicide in a Religious and Cross-Cultural Perspective," pp. 3–80.
3. On social inequalities and suicide in Finland, see Netta Mäki 2010, whose Ph.D. dissertation clearly shows the relationship between socioeconomic position and suicide. On the positive correlation between unemployment and suicide in the United States, see Kposowa 2001. Her other works also show a positive correlation between low professional status and suicide; see Kposowa 1999.
4. According to the definition of American Psychiatric Association (2003: 4) "Suicide: self-inflicted death with evidence (either implicit or explicit) that the person intended to die."
5. For near-death experiences, see also, e.g., Tem Horwitz 1998.
6. For a recent review on the philosophical literature on suicide, see, e.g., Cholbi 2009.
7. For a comparative study, see Kivimäki et al. 2007.
8. About these themes, see esp. chapter 1 below and Macdonald 2007.
9. On ambivalence, see notably Shneidman 1976, Shneidman 1996. According to him, ambivalence is present in the mind of a suicidal person with even the strongest death wish. This is, of course, an important point for preventive work and suicide therapy.
10. About psychoculture, see notably Lasch 1979; Sedgwick 1982; Marsh 2010.
11. For a review of genetics of suicide, see Voracek and Loibl 2007. In Finland, an international research team and the NIAAA (National Institute of Alcohol Abuse and Alcoholism), led by Professor Daniel Goldman, Finnish partners from the Finnish Twin Registry, and Finnish forensic psychiatrists, have detected a genetic variant of a brain receptor molecule that may contribute to violently impulsive behavior when people who carry it are under the influence of alcohol. However, they conclude, the genetic variant cannot explain a large fraction of the overall variance of aggressive behavior. See Bevilagcua et al. 2010.
12. ICD = International Classification of Disease. http://apps.who.int/classifications/icd10/browse/2010/en

13. Especially in Finland, more than, e.g., in the other Nordic countries, alcohol use is connected with homicide and suicide; see Lehti and Kivivuori 2005.
14. A controversial example is suicide bombing, which in the Muslim context is regarded as *jihad*—an act of martyrdom—and not suicide, *intihar.* See Dabbagh 2005 and 2012.
15. The phenomenon of suicide bombing has challenged psychiatric conceptualizations of suicide. In their article "A Deadly Contagion," the psychologists Marsden and Attia (2005: 153) emphasize that "suicide bombers cannot be categorized as mentally ill. Suicide bombing is merely a coordinated community response that fits a context of violence, aggression and revenge." Recent discussions on suicide bombing highlight social structural problems and violence, e.g., Singh 2011, Rajan 2011.
16. Japan, for example, has a reputation of being a culture of suicide. The cultural history of suicide in Japan has been discussed, e.g., in Pinguet 1984. It can be argued, to the contrary, that the Japanese seppuku and hara-kiri are forms of collective death sentences rather than suicides.
17. Since Durkheim, these questions have been widely discussed in suicide research for more than a century, e.g., Shneidman and Farberow 1957; Shneidman 1976; Douglas 1973. For comprehensive overviews, see, e.g., Lester 2005; Maris et al. 2001; Wasserman and Wasserman 2009.
18. Especially puzzling and shocking are the suicides committed by concentration camp survivors. Shock upon reading about such cases was an important motivation for Lisa Lieberman's (2003) study of the Western cultural history of suicide.

REFERENCES

American Psychiatric Association. 2003. "Practice Guidelines for the Assessment and Treatment of Patients with Suicidal Behaviors." *American Journal of Psychiatry* 160 (suppl.): 1–60.

Baechler, Jean. 1999. *Suicides.* Oxford: Basic Blackwell.

Bevilagcua, Laura, Stephanie Doly, and Jaakko Kaprio et al. 2010. "The Population-Specific HTR2B Stop Codon Predisposes to Severe Impulsivity." *Nature* 468 (7327): 1061–1066.

Blauner, Susan Rose. 2002. *How I Stayed Alive When My Brain Was Trying to Kill Me: One Person's Guide to Suicide Prevention.* New York: HarperCollins.

Bondy, B., and A. Buttler. 2006. "Genetics of Suicide." *Molecular Psychiatry* 11: 336–351.

Cholbi, Michael. 2009. "Suicide." *The Stanford Encyclopedia of Philosophy* (Fall 2009), ed. Edward N. Zalta. http://plato.stanford.edu/archives/fall2009/entries/suicide/.

Clemens of Alexandria. 1960. *Stromata: Clemens Alexandrinus*, vol. 2. Ed. O. Stählin, L. Früchtel, and U. Treu. Berlin: Akademie-Verlag.

Dabbagh, Nadia. 2005. *Suicide in Palestine: Narratives of Despair.* Northampton, England: Olive Branch Press.

——. 2012. "Behind the Statistics: The Ethnography of Suicide in Palestine." *Culture, Medicine and Psychiatry* 36 (1): 286–305.

"Definition and Typology of Violence." 2012. *Violence Prevention Alliance.* http://www.who.int/violenceprevention/approach/definition/en/index.html.

Desjarlais, Robert, Leon Eisenberg, Byron Good, and Arthur Kleinman. 1995. "World Mental Health: Problems and Priorities in Low-Income Countries." *Culture, Medicine and Psychiatry* 36 (2): 68–86.

Devereux, Gilles. 1961. *Mohave Ethnopsychiatry and Suicide: The Psychiatric Knowledge and the Psychic Disturbances of an Indian Tribe.* Washington, DC: Smithsonian Institute Press.

Douglas, Jack. 1973 [1967]. *The Social Meanings of Suicide.* Princeton: Princeton University Press.

Dwivedi, Y., ed. 2012. *The Neurobiological Basis of Suicide.* Boca Raton, FL: CRC Press.

Fei, Wu. 2010. *Suicide and Justice: A Chinese Perspective.* London and New York: Routledge.

Fenichel, Otto. 1990. *The Psychoanalytic Theory of Neurosis.* London: Routledge.

Firth, Raymond. 1961. *We, The Tikopia: Suicide and Risk-Taking in Tikopia Society.* London: George Allen & Unwin.

Freud, Sigmund. 1915. "Instincts and their Vicissitudes." In *The Standard Edition of the Complete Psychological Works of Sigmund Freud*, vol. 14, ed. and trans. J. Strachey. London: Hogarth Press, pp. 125–245.

——. 1917. "Mourning and Melancholy." In *The Standard Edition of the Complete Psychological Works of Sigmund Freud*, vol. 14, ed. and trans. J. Strachey. London: Hogarth Press, pp. 243–258.

——. 1920. "Beyond the Pleasure Principle." In *The Standard Edition of the Complete Psychological Works of Sigmund Freud*, vol. 18, ed. and trans. J. Strachey. London: Hogarth Press, pp. 3–64.

Griffin, Miriam. 1986. "Philosophy, Cato, and Roman Suicide I." *Greece & Rome* 33 (1): 64–77.

Horwitz, Tem. 1998. "My Death." In *Death and Philosophy*, ed. Jeff Malpas and Robert C. Solomon. London: Routledge, pp. 5–15.

Kivimäki, Martti, D. Gunnel, D. A. Lawlor, G. Dawey Smith, and Timo Klaukka. 2007. "Social Inequalities in Antidepressant Treatment and Mortality: A Longitudinal Register Study." *Psychological Medicine* 37: 373–382.

Kivivuori, Janne, and Martti Lehti. 2006. "The Social Composition of Homicide in Finland, 1960–2000." *Acta Sociologica* 49 (1): 67–82.

Klaukka, Timo, Juhana Idänpään-Heikkilä, and Pentti Neuvonen. 2005. "Keskustelu masennuslääkkeiden turvallisuudesta jatkuu." *Suomen Lääkärilehti* 60: 3874–3876.

Klein, Melanie. 1957. "Envy and Gratitude." In *Envy and Gratitude, and Other Works 1946–1963.* London: Hogarth Press, 1975.

Kleinman, Arthur. 2007. *What Really Matters: Living a Moral Life amidst of Uncertainty and Danger*. New York: Oxford University Press.
Kposowa, Augustine. 1999. "Suicide Mortality in the United States: Differentials by Industrial and Occupational Groups." *American Journal of Industrial Medicine* 36: 645–652.
——. 2001. "Unemployment and Suicide: A Cohort Analysis of Social Factors Predicting Suicide in the US National Mortality Study." *Psychological Medicine* 31: 127–138.
Kral, Michael J. 2012. "Postcolonial Suicide Among Inuit in Arctic Canada." *Culture, Medicine, and Psychiatry* 36 (2): 306–325.
Lasch, Christopher. 1979. *The Culture of Narcissism*. New York: Norton.
Lehti, Martti, and Janne Kivivuori. 2005. "Alcohol-Related Violence as an Explanation for the Difference between Homicide Rates in Finland and the Other Nordic Countries." *Nordisk Alkohol och Narkotikatidskrift* 22: 7–24.
Lester, David. 2005. *Thinking about Suicide: Perspectives on Suicide*. New York: Nova Science.
Lieberman, Lisa. 2003. *Leaving You: The Cultural Meaning of Suicide*. Chicago: Ivan R. Dee.
Lorant, V., A. E. Kunst, M. Huisman, G. Costa, and J. Mackenbach. 2005. "Socio-Economic Inequalities in Suicide: a European Comparative Study." *British Journal of Psychiatry* 187: 49–54.
Macdonald, Charles J.-H. 2007. *Uncultural Behavior*. Honolulu: University of Hawaii Press.
Mäki Netta. 2010. *Not in All Walks of Life? Social Differences in Suicide Mortality*. Ph.D. diss., University of Helsinki. Research Reports, Department of Sociology No. 262.
Maris, Ronald W., and Alan Berman et al., eds. 2001. *Comprehensive Textbook on Suicidology*. New York: Guildford Press.
Marsden, Paul, and Sharon Attia. 2005. "A Deadly Contagion." *The Psychologist* 18 (3): 152–155.
Marsh, Ian. 2010. *Suicide: Foucault, History and Truth*. Cambridge: Cambridge University Press.
Menninger, Karl. 1937. *The Human Mind*. New York: Alfred A. Knopf.
Messner, Steven, and Richard Rosenfeld. 1999. "Social Structure and Homicide: Theory and Research." In *Homicide: A Sourcebook of Social Research*, ed. Dwayne Smith and Albert Zahn. Thousand Oaks, CA: Sage, pp. 27–41.
Minois, Georges. 1999. *History of Suicide: Voluntary Death in Western Culture*. Baltimore: The Johns Hopkins University Press.
Nikunen, Minna. 2011. "Murder-Suicide in the News: Doing Routine and the Drama." *European Journal of Cultural Studies* 14 (1): 81–101.
Pinguet, Maurice. 1984. *La mort volontaire au Japon*. Paris: Gallimard.
Rajan, Julie. 2011. *Women Suicide Bombers: Narratives of Violence*. New York: Routledge.

Savolainen, Jukka, Martti Lehti, and Janne Kivivuori. 2008. "Historical Origins of a Cross-National Puzzle: Homicide in Finland 1750 to 2000." *Homicide Studies* 12: 67–88.
Schuman, Gary. 1992–93. "Suicide and the Life Insurance Contract: Was the Insured Sane or Insane? That Is the Question—Or Is It?" *Tort and Insurance Law Journal* 28: 745–746.
Sedgwick, Peter. 1982. *PsychoPolitics*. London: Pluto Press.
Shneidman, Edwin, ed. 1976. *Suicidology: Contemporary Developments*. New York: Grune & Stratton.
——. 1996. *The Suicidal Mind*. New York: Oxford University Press.
Shneidman, Edwin, and Norman Farberow. 1957. *The Cry for Help*. New York: MacGraw Hill.
Singh, Rashmi. 2011. *Hamas and Suicide Terrorism*. London: Routledge.
Sosiaali- ja terveyshallitus. 1992. *Itsemurhan voi ehkäistä: Itsemurhien ehkäisyn tavoite- ja toimintaohjelma*. Helsinki: Valtion painatuskeskus.
Staples, James, and Tom Widger. 2012. "Situating Suicide as an Anthropological Problem: Ethnographic Approaches to Understanding Self-Harm and Self-Inflicted Death." *Culture, Medicine, and Psychiatry* 36 (2): 183–203.
Värnik, Airi, K. Kõlves, and Danuta Wasserman. 2005. "Suicide among Russians in Estonia."*British Medical Journal* 330: 176–177.
Voracek, Martin, and L. M. Loibl. 2007. "Genetics of Suicide: A Systematic Review of Twin Studies." *Wien Klinische Wochenschrift* 119: 463–475.
Wasserman, Danuta, and Airi Värnik. 1998. "Suicide Preventive Effects of Perestroika in the Former USSR." *Acta Psychiatrica Scandinavica* (suppl.) 394: 1–41.
Wasserman, Danuta, and Camilla Wasserman, eds. 2009. *The Oxford Textbook on Suicidology*. Oxford: Oxford University Press.
WHO. 2004. "Distribution of Suicide Rates by Gender and Age." http://www.who.int/mental_health/prevention/suicide/suicide_rates_chart/en/
——. 2005. "Suicide Rates per 100,000 by Country, Year and Sex (Table) Most Recent Year Available; as of 2011." http://www.who.int/mental_health/prevention/suicide_rates/en/index.html.
——. 2012. "Suicide Prevention." http://www.who.int/mental_health/prevention/en/
Wolfgang, Marvin, and Franco Ferracuti. 1967. *Subculture of Violence: Toward an Integrated Theory in Criminology*. London: Tavistock.
Zalsman Gil, A. Frisch, A. Apter, and A. Weizman. 2002. "Genetics of Suicidal Behavior: Candidate Association Genetic Approach." *The Israel Journal of Psychiatry and Related Sciences* 39 (4): 252–261.

Part I

Suicide

Cross-Cultural Perspectives

Chapter 1

The Construction of the Suicidal Self in Phenomenological Psychology

Charles J.-H. Macdonald and Jean Naudin

INTRODUCTION

Anthropologists have met with difficulties using their conceptual toolbox while approaching the problem of suicide (see Verrier 1943; Bohannan 1960; Devereux 1961; Cátedra 1992; Eveno 2003; Macdonald 2007). One is that notions like role, status, cultural values, and the like may be conceptually inadequate when trying to make sense of suicidal behavior. Another problem is generalizing certain specific psychodynamic profiles to a whole culture or society (Macdonald 2003, 2007). In other words, these researchers have faced the usual challenge of making sense of the double conundrum of suicide: its statistical stability and its individual unpredictability. The phenomenon of suicide must indeed be approached from two different angles: quantitative, statistical, and sociological on the one hand, and qualitative, interpretive, and psychological on the other. These approaches may overlap somewhat but are never completely identical (see below).

In a previous study on suicide among an indigenous group in the southern Philippines, Macdonald (2007) addressed the first question: why does a section of a population present a uniquely high rate of suicide (from 130 to 170 per 100,000) whereas the rest of the (culturally) same population does not (their suicide rate is close to zero)? Macdonald concluded that no single psychological profile or type could account for all the recorded suicide cases; nor were the operational cultural norms or values, in this particular society at least, completely decisive in making sense of the high rate of suicide (Macdonald 2007: 266–268). In other words, there was neither a simple psychological explanation for suicide nor a way to "explain" its anomalous occurrence in terms of cultural values, social rules, or even the social context of the time. Following Baechler (1975), Macdonald postulated the existence of an additional x-factor and hypothesized that this factor could be genetic, possibly involving serotoninergic imbalance as well as cognitive and emotional deficiency (see Mann 2003; Courtet et al. 2004; Jollant et al. 2005). Although the etiology of suicide was seen as overdetermined by cultural, historical and psychological variables, there was room left to experiment with another approach accounting for an inherited predisposition to suicidal behavior. No approach should be seen as excluding others. Suicide is indeed a very complex phenomenon calling for a complex and multivariate explanation.

This is why this essay will take yet another tack and make suggestions based on concepts provided by phenomenological psychology.[1] We will thus analyze one case of suicide through the narrative presented by another member of the community. It will yield a highly idiosyncratic picture, but we believe that some of its traits and dimensions can be somewhat generalized to other recorded cases, using the concept of "melancholy type" (*Typus Melancholicus*) derived from Tellenbach's work (1987). This concept has proved relevant in a transcultural perspective (see below).

We will borrow yet another idea stemming from the work of phenomenological psychiatry: the notion of "narrative analysis" or "co-entanglement of histories," taken from Binswanger's and Shapp's philosophies (Naudin and Azorin 1998) and from Naudin (Naudin et al. 1995). This leads to another definition of culture, one based on the dynamics of entangled narratives through which the subject projects himself in the world and thus defines his or her own identity. It points to the relational nature and interdependence of individual cases, and stresses the link between one case and others in the history of the community. In the sense that a particular culture is a skein of (hi)stories—the history of all individual histories in an ongoing and plural narrative experience—suicide becomes part of the culture of the group.

Therefore this chapter aims at exploring a different interpretive dimension, in no way exclusive of other cultural, psychological, psychiatric, and genetic approaches mentioned before. Both of the conceptual grids examined in the course of this chapter—one based on a type, the other on a process—are grounded in phenomenological psychology and/or psychiatry.

THE SUICIDE OF SAQAY

Here we investigate a particular instance of suicide that occurred in March 2002 among the Palawan people, an indigenous cultural community of the Southern Philippines.[2] Saqay had committed suicide, and his nephew Pirmin narrated the events leading to it. In summarizing this story, we will scrutinize the way the narrator told it because the telling of such a story is part of the object we are investigating: not only how we (foreign investigators) interpret the story, but also how people themselves interpret it. We investigate a fact (someone has committed suicide) and the native interpretation of the fact as well.

> Pirmin started by saying: "I shall start from the beginning. Saqay told Pirdisiu, his son: help me sell my coconut grove . . ." Pirmin then goes on about detailing a transaction that eventually does not take place as Pirdisiu, Saqay's son, is opposed to the sale. The narrator gives numerous details about the amount requested for the land, the would-be buyer (a Christian lowlander). As is usual the narrative includes excerpts of dialogues taking place between father and son. At some point Saqay is reported as saying that he "might commit suicide" if only he had the strength or will power to do it. At this point the narrator comments on Saqay's mental disposition concerning this transaction. He was doing it "like against his own will." Eventually then the sale does not take place, the meeting with the prospective buyer is canceled by one of Saqay's sons. This causes Saqay to be aggravated. He summons his sons in his house the next day. The narrator has this so say about Saqay: "He was like that, even before his wife's death. He was worrying about everything." Saqay said: "Pirdisiu, I have not consoled myself from the demise of your mother. This sale is just making it worse (deepening my grief)." The narrator comments: "Yes indeed he was worrying. He had promised his wife to join her in death." So the next day Pirdisiu goes to see his father at his bidding and finds the door locked. He is puzzled since his father never locked the door. He waits and waits until other people come and join him: his sister, his brother-in-law and his nephew. They decide to break the door open and they find the dead body of Saqay. He is found in a kneeling or crouching position, covered with a blanket, with a rope around the neck. They ascertain his death by touching his body which is "cold as lead." The narrator repeats that Saqay was covered with a blanket. Pirdisiu goes back home and entrusts his brother with the funeral proceedings. At this point, says the narrator, he was informed by neighbors about the death of Saqay, his uncle. The neighbor says: "Your uncle killed himself. Go and speak to Pirdisiu." So Pirmin goes and fetches Pirdisiu. He tries to convince him not to quarrel with his brother (the two

> brothers apparently had a quarrel about the sale of the coconut grove). Pirdisiu agrees but in spite of that he and his brother exchange bitter words. The narrator comments again on Saqay's frame of mind by quoting a dialogue he had with his children. When Saqay's wife died, he said: "I do not have the strength to hang myself and to join her, but I shall wait. In two years time we have an appointment she and I." Thus after his wife's death he went regularly to visit his wife's grave on a hill where she was interred. He brought food, cassava, rice, sweet potatoes. "Why," asked the children, "why do you bring all this food to a dead person?" "Just shut up!" he answered. The narrator insists: Saqay brought his wife bananas, clothes, everything. He put that on his wife's grave. He had constructed a lean-to (or a shed) where he slept sometimes. Eventually he even built a little house next to his wife's tomb. At one point he asked his children (Pirdisiu and his brother): "Has your mother died two years ago?" "Not yet" they said "why do you ask?" "Because I cannot endure it anymore. I cannot forget your mother, I see her in my dreams. We are together but it is intolerable. Why?" So, says the narrator, he could not be consoled. The longing to be close to her was always with him. After two years had lapsed he told his sons: "Two years now have lapsed since your mother's death." Saqay did not add any further comment. He did not say he had an appointment with his wife. Two years. He just killed himself. He found the courage to do it. (Field notes, Macdonald 2007)

TYPUS MELANCHOLICUS

Phenomenological psychology offers a notion that might be adequately used in this particular case. It is the "melancholy type" or *Typus Melancholicus*. This type (defined as a lasting personality disposition) has been observed in a number of well-documented clinical cases. Tellenbach characterizes it by the following traits: above all a great concern for other people, meticulousness and attention in dealings, and a sense of duty and accountability for his or her own actions, together with constant worry, feelings of guilt, and high expectations of him- or herself (Tellenbach 1987: 398). Other traits that define the type are steadfastness, caution, submissiveness, conventionality, and unimaginativeness (399). Being both demanding of him- or herself and timid, the melancholy type is prey to emotional insecurity, which is transcended by pursuing high ideals. In any case this subject is bound by approved norms of conduct and oriented to others, valuing other people's points of view above his or her own. At certain points Pirmin's narrative indicates similar traits in Saqay's personality, particularly emotional insecurity (he is a "constant worrier"), submissiveness to his son's demands, careful planning of the sale of his land, steadfastness in his determination to sell the land in spite of his misgivings (he did it as though "against his own will").

In Macdonald's study of suicide among the Palawan people, similar observations in several cases are reminiscent of the melancholy type, to quote:

> A decision to die as a result of rational calculation seems to be a common trait among all suicides connected with old age and illness. . . . I am however linking these cases with those that apparently result from a similar kind of protracted impairment, but in emotional rather than physical terms. Suicide in these cases is planned far in advance . . . (Macdonald 2007: 218)

Saqay had the idea of joining his wife in death for many years. The manner in which his suicide was carried out and the planned agenda and considerate manner that characterized the act seem also to reflect a personality type defined as melancholy: humble, considerate, and introverted, with a keen sense of duty and propriety. Many other older people have, like Saqay, carried out their own deaths according to careful plans. They bid farewell to their children and loved ones (like Saqay, who summoned his sons the day before he committed suicide) but were careful not to reveal their intentions. The common threads in these cases together are age, premeditation, rationality, and consideration of others (Macdonald 2007: 218). Fourteen out of eighty-seven cases fit this profile.

Another, similar case—Merensinu's suicide—is worth mention. It happened a long time ago, in the 1950s. This gentleman, a senior member of his community, had an extramarital affair that came to light, exposing him as an adulterer. His own daughters confronted him and berated him for his conduct. How could he, a respected elder and judge in customary law, be found guilty of such behavior? He confessed to adultery and, having admitted his guilt, proceeded to end his own life in a way that is both revealing and typical. He first visited his mistress's son-in-law and asked him to put a stop to the gossip circulating about the affair. According to our informant Merensinu, in making this visit he probably intended to address a final farewell to his paramour. Then he went into the forest and found an isolated spot, where he sat by himself and had a smoke. After smoking he hanged himself.[3] All traits characteristic of the melancholy type are easily recognizable: an acute sense of his responsibility and guilt, and a very carefully planned suicide project, unannounced and carried out in a discreet and solitary manner. All this reveals a character who is detached, resigned, calm, and determined.

The *Typus Melancholicus* thus appears as a valid psychological class or profile not only in Western culture, but also in an "exotic" culture such as the Palawan in the Philippines. It seems to apply equally well to a number of other cultures. One is the culture of the Vaqueiros of Northern Spain described at length by Cátedra (1992). It seems an equally adequate description for recurrent cases among the Alaska Inuit (Eskimos) (Hippler 1969) and Semai from Peninsular Malaysia (Dentan 2000). These three different cultures also display unusually high suicide rates.

Among the Vaqueiros who live in the Cantabric mountains, the anthropologist Cátedra notes that " . . . suicide becomes an act with a strong moral content" (1992: 173). Further on she describes the indigenous notion of *aburrimiento*, which the informants themselves use to explain suicide (202). It amounts to a mental state of detachment and loss of interest in the concerns of daily life, verging on a state of complete repulsion. This state is akin to another termed *arrepentimiento* in the vernacular, glossed as "renouncement." *Aburrimiento* is also characterized by a condition described as "exhaustion, impotency, and passivity" (351). Both the moral content and the general passivity and diminished vitality that characterize this state can readily be included in the *Typus Melancholicus*, as opposed to the more vital and active *Typus Maniacus*.

Among the Northern Alaska Inuit (Eskimos), the suicide rate quoted by Hippler (1969: 1080) is 41.7 per 100,000 people–that is, very high. Hippler's characterization of the Inuit cultural personality emphasizes a "fatalistic optimism" that combines an attitude of passive tolerance with much concealed anxiety (Hippler 1974: 454). This personality type makes frustration particularly difficult to bear, according to Hippler. Other traits show the Inuit type to be very similar to the Palawan culture and personality type, particularly the general egalitarianism and nonviolence characteristic of both cultures; the socialization process, which is extremely "nurturing" in that great attention is devoted to protecting and caring for infants; and the great respect for personal autonomy. The melancholy type could be well accommodated to such a cultural environment.

It is fascinating to find a very similar anthropological description of the modal personality of the Semai of Peninsular Malaysia, including a number of traits reminiscent of the Inuit personality (Dentan 2000). The Semai's proneness to suicidal behavior is noted also. The author uses the phrase "learned helplessness" (32) to refer to dispositions like passivity, nonaggression, or a feeling of impotence. All this resembles the passivity and fatalism characteristic of the Inuit according to Hippler. It is also strongly reminiscent of what has been said of the Vaqueiros and their renouncement of action.

Thus, very similar patterns apply to four completely different, historically unconnected cultures in distant parts of the world and completely different environments, following distinct and dissimilar ways of life. We can therefore hypothesize the transcultural existence of a psychological profile or type like the one Tellenbach defined. Individuals belonging to this type are likely candidates for suicide—at least, the kind of premeditated, rational, ethical suicide performed by an altruistic subject deeply concerned with conformity to accepted norms. Actual suicides are the result of the confluence of a type and a situation (a structure and an event). Whereas events cannot be programmed, actions dictated by a personality type may be seen as programmed. When the modal personality is the potentially suicide-prone "melancholy type," one could expect a higher frequency of suicides in the culture under consideration. This line of reasoning is more or less followed by anthropologists or ethno-psychiatrists who, like Devereux (1961), try to make sense of the logic inherent in suicidal behavior and apply this logic to the culture as a whole. Here, in fact, we face a classic problem in anthropology: the temptation to generalize a model to all.

Despite the good fits between the case and the type, not all suicides fit the type. Out of 87 cases in the Palawan situation, for example, only 14 fit the type at all; impulsive suicide by teenagers accounts for 17. Angry and passionate emotions (e.g., resulting from forbidden love) characterize 13 other cases, and 10 of the same 87 suicides were triggered by grief (e.g., upon the death of a child). The melancholy type definitely has weight in the overall balance of all cases but accounts for no more than 16 per cent of all cases. Angry and passionate suicides, and especially impulsive suicidal acts by teenagers, are at the opposite end of the psychological spectrum, committed often by young people in a rash and unpremeditated fashion.

Moreover the modal personality cannot be defined, if at all, as melancholy; if it were, the great number of necessary exceptions would empty the concept of empirical content. We should therefore conclude that the melancholy type has valid but limited explanatory force, and that other notions and models may be more helpful at the level of the culture as a whole. Phenomenological psychology may yet provide such concepts.

SUICIDE AND CO-ENTANGLEMENT OF (HI)STORIES

Let us first return to the story of Saqay. The organization of the narrative and the way events were told are revealing. Their exact sequence is respected in the summary above. First we ask why the narrator gives so much salience to the sale of the coconut grove, opening with what appears to be a secondary appendage to the story. The "true" story revolves around the death of Saqay's wife, his widowhood, his inconsolable grief. However, the attempt to sell Saqay's land–in a complicated transaction involving a lowlander, a quarrel between two brothers, and the aggravation resulting from this family conflict–immediately precedes the suicidal act and has a chronological right to be included in the whole story. This entanglement of narrative threads in the narrator's text merits further investigation.

A first element is the detailed description of Saqay's personality as engaged in the transaction. He sells his land "as against his will", *tijat santang negselsel*, and worries, *pegsususaan*, about everything. He wishes for death. These traits, mixed with everyday dealings and the transaction at hand, said to increase his state of unhappiness, introduce the final suicide sequence, which does not come unannounced. Another formal aspect of the narrative is the use of direct quotations (He said: " . . ."). Direct quotations (a narrator reporting another person's speech in direct style) is a typical feature of Palawan rhetorics. The narrator, a witness to Saqay's actions, makes himself credible through such metapragmatic utterances (he qualifies his speech as trustworthy). By doing so he also entangles himself in Saqay's story. He seems to say that he was a chief witness to his uncle's demise and that the discourse about the land sale is indeed of primary importance in understanding Saqay's suicide.

The story as a whole has three main narrative segments: a land sale, a quarrel between brothers and between a son and his father about the sale, and the mourning of a widower. A fourth section is the discovery of Saqay's dead body, a quite visual and tactile experience. The body is "cold as lead," found in a crouching position typical of suicides by anoxia. This way of killing oneself is both unobtrusive and apparently painless. The suicide leans into the rope and passes out. Another important detail is present: Saqay took care to cover himself with a blanket. Again, this points to a suicide project planned and carried out with care. After locking his door, the victim covered himself–probably out of modesty, lest his sons and relatives see his naked body.

Looking at the narrative's concluding thread, Saqay's mourning, one is overwhelmed by the inescapability of the victim's fate. His death seems the inevitable result of his inconsolable grief, his obsessive closeness to the grave, and his commitment to meet his departed wife at the appointed time. One therefore may wonder why the other narrative threads are present, or why they are even mentioned at all. The land sale or disagreements with his sons did not, after all, carry much weight in motivational terms. So why is Saqay's story presented with these apparently pointless details? To provide an answer, we use the notion of "connections of meanings creating ties of intentionality between lived experiences" (Naudin et al. 1995: 577) and "co-entanglement of (hi)stories" (Naudin, et al. 1998: 581). These concepts might lead to a better understanding of Saqay's story and many others too.

How do we make sense of these various (hi)stories or narrative threads; how do they coalesce meaningfully? In other words, how do we interpret Saqay's experience, especially through Pirmin's account of it? Our starting point is the idea that consciousness is structured through a narrative process involving (hi)stories told by the self and involving stories told by others who are connected or connecting in some way with the self. In this perspective, the self becomes "entangled" in other people's (hi)stories. At this point we should take pains to distinguish clearly between a story as a text and a story as an unfolding living process. A text is closed: it has a beginning and an end; it is a fixed static entity. Narration, on the other hand, is an open process in flux with neither ending nor beginning, as the narrator constantly reinterprets the past. Following Schapp (Naudin and Azorin 1998: 228), "experiencing means establishing connections amidst a (hi)story: it means being 'entangled,' namely always sketching, grasping in its heart, closing, or following a narrative." (Hi)stories' connection within a huge web or skein of narratives can be summarized by the proposition "there is no isolated (hi) story" (223). This mass of (hi)stories told by oneself to oneself is not entirely chaotic or devoid of internal organization. It has unity and a direction of growth (like a tree). It has a horizon, a number of possible outcomes. It is also internally differentiated. Some narrative threads are more meaningful than others.

Let us say, then, that Pirmin the narrator understands the (hi)story of Saqay as the unfolding of a narrative process wherein Saqay is entangled in a manifold (hi)story, including himself, his wife, his sons, his neighbors, and many others who do not appear in Pirmin's short account, including people Saqay knew of, like Merensinu and others, who experienced loss and committed suicide. In this process of consciousness, there occurs something that Naudin calls "radical entanglement," in which the patient cannot "break the charm" or the spell (Naudin and Azorin 1998: 229). It is a "submission to a theme" (229). Saqay has been "radically entangled" in a skein of narrative threads with the dominant theme of grief that leads to suicide. The suicidal theme looms large on the horizon of Saqay's narrative consciousness. It is actually another way to define personal identity—a dynamic, self-affirming, self-projecting way, resting on a many-stranded narrative process. From the point of view of the narrator, Pirmin, there is a hierarchy in the time structure. The sale of the coconut grove comes first because it immediately precedes the suicide. This (hi)story frames Saqay's death and explains it somewhat: the sale of the land and the conflict with his son deepen his grief.

But the grief itself belongs to another narrative thread, the loss and the mourning following Saqay's wife's death. The entanglement is quite obvious: Saqay is a worrier, and he is also seeking death. The threads are intertwined. They are entangled in Pirmin's narrative as well, making it difficult to determine which is the most significant.

This particular approach differs from the more classical approach of the etiology of suicide because we do not think in terms of causality. Saqay's widowhood did not cause him to become suicidal; aggravations linked to the land transaction did not cause him to hang himself. But they are all entwined and entangled. We see this as a more profitable approach to the etiology of suicidal behavior because it enables one to discard sociological interpretations based on roles, statuses, and structural values.

Clearly Pirmin is aware of the mutual implication, the entanglement of (hi)stories that result in Saqay's demise. If we had more information, we could thus trace back many more narrative threads in which Saqay was entangled and from which his identity emerged. As a living experience, the narrative process is, to reiterate, not a closed and finished "story" but an unending process of self-invention through connections of meanings. A classic and popular way to interpret a suicide story is to tell it via a sequence of events and situations (loss, mourning, rejection, solitude, poverty, etc.). The accumulation of events/situations and the sequential logic of the whole result in the final suicidal act. So-and-so killed himself, we say, remarking, "Mind you, he had lost a son, his wife just died, and he got sick!" We understand suicide as being caused, in a way, by loss, grief, mourning, and sickness, in an arithmetic of unhappiness.

This is a misconstruction on two counts. First, the life story is retro-injected with the final event (suicide), which in hindsight transforms a regular life story into a life geared toward suicide (Macdonald 2007: 227). Had the final event not been a suicidal act, then the whole construction would fall apart as a suicidal story. Second, too much weight is attached to events in themselves. It is, of course, Saqay's consciousness in its intentionality and his project of self as an entanglement of (hi)stories that make these events potentially suicidogenic. Saqay was not a candidate for suicide to begin with, nor did exterior facts determine his becoming suicidal. Saqay was a subject gifted with intentionality and acting through a complex narrative process he was entangled in. Suicide eventually became prominent on the horizon of this narrative process, undoubtedly in part because of the presence of narrative threads including other suicides, as in this particular community suicide happens with some degree of frequency (Macdonald 2007: 199–205). If it is so that other suicidal (hi)stories are part of Saqay's own, then we have found a crucial connection of meanings in our quest regarding not only

Saqay and the highly idiosyncratic profile he and a few others may present, but also the way suicide propagates itself so that individual suicides eventually accrue into suicide rates. Let us therefore return to the general question of suicide and how we "explain" it.

IS A CULTURAL EXPLANATION OF SUICIDE POSSIBLE?

Discussion of suicide in the social sciences deals with two different objects under the same name (see Introduction above). One is suicidal behavior, which we investigate by looking at the subject's biography and constructing a psychodynamic process that explains the final act of inflicting death upon the self. Such an investigation is the domain of psychology and psychiatry, and it is what we have tried to do so far. The other, entirely different object of scrutiny is suicide rates. These are abstract, statistical objects. What makes suicide rates so interesting, as a desirable object of investigation for sociologists, is that for given populations, they remain relatively stable over years. Social scientists trying to explain this stability using factors such as age, sex, occupation, religious affiliation, status, residence, income, and so on have been somewhat successful: their work has provided us with reasonable predictions of specific suicide rates, showing that in France, for instance, unemployed widowers over fifty years of age are more likely to end their own lives than are young, employed, married females (Baudelot and Establet 2006).

The real problem, however, is meaningful connection of these two aspects or questions. Psychodynamics and psychiatric diagnosis are usually extremely idiosyncratic because they probe deep into the subject's psyche; social scientists, on the other hand, use relatively few, general variables (age, sex, status, etc.). We like to think that both are connected, and that our intuitive view of this is vindicated—after all, is an old man, poor and alone, not more likely to commit suicide than a young, affluent housewife? We are thus convinced that social structural variables match psychological variables. For a topic like suicide, appearances are misleading, inasmuch as an intuitive reading of a situation conceals key elements at work in creating suicidal vulnerability. Only a few of all poor, elderly widowers will commit suicide, because only these few are made more vulnerable by invisible psychiatric factors. External factors such as poverty and solitude, combined with an endogenous vulnerability, may together explain the act of inflicting death upon oneself.

Saqay's suicide took place in a community that has been studied for over thirty-five years. It is only a small section of a larger cultural indigenous group (an ethno-linguistic group) but, as mentioned, it stands out for its extraordinary suicide rate, calculated over the years to be between 130 and 170 per 100,000 (Macdonald 2003, 2007: 204–205). The problem we have faced, as social scientists trying to make sense of this highly unusual situation, is that this community (of around 3,000 persons) is, in nearly every aspect—culture, way of life, values—virtually identical to all other Palawan communities, which by contrast have suicide rates close to zero. Still, regardless of whether the usual cultural traits and social structural variables operated as a way of explanation, one thing was sure: for generations, people in this particular community had committed suicide. It was a stable phenomenon. Could we not explain suicide with suicide?

Saqay grew up in an environment where suicides happened and were reported to him. We can be sure of that. They might have been elderly people (like Merensinu, whom Saqay almost certainly knew of), or even relatives of Saqay. Chances are that anyone growing up in this community will be told that a neighbor, a relative, someone of good standing, has killed him- or herself. In this culture people do not look favorably upon suicide. They think, much as many of us do, that it is a wasteful, somewhat irrational, stupid thing to do. But although they definitely disapprove of it, they are not in the habit of judging others harshly, being in general very tolerant. Yet despite this negative judgment, suicides are frequent. So again, a cultural value (to commit suicide is bad) seems of very little worth in persuading people not to kill themselves. It is probable, however, that the sheer existence of actual cases of suicide in the immediate human environment of the subject makes suicide a deeply *internalized option* in the mind (that is to say, in the [hi]story, and in its co-entanglement with other [hi]stories) of the subject. Society's explicit edict (suicide is bad) is not effective. What is at work here belongs to a deeper stratum of the psyche.

Suicide, therefore, is what it has always been reported to be: a "contagious" phenomenon. Recent research on suicide confirms this (see for instance Rubinstein 2002). The mechanism at work is something we might call "imitation." But how does this mechanism function, and to what extent can we speak of imitation? Is it mere fascination, being enthralled by a role model—young Werther, perhaps, or one's peers? The difficulty lies in the kind of cognitive model used. Some anthropologists (e.g., Sperber 1996; Atran 2003) have successfully claimed that logical properties, inherent to representations, cause these representations to be imitated, spread, and maintained in a community. Inferential properties linked with certain ideas make these ideas more successful than others. But our case does not really concern ideas or values with a propositional content. We are dealing with something outside of discourse in its propositional and volitional reality.

Suppose that A had an uncle who committed suicide because he was inconsolable upon losing the wife he cherished. Now A's wife, whom A loves, dies, and A is inconsolable. Will A say: "My uncle had a wife who died. He was inconsolable. He killed himself. I had a wife who died. I am inconsolable. *Therefore*, I will kill myself"? Such an argument seems beside the point. A is unlikely to kill himself through a process of logical reasoning. More likely, in our view, is that he will do it through a process of "radical entanglement" such as that depicted above. Other lines of reasoning come to mind. One goes like this: culture X posits a threshold of pain beyond which one is not supposed to go on living. Here again, a subject can be imagined as evaluating his position respective to this level or threshold of pain or unhappiness and, through a deductive process, deciding in his heart that he will have to kill himself. Yet such a sequence of events is unlikely, even though people make it appear so. One would more probably exclaim: "I will do as my uncle did, and hang myself!" or "Life is not worth living anymore!" or "I cannot endure it any more, I will kill myself." The latter is actually a quite typical declaration, or proposition, found in suicide notes in Finland (Utriainen and Honkasalo 1996). Contrary to appearances, however, these propositions do not seem to be the foundation for suicide. Let us never forget that only a few people commit suicide, and that pain, stress, and unhappiness per se are not causes for dying. To be sure, pain and stress are relevant factors, but there is always something else, possibly Baechler's x-factor (1975), that is ultimately accountable for the finalization of the suicidal process.

In this essay we restrict ourselves to the hypothesis that intentionality and co-entanglement in (hi)stories are the likeliest foundation of the suicidal act. We can speak of imitation, but not the kind that would result from a rational, conscious validation of a propositional truth. It is improbable that the suicidal subject would examine a proposition and, on the basis of an inference, decide to end his life. He will commit suicide because his whole identity is defined by a project surging from the entanglement of his and others (hi)stories. Suicide has become the dominant narrative theme on the horizon of his life. He cannot "break the spell." His identity includes suicide as an aspect of self and a result of his entanglement in other (hi)stories. So did Saqay's narrative identity, in its tragic and inescapable fate.

Despite its limitations, this kind of interpretation holds an advantage. If cultural edicts, values, institutions (like justice), propositional representations, official discourse, and the various other cultural artifacts do not operate at the depth of consciousness required to motivate actors to do what they do, then maybe this property of the structure of consciousness—that is, co-entanglement—will help explain numerous actions, especially those that run contrary to the established values of society. We do not delve into structural values, role and status as culturally constructed. Instead, we focus on the skein—the web of entangled (hi)stories that create the identity of a subject who appears to be deeply socialized by "unsocial" or "uncultural" values that have been used to construct the self's narrative identity.

CONCLUDING REMARKS

In the first part of this essay, we examined the concept of *Typus Melancholicus*, which intriguingly seems to be validated in several distinct cultural settings. Therefore we concluded that certain "profiles" or types may possess transcultural validity, regardless of their varied expressions and unequal importance in cultural terms, or of whether or not we posit the existence of a modal personality. The same basic psychodynamic factors may operate in totally different cultures. This weakens the position of radical relativism somewhat but also partly undermines the classic socio-anthropological approach via social structural variables. What goes on at the deeper, determining level of consciousness should be approached from a different perspective, using other intellectual tools. Such was our endeavor in the first section of the chapter.

The second part of this chapter was devoted to exploring another concept borrowed from phenomenological psychology, that of co-entanglement of (hi)stories within a narrative process of identity formation. It could be used, we argued, to interpret suicidal acts by helping explain why suicide becomes an element in the construction of self. Such an approach may shed new light on what anthropologists have so much difficulty defining: culture and identity. If personal identity is just that—a co-entanglement of (hi)stories, a skein of narratives produced by the individual telling himself who he is through his and other peoples' (hi)stories, weaving his narrative identity with the threads of other people's narratives—then cultural identity appears to be the super-skein of all the narrative threads available to individual subjects in the community. Narrative threads cross borders between the actual and the fictional. Those found in myths, tales, and legends are woven into the same cloth as those based in the life histories of relatives and neighbors. A culture too may thus be understood as a co-entanglement of (hi)stories, similar to an individual but much more complex.

From a different angle, we could argue that this approach reconciles the intractable conundrum of individual cases, in their highly idiosyncratic and unique complexity, with the uniform and compact body of cultural values and structural norms. But predictability is never complete. The entanglement of histories, in its sheer multiplicity of narratives, makes a web too intricate to be deciphered from the outside, without intimate knowledge of each person's history, connections, and disposition. So this approach is of little avail in predicting who will commit suicide next. What it does offer is a rich and firm ground in which to anchor individual cases. Let us conclude that even if Saqay was predisposed by both melancholy and serotonin, his final decision was part of the total history of the community and was also, in a way, the enacted memory of the group.

NOTES

1. The focus of phenomenological psychology is a "return to the things themselves," as the founder of phenomenological philosophy, Edmund Husserl, phrased it. It characterizes an approach based on the study of experience, subjectivity, immediate intuition of the world, and how the world appears to people. It aims, through description of concrete experiences and the participant's narratives, to illuminate the lived world of the participant (Naudin, Pringuey, and Azorin 1998).
2. The Palawan indigenous community is located in the southern part of Palawan Island, Philippines. Traditionally, their main source of livelihood was shifting agriculture supplemented by various extractive activities (fishing, hunting, gathering, and now wage labor to some extent). The 45,000 Palawan people live in small, scattered communities with no central government. They are nonviolent and egalitarian; they settle dispute through litigation and a system of customary law ensuring peaceful relations among equals. Personal autonomy is highly valued, and morality centers on the concept of "sympathy" or "compassion" (*ingasiq*) (see Macdonald 2007). Displays of aggressive feelings and violent behavior are valued negatively. Interpersonal relations are dominated by an ethos of sharing, peaceableness, and joyous companionship. Case studies show little statistical connection between aggressive or violent acts and suicide.
3. The sequence of events was reconstructed after the fact on the basis of material evidence: leaves that he sat on, cigarette butts, etc.

REFERENCES

Atran, Scott. 2003. "Théorie cognitive de la culture: Une alternative évolutionniste à la sociobiologie et à la sélection collective." *L'Homme* 166: 107–144.

Baechler, Jean. 1975. *Les Suicides*. Paris: Calmann-Lévy.

Baudelot, Christian and Roger Establet. 2006. *Suicide, l'envers de notre monde*. Paris: Seuil.

Bohannan, Paul, ed. 1960. *African Homicide and Suicide*. Princeton, NJ: Princeton University Press.

Cátedra, María. 1992. *This World, Other Worlds: Sickness, Suicide, Death, and the Afterlife among the Vaqueiros de Alzada of Spain.* Chicago and London: The University of Chicago Press.

Courtet, P., M.-C. Picot, F. Bellivier, S. Torres, F. Jollant, C. Michelon, D. Castelnau, B. Astruc, C. Buresi, and A. Malafosse. 2004. "Serotonin Transporter Gene May be Involved in Short-Term Risk of Subsequent Suicide Attempts." *Biological Psychiatry* 55: 46–51.

Dentan, Robert K. 2000. "This Is Passion and Where It Goes: Despair and Suicide among Semai, a Nonviolent People of West Malaysia." *Moussons* 2: 31–56.

Devereux, Georges. 1961. *Mohave Ethnopsychiatry and Suicide: The Psychiatric Knowledge and the Psychic Disturbances of an Indian Tribe.* Washington, D.C.: United States Government Printing Office.

Eveno, Stéphanie. 2003. *Le suicide et la Mort chez les Mamit-Innuat.* Paris: L'Harmattan.

Hippler, Arthur E. 1969. "Fusion and Frustration: Dimensions in the Cross-Cultural Ethnopsychology of Suicide." *American Anthropologist* 71: 1074–1087.

———. 1974. "The North Alaska Eskimos: A Culture and Personality Perspective." *American Ethnologist* 1: 449–469.

Jollant F., F. Bellivier, M. Leboyer, B. Astruc, S. Torres, R. Verdier, D. Castelnau, A. Malafosse, and P. Courtet. 2005. "Impaired Decision Making in Suicide Attempters." *American Journal of Psychiatry* 162 (2): 304–310.

Macdonald, Charles. 2003. "Urug: An Anthropological Investigation on Suicide in Palawan, Philippines." *Tonan Ajia Kenkyu* (*Southeast Asian Studies*) 40: 419–443.

———. 2007. *Uncultural Behavior: An Anthropological Investigation on Suicide in the Southern Philippines.* Honolulu: University of Hawaii Press.

Mann, J. John. 2003. "Neurobiology of suicidal behaviour." *Nature Reviews Neuroscience* 4 (10): 819–828.

Naudin, Jean, J. M. Azorin, L. Giudicelli, and D. Dassa. 1995. "Binswanger avec Schapp: analyse existentielle ou analyse narrative." *L'Evolution Psychiatrique* 60 (3): 575–591.

Naudin, J., J. Henry, M. Maure Raymondet, and J. M. Azorin. 1997. "Comment explorer la 'théorie de l'esprit' chez les schizophrènes? Intentionnalité pulsionnelle et développement." *L'Evolution Psychiatrique* 62 (2): 315–326.

Naudin, Jean, and Jean Michel Azorin. 1998. "Binswanger & Schapp: Existential Analysis or Narrative Analysis?" *Journal of Phenomenological Psychology* 29 (2): 212–230.

Naudin, Jean, Dominique Pringuey, and Jean Michel Azorin. 1998. "Phénoménologie et analyse existentielle." In *Encyclopédie Médico-Chirurgicale*, 37-815-A-10. Paris: Elsevier.

Rubinstein, Donald H. 2002. "Youth Suicide and Social Change in Micronesia." *Kagoshima University Research Center for the Pacific Islands Occasional Papers* 36: 33–41.

Sperber, Dan. 1996. *La contagion des idées.* Paris: Odile Jacob.

Tellenbach, Hubertus. 1987. "Sur l'histoire du concept 'Typus Melancholicus' et sur les conséquences pour la conception d'un 'Typus Maniacus.'" *Psychologie Médicale* 19 (3): 397–400.

Utriainen, Terhi, and Marja-Liisa Honkasalo. 1996. "Women Writing their Death and Dying: Semiotic Perspectives on Women's Suicide Notes." *Semiotica* 109: 195–220.

Verrier, Elwin. (1943) 1991. *Maria Murder and Suicide.* 2nd ed. Delhi: Oxford University Press.

Chapter 2

When It Is Worth the Trouble to Die

The Cultural Valuation of Suicide

María Cátedra

INTRODUCTION

Suicide is a cultural and human topic. In no known human society or culture is suicide absent (Maris 1981; Lester 2004). Some authors–Durkheim, for example–have stated that suicide, like crime, is necessary in society and linked to the basic conditions of social life. It has even been suggested that suicide "may function to remove the genes of defective people (those who are psychiatrically disturbed for example) and those past child-bearing age from society" (Lester 2004: 65). The problem with those theories, however, is that suicide is not a crime or a disease but belongs to the sphere of human action.

At the population level, suicide rates vary from the Egyptian 0.1 (per 100,000 per year) to 45.0 in Hungary for the period 1979–81 (Lester 2004, 2006). According to Bertolote and Fleischmann (2009: 91, 94), in 2002 almost a third of all cases of suicide found worldwide were in China and India, followed by Northern and Eastern Europe (Lithuania, the Russian Federation, Belarus, Finland, Hungary). Within Europe there are striking differences as well: a low suicide rate in Southern Europe and a high rate in Northern Europe and Scandinavia. Therefore suicide rates are influenced by persistent cross-national differences, including traditions, customs, religions, social attitudes, and climate. However, the different countries' suicide rates tend to be relatively stable over time,[1] and this stability becomes even clearer when diverse geographic regions or groups are compared (Lester 1997). How can we explain the stability? Culture may strongly affect the incidence, circumstances and methods, acceptance or disapproval, reasons, and meaning of suicide. Just a couple of classical examples–*suttee* in Indian or *seppuku* in Japan–attest to this. The high frequency of suicide and the honorableness of the act among the upper classes of ancient Rome, the tradition of suicide in Japan, and the importance of death by suicide in the European Romantic movement would suggest that the individual often reflects the attitudes of the culture with respect to suicide, death, and the otherworld other life (Cátedra 1992). Yet scholarly research on suicide seems to overlook the import of the cosmology of death and cultural assumptions concerning the afterworld. Meanwhile, the meaning of suicide, which has changed rather dramatically throughout history, has been increasingly medicalized and psychiatrized in modern times, even though some understand it as a psychotic act or even a human right (Bille-Brahe 2000).

Sociological and Psychological Research on Suicide

The two main classical fields of research on suicide are sociology and psychoanalysis. Durkheim's well-known, excellent book (1897), by showing the social dimension of what appears to be an individual and private act, initiated the sociological study of suicide. Although sociologists today, as Taylor (1990) and Moksony (1990) pointed out, have failed to demonstrate the influence of *society* on suicide, they have produced a body of research on the impact of social variables as causal agents in themselves on the suicide rate of individuals in the society. In any case, despite criticism, any new analysis of the topic revisits Durkheim's *Le Suicide* (Stack 2000; La Fontaine 2012).

Jack D. Douglas's innovative book (1973) presents the main critique of the Durkhemian method from what we would today call a "deconstructive perspective" on the analysis of official statistics, the main data used by sociologists. At the time, the book was a brave foray into a milieu in which statistics were seen almost as sacred. Douglas pointed out the lack of consensus on the definition of the word suicide, either in terms of the objective criteria used to classify a death as a suicide or regarding the investigative procedures to determine whether these criteria are met. He argued that many cultural factors, such as religion, influence the collected data: for example, Roman Catholics disapprove of suicide and therefore tend to conceal it. Today the reliability of international suicide data is widely questioned, and European death registration practices are so variable that the same criticism is still pertinent. The problem of registration is even more pressing in the case of third world countries (Desjarlais et al. 1995; Hjelmeland et al. 2006). However, Douglas went even closer to anthropology by pointing out that the members of a culture adapt the terms used to construct meanings for suicidal behavior.[2] In other words, the incidence and circumstances of suicidal behavior are a social construction. I have benefited from Douglas's analysis in my own work on the Vaqueiros.

An interesting alternative research question would involve suicide's impact on society. In some ways suicide is a revolutionary tool because it reflects negatively on the state, religion, and health system. It undermines the power of the social system, emphasizing the rights of the individual over those of the larger society. Viewed as an index of poverty or misery, it draws attention to social ills and helps to define normality for the society (Lester 2004).

Over the past few decades, anthropologists have dealt with suicide in various cultures.[3] In most Western cultures suicide has strong negative moral connotations, which might have prevented an objective approach to it as a cultural phenomenon. By the same token, psychologists and sociologists have focused on suicide prevention. Nevertheless, one task of a cultural anthropologist studying suicide is to explore the nature of the morality attached to it, rather than take any normative assumptions for granted.

Finally, although suicide as an act of *self*-destruction has attracted much inquiry, little attention has been devoted to the meaning of *death*. Suicide is on one level an individual and social act; however, as a *form of death* it is a cultural one. This is the guiding assumption of my fieldwork on the Vaqueiros.

SUICIDE AMONG THE VAQUEIROS

I started my fieldwork among the Vaqueiros in 1971, in several hamlets in Western Asturias in the far North of Spain. The Vaqueiros are a transhumant cattle-raising people who were considered a marginated group in the 1970s. They lived on the slopes of low mountains in small communities (*brañas*) of about ten households, each sheltering two or three generations. The household was almost completely inherited by the eldest son, who became the *amo* (master, owner) upon his father's death; women generally entered the household by marrying the heir, whose siblings had to either leave or remain single and work in the household. I quickly realized that the Vaqueiros regarded suicide not as a strange, inconceivable, or isolated act, but rather as something traditional and familiar. They also had a name for suicide by hanging, *el cordelín* (diminutive name). In addition to the results of my fieldwork, my data include a study by a judge, Soto Vázquez, who also statistically confirmed the high frequency of suicide in the Vaqueiro region (see table 2.1).

My ethnographic account of the cultural construction of death, sickness, suicide, burial, and afterlife among the Vaqueiros de Alzada of Asturias, Spain, is based on fieldwork (Cátedra 1992), whose theoretical framework relies on the claim that the contrast between suicide and natural death is important to understanding both. Suicide thus should not be studied in isolation but within its wider context as a form of death. Further, my aim has been to understand suicide not as a pathology, but as something culturally construed that is part of the local belief system. As a cultural account, my ethnography focuses particularly on the implicit cosmology of death, in which an intricate complex of symbols and sentiments attend the passage to another world.

The Problem from the Outside

In 1965, the local judge Soto Vázquez published the article "El suicidio entre los 'Vaqueiros de Alzada' Asturianos" in an Asturian scholarly journal, presenting three findings:

1. The number of suicides among the Vaqueiros is proportionally much higher than that of their neighbors.
2. The percentage of suicides among Vaqueiro women is much higher than that in local or national statistics for women.
3. The number of suicides for absolutely unknown reasons is also higher among the Vaqueiros.

Soto Vázquez based his work on the judicial archives of the three districts where most of the Vaqueiros lived from 1940 to 1964. Over this period in this zone, out of a total of 273 suicides, 111 were Vaqueiros (including 6 failed attempts). Of the three townships' total population of 110,000, Soto Vázquez counted 7,000 individuals as Vaqueiros and then doubled this figure because the exact number of Vaqueiros could not be determined. In my opinion, this doubling was clearly excessive;[4] it supposes a total of 14,000 Vaqueiros, which would be one seventh of the area's total population. However, even in this case the Vaqueiros would account for two fifths of the total number of suicides (Soto Vázquez 1965: 85).

Vaqueiros who end their own lives do so mainly by hanging, and to a lesser extent by drowning themselves and jumping from heights. They typically want a death that is quick and certain. Soto Vázquez found no false attempts at suicide, though some were exhibitionistic. He recorded direct testimonies of those who failed in their attempts or survived long enough to give their reasons. Of these six Vaqueiros, two men named family problems and physical incapacity to work due to sickness as reasons, whereas two women referred to mental illness and fear of legal prosecution. The remaining two cases presented an interesting reason:

> . . . and even unexplainable references to *aburrimiento* (boredom, loss of interest) in the other two cases, both of persons aged 62, in which there was not even an attempt to present a coherent explanation, limiting themselves to declare they had committed the suicide "*because they took the notion to do it*" (*porque les había dado por hacerlo*). (1965: 177, emphasis added)

As for the causes of the suicides, Soto Vázquez drew up a table presenting the 158 cases for which he had complete information, excluding two subjects under sixteen years of age. When two or more reasons were given, he placed the person in the category of the motive that seemed the strongest.

Although Soto Vázquez regards the figures for mental illness as normal for both the Vaquerios and the surrounding population, both groups, he draws attention to the high percentage of "unknown" motives among the Vaqueiros (about 20 percent of all suicides). According to Soto Vázquez, the Vaqueiros' suicides differ from those among the rest of the population in that they are psychotic, whereas among non-Vaqueiros the distinguishing feature is neurosis. He goes on to point out the comparatively high percentage of older Vaqueiro men referring to physical disability (see table 2.1). Further, he compares the age of suicide among Vaqueiros and non-Vaqueiros, focusing on young (aged 21–30) women's 43 percent share of Vaqueiro women's suicides, compared to the 31 percent accounted for by older women (aged 51–70). Among men, he found 12 cases in the 42–50 age group and 10 in the group aged 61–70. He notes too that the rate for Vaqueiro women in general is especially high (4 for every 5 men), while that among the other residents of the area is barely half the men (59/103).

Soto Vázquez attempts finally to offer an explanation of the suicides, referring to two contrasting hypotheses: the "characterological biotype," and the environment in which the group lives. Convinced that there is no somatic or psychological degeneration that would explain the abnormal frequency of suicide or the apparent lack of reason for it, he reaches the conclusion that his hypotheses are not alternatives, but rather complementary: "The root of the matter, as we see it, lies in the sociological influences of isolation and the real (although now decreasing) inferiority complex . . . combined with certain constitutional throwbacks or reversions (*atavismos*), which are not pathological, but merely traditional" (1965: 87).

Table 2.1. Classification of Suicides According to Motive and Age

Male Vaqueiros

Motive for suicide	*Ages of individuals*	*Total*
Mental illness	18, 24, 25, 26, 28, 35, 44, 48, 48, 55, 62, DK	12
Serious physical illness	46, 59?, 60, 61, 62, 65, 65?, 70, 70?, 71, 74?, 75, 80	13
Serious economic conflicts	25?, 44?, 48?, 65, 84?	5
Serious family or marital problems	43, 61F?	2
Misadventures in love or jealousy	20?, 30	2
Poverty	41, 51	2
Fear of legal prosecution	85	1
Severe melancholy	42	1
Great nervous stress	27	1
Unknown	24, 40, 42, 42, 45, 54, 62, 65, 77	9
		48

Female Vaqueiros

Motive for suicide	*Ages of individuals*	*Total*
Mental illness	22?, 28, 29, 30, 50, 54, 58, 69, DK	9
Serious family or marital problems	17?, 20, 23, 29, 40, 60	6
Serious physical illness	50, 54?, 58	3
Misadventures in love or jealousy	25, 27, 28	3
Serious economic conflicts	62, 63	2
Severe melancholy	45?, 62?	2
Fear of legal prosecution	41F	1
Unknown	17, 22, 22, 23, 24, 24, 59, 62	8
		34

Male Non-Vaqueiros

Motive for suicide	*Ages of individuals*	*Total*
Mental illness	30, 30, 31, 35, 35, 36, 40, 42, 43, 44, 49, 50, 51, 56, 61?, 63, DK, DK	18
Physical illness	14, 25, 28, 42?, 44, 77, 78, 80	8
Family problems	17, 21, 21?, 27, 31, 62, 66	7
Love or jealousy	34, 39, 39	3
Economic conflicts	58, 61, 64	3

(continued)

Table 2.1. *(continued)*

Motive for suicide	*Ages of individuals*	*Total*
Fear of legal prosecution	56, 57	2
Severe melancholy	16, DK	2
Poverty	49	1
Unknown	24, 28, 41, 75	4
		48

Female Non-Vaqueiros

Motive for suicide	*Ages of individuals*	*Total*
Mental illness	18, 31, 36, 38, 44, 46, 48, 50, 52, 52, 60, 63, 65, 87, 88	15
Physical illness	53, 62, 63, 77?, 78	5
Family or marital problems	39, 52, 59	3
Love or jealousy	22, 28	2
Poverty	35	1
Economic conflicts	40	1
Unknown	19	1
		28

Note: When age of person is not known for sure DK are used. The age followed by F means a failed suicide, and a ? indicates that the reasons for including the individual in the category were weak.

The Problem from the Inside

Unlike Soto Vázquez, who carried out his research from the outside, I shall approach the matter from the inside, from the point of view of the actors. Strictly speaking, the main protagonists are the suicides themselves, who are, obviously, inaccessible and inscrutable. Nevertheless, if culture as we understand it includes a collection of shared and transmitted meanings, then the meanings of death in general and suicide in particular are shared by the entire group of which the suicides form a part. Perhaps by analyzing the conditions in which this phenomenon occurs, or at least the reasons accepted for it in the popular perception, we can somehow understand the choice of this kind of death. This approach also avoids, as much as possible, imposing the categories, ethnocentric values, and moral considerations that frequently impede understanding of the matter.

The relevance of this *emic* perspective became evident to me on the occasion of a suicide whose entire process I was able to study, including visits by the magistrate or "the law" (*la justicia*), the wake, and the burial. The discrepancies between the local people's ideas and considerations on the one hand, and their official testimony on the other, seemed significant indeed. I not struck so much by the Vaqueiros' lying to the representatives of the law—for they did not, at least not consciously—as by the fact that the language, values, and categories they used to communicate among themselves differed from those they used with people from outside. The neighbors' comments confirmed my initial observation.

In general, spectacular suicides appear frequently in local descriptions, whereas less striking cases are forgotten or mentioned only briefly and seldom. The latter typically include those of women and bachelors, and those that occurred longest ago or farthest away. These cases come up spontaneously in conversations in the *braña*, often as illustrations of local theories on the matter. All interviewed persons easily recalled half a dozen instances of suicide, which they expanded to a dozen with a little insistence on my part. By this means I found out about 39 suicides—30 men and 9 women, of which 3 were failed attempts. Five of these took place outside the area (4 in Madrid and 1 in Buenos Aires), 2 took place in a nearby town where the suicides lived, and the rest happened in the sixteen *braña*s, the nearby vicinity, or the mountain pastures. In eleven *brañas* there had been more than 1 suicide, and for one *braña* 5 cases were cited.

As to the ways Vaqueiros end their lives—hanging, drowning, and falling from a height, in Soto Vázquez's account—my data confirmed that hanging is by far the most common method,[5] even though they use other methods away from home. Soto Vázquez's claim that Vaqueiro suicides want a quick, certain death was amply corroborated by the people of the *braña*.

However, my findings as to motives differ markedly different from those of Soto Vázquez. Methods are objective, confirmable facts, but motives are subjective estimations. This subjectivity seems more cultural than individual, for the Vaqueiros' personal opinions about a given case tend to be quite similar, although there are exceptions. There also appear to be certain biases, both theoretical and methodological, in the dossiers of the magistrates, who tend to favor the motive or motives that seem appropriate as reasons for suicide and to reject others, such as *aburrimiento*. Like everyone, the magistrates have preconceived ideas on the matter, and in gathering the generally brief testimony, they unconsciously provide cues for the witnesses, who invariably follow them. Furthermore, the suicides and their motives are, often forcibly, fitted into the categories of legal manuals, leading to facile simplifications when a combination of motives, any of which taken alone would not have led to suicide, is reduced to one category. Finally, the frequency of certain motives in the dossiers suggests that the magistrates make negative moral judgments concerning suicide; this partly explains the frequent use of the category of mental illness.

For the people of the *braña*, the magistrates represent "the law," *la justicia*, with which the best relation is no relation at all. The Vaqueiros' ignorance of the law leaves them relatively defenseless in dealings with magistrates. Vaqueiros fear coming up against "the law" because they think that sooner or later they will have to pay dearly ("the law will bring the house down"), there will be long-lasting legal complications, and most importantly, they will be punished for something. A magistrate's visit to a Vaqueiro house always arouses fear, suspicion, and anxiety. Their behavior manifests a combination of caution and a desire to ingratiate themselves with the outsiders by acting very respectful and polite. The formal testimony is taken in this context.

Therefore, Vaqueiros say they do not know why their relatives or neighbors committed suicide–which perhaps explains some of the unknown motives–or use labels or categories that do not compromise them, for example, insanity. They also systematically suppress motives like family disputes, which might morally (or legally) implicate Vaqueiro survivors. Moreover, they magnify or reduce motives at will, converting what was a "serious marital dispute" into a "minor argument," or, inversely, a quiet or taciturn personality into someone who "suffers from nerves" (the equivalent of mental illness). In casual conversations and among friends (especially those outside the family circle), these defenses are unnecessary, and the comments are quite different.

Prosecution of Justice

The suicides that are easiest to explain result from exceptional circumstances, such as the Spanish Civil War or commission of crimes punishable by the state. Of the few Vaqueiros who joined one of the two sides in the war, those on the losing side ended their lives at the end of the war to avoid reprisal. One case is reported to have occurred because of a supposed membership in a secret society, the Masons. A third man who had tried to kill one of his neighbors committed suicide to avoid his trial and probable imprisonment. These three cases have in common the fear of legal prosecution. It is generally agreed that death in the *braña* is preferable to life in jail, for a Vaqueiro feels impotent and defenseless before the law. Suicide is considered a reasonable expiation or corrective for a crime or a wrong decision. To justify these suicides, the Vaqueiros would simply say "There was a reason for it."

Cancer

Physical illness or infirmity is one of the few self-explanatory causes of suicide, and cancer is the prototype of such an illness. In such cases, suicide becomes "logical" even among persons who are sensible and normal. The disease itself weakens one's resistance and puts one in a frame of mind suggesting suicide. However, not just any illness is considered sufficient justification for suicide–not even cancer, if drugs can ward off the pain. Then again, in addition to their own pain, the terminally ill suffer from the trouble they cause their relatives.

Suicides due to illness are thus the ones most easily understood by the people of the *braña*, especially when there is no hope of cure or the sick person is very old. Yet the actual number of such suicides is quite low. As one person told me, "Yes, there are those who do it so as not to suffer, but very few, it seems to me." The hypothesis of illness is often considered, especially when speaking with outsiders, but in the cases I studied it appears as the reason for suicide in only four cases, two of which were unsuccessful. In the two successful attempts, the motive also seems to have been combined with a desire to avoid the medical expense of continued care. Interestingly, people often use the phrase "That is *aburrimiento*" to refer to such cases. Both people who failed in their attempts said they had thought they had cancer, apparently mistakenly. This suspicion is common because family members rarely inform a sick person of a diagnosis of cancer for fear of how they will react. These particular cases may also have involved mental instability.

Therefore, suicide is considered humanly reasonable in cases of chronic or painful illness in a society where the use of painkillers has traditionally been unknown. It may even be said that friends and relatives of the suicide not only consider this type of death rational, but also value it positively as a moral act. A household member's illness can mean the loss of household savings and accumulation of substantial debt, especially when treatment is long and costly. The possibility of suffering, combined with that of making others suffer, can thus be less tolerable than the idea of death.

The Household and the Inheritance System

According to Soto Vázquez, physical illness is the motive for the greatest number of suicides among male Vaqueiros (27 percent), whereas this motive is much rarer among women (8 percent). By contrast, he holds, marital or family disputes are a significant cause of female suicide (second only to mental illness) but a minor cause for men (18 percent for women, 4 percent for men). At first glance, these figures do seem to point to a significant difference between the sexes. If we compare Soto Vázquez's average ages for male Vaqueiros who end their lives because of illness and female Vaqueiros who do it for domestic reasons, we find that the former are more than twice as old as the latter.[6] Soto Vázquez found that these figures meant that suicides surged among Vaqueiro women aged 21–30 and that physical sickness motivates suicide for older Vaqueiro men.

My material, however, indicates that a motive I term "family and conjugal disputes" affects quite a large proportion of suicides. Of the 34 suicides for which some motive was reported to me, more than a third involved this motive explicitly, and it appeared implicitly for at least 5 others. Given that the homestead is the basic institution of work and living, the Vaqueiros regard many suicides as originating in the tensions and conflicts inherent in it. The household resolves certain problems, but it also creates others that, in extreme cases and with certain kinds of persons, result in this kind of death. Suicide can thus be a critical indicator of the negative aspects of the cultural and social system, illuminating its weak points and dark corners.

Suicides attributed to family disputes are most typical among those who are most defenseless within the household organization and occupy the weakest position according to the rules of inheritance. The smooth, "natural" death of the *amo* (householder), which offers the expectation of a transition in administrative control, differs greatly from the deaths of those who are not *amos*: the spouse, uncles, or "other old folks of the house."

Women in Vaqueiro Society

The *amo* may be male or female but is typically a man; thus the spouse is typically a woman. The first-born son or *mayorazo* normally inherits the house. A necessary condition is that he "marries in the house," often with the active involvement or at least the approval of his parents. A woman thus enters her new home by marriage. Although there is some kind of dowry, a daughter in law's position is relatively unprivileged. Mother-in-law and daughter-in-law do not mix (*cuecen mal*), it is said, and competition and confrontations are common. Some women remember the selective distribution of food in times of hunger, when the *amo*'s wife kept supplies locked up and the smallest portion went to the "newcomer" (*la nueva*). Even those who are treated well report the way their fathers-in-law say, "Eat what you want," as though it were a favor. In both cases the "newcomer" remembers her natal home with nostalgia. Even today young women say, "When you come from outside and you want to live in peace, you have to keep quiet a lot, eh? Keep quiet and work."

And they do work—a lot. Many young men leave the house to earn wages as laborers in the area (e.g., in pine plantations), leaving much of the work at the house and farm to their wives. The mother-in-law will at most take care of smaller domestic animals and light housework, while the young wife does the hardest work in the pastures and fields. This work limits the young couple's excursions to fairs and fiestas in the area, which they may attend only if the *amo* and his wife do not want to. On these occasions, they must ask the *amo* for permission to spend money, since they do not dispose of money of their own. All other necessities, including clothes, must be obtained in the same way.

This dependence and the tensions it generates can result in the young couple—either of their own accord or by the older couple's decision—abandoning the home and emigrating to the city with very little capital, even after having worked many years in the household. Such a decision is taken only in extreme circumstances. If the household is "good," that is, has enough land, the preferred son will try as much as possible to avoid clashing with his parents—even allying himself with them against his wife—since another brother could easily take his place. Life can thus be very hard for the newcomer.

On the other hand, if a newcomer is widowed while the old *amo* is still living, the control of the house will pass directly to her son on condition that she does not remarry. If she has no children, a brother of her husband may become the heir, and he may marry her if he is single and his parents get along well with her. But if there have been conflicts, the widow must return to the home of her parents and her own preferred brother. Such cases highlight the newcomer's precarious position, which lasts until the old *amo* dies or becomes physically disabled, whereupon the power passes to her husband—something that tends to coincide with the marriage of her son. Then she assumes the position of mother-in-law, often taking revenge on her young daughter-in-law. She loses all her power when her husband dies, since the power then passes to her son. If he does not maintain a fine equilibrium between his mother and his wife, then one of the two, frequently the mother, will suffer the consequences. Older women often worry that the newcomers "won't be good to them," and the lack of allies is often aggravated by these women's age. If life becomes intolerable, they do not have the alternative of going elsewhere, as young women or couples do.

The situation changes drastically if the preferred child is a daughter. The *ama* acquires many of the social characteristics of the male. Some of these women sell and buy cattle, take charge of the household—including the distribution of its money—and get their husbands to do work normally considered feminine. I knew one *ama* who said, when arguing with her husband: "You, since you brought nothing, will take nothing away. Take your jacket and go back over the mountain" (to his home *braña*). In such cases it is not only the *ama*'s husband who is at a disadvantage: so are her son and, especially, her daughter-in-law. A clash with a mother-in-law could mean the loss of a husband's inheritance in favor of one of his siblings. It is also difficult for an *ama* to accept that her own daughters have to leave the house so that an "outsider" can enter by marriage.

It is thus clear that within the household, certain kinds of persons are more susceptible to suicide. For the *amo*, the transmission of the property means not only security in old age, but also the guarantee of acceptable treatment, for he can choose the child he prefers as heir and control him or her by threatening to change the will. Lacking this weapon, the other inhabitants of the house are defenseless in conflicts. The "disinherited" persons usually include women, who very rarely become *ama*s. The age at which women are at highest risk of committing suicide, according to Soto Vázquez (i.e., 21–30), corresponds to the age when the newcomer is adjusting to her new house and to her difficult roles as a daughter-in-law, wife, and mother.

This adaptation marks a sharp change from the preceding period, "*la mocedad*" (from around age 14 to 20), usually remembered as the happiest time of life. A time of courtship and frequent dances and fairs, *la mocedad* is also a critical period of making a choice that determines one's entire future. A *mayorazo* from a good home with few relatives is a good match. Candidates must be weighed carefully, but if a girl waits too long, she runs the risk of remaining single or wasting her time. A Vaqueiro woman in her late twenties is in danger of becoming an old maid (*moza vieja*) and becomes less choosy. Marriage means the end of diversions and the beginning of hard work, many obligations and few rights. I heard many mature women lament their choice of mates and conflicts with mother- and sisters-in-law in the new house and vividly remember their sorrow at leaving home. Even after many years of residence in the new house, they use "my house" to refer to the house in which they were born, in contrast to "this house."

The high suicide rate among women in their twenties must be understood in this context. Significantly, however, examples of this type were lacking among the local cases of suicide spontaneously brought up in conversation, even though the hardship and "life problems" at this age are spoken of. I think there are two reasons for this avoidance. The first is that such suicides are most intolerable in the local perception because they involve the disappearance of young people "in their prime of life" for reasons that all Vaqueiros feel somewhat guilty about. By the same token, suicides of older people are less morally unjust and more talked about. In a couple of cases, suicides of young women were ascribed to "nerves," even though it was recognized that there also had been conflicts in the house. It seems that many women of this age have something wrong with "the nerves." Once this condition is diagnosed, the other household members' behavior toward the newcomer tends to improve.

A second reason why female suicides were not brought up in conversation is women's lack of salience in the culture. According to Soto Vázquez, Vaqueiro women commit suicide almost as much as men (49 cases compared to 62). But of the suicides mentioned to me, only 9 women were cited, compared to 30 men. Women's suicides seem to be less noteworthy than the suicides of *amos*, probably because of the women's low status. In this respect women, especially childless women, resemble the bachelor uncle or any other "old people of the house." The contrast between women and *amos* is reproduced in the greater or lesser publicity and attendance of the respective funerals and post-mortem rituals. In the legal sense, all women who are not *amas* are "nobodies" in the house, at least until they have children, and even then their rights depend on their sons.

Old Uncles

Even less enviable is the situation of uncles and other "old people of the house," a term that includes very different kinds of people. Most of them are siblings of the *amo*, for example, a widow who had to go back to her natal house because she did not get along with her in-laws. Upon the death of their parents, these women become unpaid servants to their preferred sibling and his (or her) spouse. There may also be other siblings who have not left the household, hoping against hope that the inheritance may be changed in their favor, and others who, although once preferred, waited too long to marry and lost their chance to a sibling who married in the house. A brother of a preferred son will have difficulty marrying and remaining in the area, unless he marries a preferred daughter or someone takes on the new couple as heirs (*heredeiros*), which is relatively infrequent. Apart from such cases, those not preferred must use their small portion of the inheritance to emigrate with their spouses. If such siblings do not marry they may remain in the house, but only if they renounce their inheritance in favor of the preferred sibling.

While they are young, these aunts and uncles of the house may work outside it, and if the situation is tense, they may decide to leave. But as they get older, they have fewer alternatives. The old uncles often did the most disagreeable tasks and had no say in family decisions. Sometimes they even ate separately from the rest of the family. Their position in the house was identical to that of servants, who cannot return to their parents' house and in old age lose their wages in exchange for terminal care. As part of the household, they become the butt of the youngest members' remarks and practical jokes. The more benign *amo*s and *ama*s tell children that aged servants merit respect "because of all that they have done for the house."

Given these structural tensions caused by the inheritance system, some suicides take on a new meaning. The Vaqueiros themselves are aware of the frequency of disputes between mothers-in-law and daughters-in-law, the weak position of old people in the house, and the ways these situations relate to the decision to commit suicide. Of suicides reported to me, four were motivated by conflicts between mother-in-law and daughter-in-law, mother and son, or even father-in-law and son-in-law. In no case did the suicide own the house, and this was explicitly stated.

The suicides of "old people of the house" do not spark much commentary, just as their "natural" deaths cause little mourning and few attend their funerals. It might be said that these people's disappearance is ignored because of the slight social significance attached to "dead branches" of the family tree. Their weak position in the house is matched by their almost anonymous deaths. Some suicides among the Vaqueiros are likely of this kind, but I do not include them because of lack of information. I do have considerable information about the following case, though, because it happened during my time in the field.

Carlos[7] was a non-preferred son who joined the house of a widow with several young children as a servant when he was twenty-five or thirty. He helped raise the children and cohabited with the *ama*, and over time he came to be considered a family member. After about forty years, the widow went with her children to the city to have an operation. After the operation, not only did she not return to the *braña*, but she appeared to have no intention of doing so. Carlos took charge of all of the work in the house with the help of a young, mentally retarded servant. All this time he anxiously awaited the return of the *ama* and her children, since he was used to obeying and disliked the responsibility of buying and selling cattle, killing pigs, and so on, especially because, it was said, he was illiterate. When a relative of the widow in the *braña* called him an idiot, he replied: "Yes, you say I am an idiot, and you still give me all the work to do." He also complained that he was "nobody" in the house. It was rumored that the house would be closed and he would end his days in a rest home. The night before his suicide, Carlos said things like, "Tonight I will go to bed, but tomorrow . . ." and "Let's go to bed, there won't be another day . . ." He made his preparations, locking the room where he kept his small savings, feeding the animals, and even leaving ready the corn flour they would need the next day. Then he sent the young servant to work with some neighbors so he would not discover the body. He hanged himself in the stable near the house, with a rope and several knots.[8]

When the magistrate and the civil guard came, the widow's relatives received them and busied themselves, along with neighbors, getting the body down and testifying. People declared that the deceased had no problems, was normal, had a disease of the urinary tract, and that "they don't know why he hung himself." Once the authorities had left, the funeral, like any other, took its normal course.

Immediately afterward, rumors began to circulate. In private, the alleged illness was not considered a reason for suicide, since the deceased had gone to a specialist who merely said that his urine "was dirty," and that it wasn't serious. The family of the *ama* repeated insistently that there were ample provisions in the house for his use.[9] To support their words they opened the pantry: "Look, he had everything; soup, coffee; he was the boss; four hams, one open." A neighbor spoke up, "He said, 'I didn't even touch it. The *ama* might need it when she comes back.' He didn't want to cut into it." Obviously these affirmations and their emphasis were an attempt to head off possible accusations of lack of care—attempts that the neighbors' comments, some milder, some quite severe, brought out.

Amos

Persons with no inheritance are not the only ones affected by the tensions of the Vaqueiro household. *Amo*s too have ended their lives because of conflict or neglect. One man who lived in discord with his wife and daughters took care, before he died, to pass the inheritance to a young son. Besides trouble with family, loneliness is another explanation for suicides. The suicide of an old widowed *amo* whose children have all emigrated is commonly, according to local opinion, due to loneliness. Some men also find their role as *amo* too much to bear. They are responsible for the prosperity and perpetuation of the household, and a serious economic blunder or error in foresight can leave the house without a successor, leading to great remorse and personal anguish. Failing to ensure the household's prosperity or perpetuate the succession implies mistakes on the part of the *amo* for not knowing how to run the house, or not having exercised enough authority. Both tasks demand an assertive personality, at times even toughness and aggressiveness, given the difficulties of the Vaqueiro environment and the conflictual social organization of the household and the *braña*. The need to defend one's interests within the family extends to the *braña*, where some households take advantage of the others' weakness to expand their territory (at times in the crudest ways, by moving boundary markers or appropriating disputed fields). The role of the *amo*, with its implicit responsibility, is the opposite of that of the bachelor uncle who has to work and obey. Some people are not at ease in their respective positions, and for some of them, suicide is a way out.

Some suicides of *amo*s are due to debts. Today the poorest houses of the region have been depopulated by the emigration of their members or because their *amo*s were unable to marry or find *heredeiro*s, even though Vaqueiros are considered to live in relative prosperity. The remaining households supposedly can afford to raise a family by local standards, but they are still vulnerable to occasional crises caused by natural disasters (a bad harvest, the death of one or more animals, etc.), social obligations (e.g., a succession of weddings or funerals), or other unusual circumstances (e.g., litigation over inheritance or the purchase of land). Such crises result in debts that are paid off slowly, with much effort. The work of the house requires good administration and great patience, so it is no surprise that ambitious or impatient Vaqueiros seek to repay their debts by other means, faster but less secure (e.g., by becoming cattle dealers) and end in trouble. Three of the suicides in my study were of this type. Economically prompted suicide of this kind is almost exclusively a masculine phenomenon, since men are usually in charge of the household economies. The suicides and their local descriptions warn *amos* not to run risks. The Vaqueiros also stigmatize untoward interest in becoming rich at the expense of others.

Two of the cases in my field work also serve to caution against marrying in old age or at disparate ages. Vaqueiros attribute certain problems to such unequal marriages, jealousy, and infidelity, but suicides for such reasons are, in my opinion, not common. These cases were referred to me with a certain perplexity, since one involved a single mother (single mothers are not socially stigmatized in the area) and another passionate behavior and crime, something very uncommon.

Suicides from motives related to the household have a strong moral content among the Vaqueiros. When describing the particular family circumstances surrounding a suicide, the *vox populi* emphasizes failures in human communication, selfishness, and the pettiness of daily interactions. A motive related to family or marital disputes reveals the conflicts and inequalities inherent in the inheritance system and its consequent distribution of roles in the household. Instead of a direct accusation or an open denunciation, Vaqueiros prefer a vague rumor, an implicit suggestion that permits them to continue living side by side with the survivors, that is, "living with the living" (*vivir con los vivos*). The suicide is sufficient to punish those who survive. In such cases, partial responsibility for the suicide is attributed to the surviving members of the household, but in a way so subtle and diffuse that, though serving to morally sanction and warn the guilty, it does not threaten their daily relations with the community. Given that all houses are organized in the same way, these diffuse accusations stand as negative models and as collective recognition of the guilt in which nearly all Vaqueiros share.

Mental Illness

In the local etiology, the mentally ill are usually said to "suffer from nerves." Some illnesses of nerves are considered permanent, and people with such permanent conditions are said to be "incomplete," crazy or crazed (*alocadas*), and "wrong in the head": "If someone is suffering some from nerves he'll hang himself for no reason at all." The association between the sickness of nerves and suicide is predictable. People who are sick in this way, whether permanently or temporarily, are more likely to suffer "a spell of craziness," "a *mania,*" "a bad hour," or a seizure (*remate*), which can lead to self-destruction. The nerves drive such people to end their lives when faced with difficulties that ordinarily would not provoke suicide, such as curable or painless disease, or a minor family problem or argument. In other words "the nerves" explain doubtful cases of suicide. Clear and diagnosed insanity is recognized as such. Meanwhile, suicides of the mentally retarded (2 cases) require no explanation at all, as these persons' behavior is always considered unpredictable.

Remarkably, in the case of mental illness the suicide is not considered to be responsible for his or her action. The same is true in cases of permanent and diagnosed craziness, particularly if the suicide has been a mental patient. There also is no implication of responsibility for suicides committed by the mentally retarded. Both types of individual are seen living outside the normal rules of reasoning, so any incident may lead them to kill themselves. It is thought that certain imagined physiological causes—violent blood and the bursting of the nerves in the head—can initiate the process of self-destruction, if others do not avoid flare-ups and arguments. Soto Vázquez found that suicides of this kind are common, but only four cases in my material can be thus classed. One might suggest that suicide does not pose a moral problem for the mentally ill or retarded: someone who is not responsible for his or her own actions cannot be blamed for the act of committing suicide (for such an analysis, see also the Introduction and chapter 3 in this collection).

Cultural Inheritance and Destiny

Another common explanation for suicide—"the inheritance"—applies when a suicide comes from a family that has had other suicides. At first glance, the inherited factor appears to be a biological trait, and some suicides are explained by this means. But other cases explained with reference to inheritance involve no genetic kinship but only affinity or membership in the same house; thus the logic can pass from biological to cultural inheritance. Likeliness to end one's life is thus a trait transmitted within the house, a kind of destiny or family fate, and as such it becomes comparable to a skill like singing or dancing, or other qualities or defects such as devoutness, studiousness, or thievery. That is why the people in the *braña* become preoccupied with family members of a suicide who show symptoms of wanting to die in the same way. This sense of imitation affects the entire Vaqueiro group. The suicide of one of its members makes people "pessimistic," and the social inheritance can affect everyone.

> People say: "What a shame, *hombre*, what a bad hour God gave him." When someone hangs himself it makes you pessimistic. You start to think, "But what really happened?" Given that you knew him, that he was a normal person, and not unstable. And someone says to you, "I'm going to end by hanging myself, eh?"—they might say it to you a long time before, years before. And you take it as a joke and then . . . (Field notes, Cátedra)

Thus the factor of inheritance implies a shift in scrutiny, from individual motives and social situations to the history of the house and its members. Vaqueiros intuitively relate personal disorders with the diachronic process of the family system, set in the confines of the house. Family precedents or repeated suicides in the same house, even the same *braña*, rather starkly affirm the eternal truth that we are all products of the past or, in local terms, "there are things that go beyond persons."

For the Vaqueiros, suicide can also be interpreted as a form of divine punishment for injustice, one of the ways God chastises not only the persons who commit sins, but also their descendents. The "fear" of God and the observance of his rules may prevent the sufferings that lead to suicide. In the final analysis, everything comes from God, including the kind of death one has, but people arouse God's wrath or benevolence with their behavior. In this way, then, the law of God is the law of humans, with whom one must live, avoiding hatred and confrontations as much as possible. This moral aspect of suicide serves as a corrective of the exploitation and bad treatment that might drive others to end their lives.

Indeed, inheritance seems to have certain deterministic aspects that turn it into destiny, which in the *braña* is held to be directed by God. Suicide is thus a moral expiation, a settling of accounts with the heavenly court, be they one's own debts or those of the prior members of the house. The household thereby seems to transmit not only certain material objects but also these old faults, which can only partly be redeemed by obeying God's commandments. For the person who commits suicide, the loss of life in itself is the punishment, and further expiation in the "other world" is not expected. After death, the only significantly different treatment of suicide consists in certain acts by the civil and religious authorities that the Vaqueiro consider to be efforts to discourage others from doing the same thing. Here is how the Vaqueiros describe these differences:

> And you know that they can't put those who commit suicide in the church either. That's right; the persons who commit suicide, hang themselves, or shoot themselves or things like that, they aren't put in the church. You know that they take dead bodies to the church. Well I went to the burial, and they didn't put it in the church. He hanged himself in a cherry tree there by the house. They say that such persons find themselves *arrepentidos*.
>
> With them it's different. Sometimes they have to go to the cemetery and so autopsy, and open their heads. I've never seen that and I hope to God I never do, because it's bad to see it, but they have to lift up the lid on the brains. (Field notes, Cátedra)

Finally, for a few suicides the people of the *braña* can find no explanation because they took place long ago or far away, or because of the discretion of the suicides themselves. ("Sometimes they find themselves *aburríos* for something they don't tell anyone about, and decide to do it.") This latter type is exemplified by a case in which people examine different hypotheses but still cannot say why the suicide occurred. In these cases blame is subtly and implicitly laid partly on the community, not just on the mysterious nature of human life. In the face of death, life prevails. One has fulfilled one's obligations to the dead, but the difficult task of living with the living remains. Some of my informants understood exactly why I was interested in this matter, and eloquently expressed their difficulty in answering:

> But look. Suicide has always existed and will keep on happening. You're hitting your head against a wall. What you want to find out is how the brain works, why they do it, how does the person who hangs know, what the brain of these people is like. Even when it happens in the village, and

> we know it; because we have to live with those who remain; we already did what we could for the one who left. (Field notes, Cátedra)

Aburrimiento

The Vaqueiros also explain some suicides in terms of *aburrimiento* (weariness). These cases include all those that lead Vaqueiros to end their lives: *braña* denizens *se aburren*, get bored, because of sickness, because they cannot defend themselves, when they see "the bad things in the houses" or "everything going wrong," because people "pick on them" in the house when they are old, because of the "problems of life" when they are young, and because of loneliness, poverty, debts, and even "the nerves." All of these negative aspects of Vaqueiro life produce, individually or in combination, a state of mind that begins with the "loss of *gracia*" (Cátedra 1989)—disinterest in life—and culminates with an abhorrence of life.

> That's it—they see that they are *aburríos* of life. No, they're not wrong in the head, no, I think they see that they are *aburríos, aburríos.*
>
> They see that they are *aburríos* of life. They see they are *aburridos* and so they say, "so, I'll do this to end and it." *Ay Dios!* They have to be in a bad way, a bad way in order to do it. (Field notes, Cátedra)

Life is *gracia*, interest in things, activity, and struggle; *aburrimiento* means being tired and irked, and loathing life. It is associated with the state of *arrepentimiento*, which in local parlance means an express renunciation of living. The Vaqueiro *arrepentido* finds no other solution but death.

> No, the one who does it is considerably *arrepentío. Arrepentío* is when one is worn out, *aburrío,* when one is not able to go out to another town, or do anything else, when one thinks about it, when one is oppressed by the idea of it, when it seems that it is the best solution, when one finds oneself forced to do it . . .
>
> When that happens it'll be because they are *arrepentíos*, they don't have another solution, and they find themselves alone, and they *se aburren* and they come to that. *Hombre*, I feel they don't have any other choice because in order for them to hang themselves they have to be really *arrepentíos.* (Field notes, Cátedra)

Just as *gracia* resumes what life is worth living for, *aburrimiento* resumes the contrary: the circumstances under which death is preferable. *Aburrimiento* is evidence of stress, conflicts, and inequalities due to the inheritance system. Violence seems somehow inevitable; the family system here, as elsewhere, is always arbitrary: it solves some problems while creating others. If the loss of grace follows a gradual and natural process of disinterest and disillusionment with life, *aburrimiento* implies that this process is hastened. Although physically alive, the *arrepentidos*, once they have lost *gracia*, can be considered socially and cognitively dead. Living, in certain circumstances, makes no sense. Death is a flight from pain and human suffering.

> Well, they are people who are cowards, who *se arrepienten*, who give up. Seeing myself in this situation. . . . Because you have to have *valor* for that . . . you have to be *arrepentío*. I don't know what they think. They think, "Perhaps if I end my life, I'll end my suffering, I won't suffer anymore." Leaving is a way of getting out of the way. (Field notes, Cátedra)

The Afterworld

Abburrimiento is one dimension of the Vaqueiros' cultural ways of understanding death. In general, they believe death begins before dying–rather early for some people, as in the case of *aburrimiento*, and later for others. Pain, age, sickness, and suffering all constitute the long, liminal glide from life to death. The route from life to death is protracted, the cultural process of death complex, the borderline between life and death vague. Vaquieros see death as a broader process than what is traditionally conceived, and they celebrate it with several rituals. Before death, the spirit of a person who is approaching death can give a premonition to close ones. Similarly, after death, the spirits of the deceased continue to participate and interfere in the world of the living. Vaquieros say that with their premonition, the spirits represent the dose of death included in life. They can be consulted in difficult cases, but sometimes they themselves need help. Communication between the worlds is not restricted to humans: animals such as cattle, dogs, and foxes are present in these processes and in the otherworld. For more detailed communication with the spirits, the Vaquieros require the assistance of a diviner. Ancestral spirits can give information on accidents or bad luck, and in this way they inhabit a world that is not really "after" but "here," or somewhere in between, as the local way of understanding does not make use of binary categories. Interestingly, the Vaquieros distinguish between the spirit as a bodily being and the "soul," *alma*, which has a more spiritual meaning. *Alma* corresponds approximately to the immortal soul of Catholicism. Here Catholicism plays quite a powerful syncretistic role, and is translated into vernacular purposes. The Vaquieros also turn to the protection of various saints. The otherworld, crowded with spirits, ancestors, animals, and saints, is as lively as this world.

Dying and becoming dead is a thick cultural process that involves an apprenticeship—a long period of domestication in which a new order of existence is learned. Such beliefs acquire meaning from the particular context in which they emerge. For anthropologists, research on suicide is a useful way of getting at the social structure of a human group, and the same applies to my study on the Vaqueiros. However, instead of asking about death to define and demarcate social groups, as is often the case in anthropological research, my emphasis is on the cultural aspect of the process: the ideas, beliefs, and attitudes about death and suicide. My approach enables understanding of contents and forms, as well as the special way Vaquieros comprehend death by suicide as the least "natural" and most "cultural" way of death. From this point of view, suicide is not a strange, aberrant, unnatural act but rather a decision that any Vaquiero might come to in certain circumstances, as the end result of a coherent process.

CONCLUDING REMARKS: SUICIDE AMONG THE VAQUEIROS

Scrutiny of the motives that lead to Vaqueiros' suicides reveals the presence of conflict in their society as well as their system of values about life and death—when and why it is worth living, and when and why it is worth ending one's life. I would like to point out that the group regards many suicides as normal, and many who commit suicide suicides are not thought sick in any way. What is more, suicide, although it may be considered a mistake, is not seen as a sin or a crime, and under certain circumstances anyone may do it.

> Suicide is something that gets into the head from thinking wrong. I'm not sure dear, what I would do, I'm not sure. It is a mistake, of course, it has to be a mistake.
>
> It seems to me to be something done backwards. That you should die when God wants it, and not before. Of course, when they're in pain, I don't know, since it never happened to me. (Field notes, Cátedra)

Elsewhere I have shown that death is no simple and obvious fact (Cátedra 1992) but must be studied in connection with pain, age, and suffering to enable a coherent understanding of the death process. Consideration of the local comprehensive worldview or cosmology is equally important. A complex, society-specific mass of beliefs, emotions, and activities adds to the organic event. Sickness and suicide are as integral to the process of death as mortuary ritual and the conditions of afterlife.

Death and suicide cannot be separated from their social context. In Vaqueiro society they mostly concern the household, but certain deaths have greater social significance than others. This is especially true for the old *amo*s, whose deaths mean a relay of generations, the transmission of property, and a periodic crisis crucial to the survival of an institution and the human beings that people it. The permanence of the house requires that the old *amo* be considered the usufructuary, one link in a chain of immortality. The ideology of the house affects the different personalities of its inhabitants, whether of the father, who should be in charge, or of the other members, who must obey in silence. The natural death of the old *amo*, attended by a well-chosen heir with a family, is evidence of success in terms, a guarantee of continuity.

Studying natural death without considering suicide, or vice versa, would be partial and insufficient. The two kinds of death provide different perspectives, the positive and negative poles of the institution of the household. Yet frequently one or another way of dying is examined in isolation, so that the community studied seems excessively dark and negative, permeated by violence and aggression, or unnaturally idyllic and happy, bound by solidarity and mutual aid. One wants to ask, "Does everybody die this way?"

Suicide is a hard topic, not only because of the fact itself but because it is multifaceted and eludes a simple or common explanation. From my perspective, focusing on the relevance of culture, the lines of thought presented below are crucial.

First, anthropology can help to overcome many myths, commonplaces, and theories of Western origin. As mentioned, Western scholars tend to impose Western categories, such as those of psychiatry, on other cultures (Colucci 2006). In the case of the Vaqueiros, outside research overtly stresses motives of supposed "mental illness," to which the Vaqueiros themselves seldom refer. From the inside cultural perspective, the most important explanations factors appeal to "family and marital problems," social exclusion, honor or social respect, and finally, an idea unique to the Vaqueiros, *aburrimiento*: the loss of the taste for life and the drive to improve one's own situation. The meaning of death in relation to the otherworld is key to understanding the liminal glide across the border of life and death and the processes by which people take suicide to be the most "cultural death". The effects of imposing Western values and theories on other cultures are observable in other contexts, for instance, the case of suicide among Native Americans. Some argue that their suicides are due to cultural conflict stemming from one of three factors: social disorganization, culture clash with the wider society, or breakdown of the family due to the culture clash. By contrast, recent research has shown that Native Americans themselves refer to sorrow over the loss of a loved one and fights with relatives and friends, and that intercultural conflict is entirely insignificant in their explanations (Lester 2004).

Next, I turn to three questions posed by Kral (1998). First, how deeply embedded is suicide in the cultural system of ideas? In other words, how do cultural messages "get under people's skin" (Strauss 1992: 1)? Here Kral asks how suicide is internalized and incorporated (as values or patterns of culture) through culture, that is, how it is extended and adopted. We are largely unaware of our schemes of knowledge about the world and ourselves. An implicit memory makes up the core of who we are: attitudes, values, beliefs, and behavior. The manner in which we die is no exception. Research should examine not only suicidal individuals but also the people who surround them, as well as well as their more comprehensive views of life and death. The meaning a bigger community attaches to something, for instance, "escape" in Western society, can affect the understanding of suicide. Second, Kral asks, who is more prone to internalize the idea of suicide, and under what personal and cultural conditions? The great myth of suicidology, namely where suicide "comes from," is perhaps not a pertinent problem—at least, not when answered in a unidimensional (biological or social) way with identified risks (e.g., problematic serotonin levels, anomia and the idea that the ultimate origin of suicide is in the person.

In sum, is it time to start asking different questions in suicidology? According to Kral, the time is ripe to seriously consider Corin's (1996) call for the use of an anthropological imagination in suicidology. It is crucial to examine cultural narratives of suicide (Honkasalo and Utriainen 1993, 1996) and their impact on individuals and groups. The proposed logic and method are highly "local" and strongly concerned with the context. As Kral (1998: 221) put it, suicide, like everything else that is complexly human, takes place in a powerful social context. Since suicide has different meanings for different cultures (Farberow 1975; La Fontaine 1975; Macdonald 2003), it would be erroneous to assume that "a suicide is a suicide" when making cross-cultural comparisons (Shneidman 1985). Meaning cannot be separated from the context of human lives, and moral attitudes, often relevant to even the epidemiology of suicide, might differentiate diverse motivations for suicide. Meaning precedes ideation and action (Boldt 1988: 95), so individuals who commit suicide do so with reference to specific cultural-normative values and attitudes. As Colucci argues (2006), to understand suicide, we need to know what it means for the person *and* for the culture.

NOTES

1. This does not apply in all cases. According to Lönnqvist (2009: 793), Finland had a high rate of suicide as well, but the trend has changed. In 1990 the rate was one of the highest, around 30 per 100,000 per year, but by 2005 it had plummeted to 18 per 100,000 per year. According to the World Health Organization, the highest rates in 2008 were in Belarus (35.1) and Lithuania (30.7). In 2009, Lithuanian suicide rates rose to 61.3 for men and to 10.4 for women.
2. "When some 'ronin' of Japan or some Asian Buddhists perform actions which lead to what American or European doctors classify as death, we must recognize that this is a classification by Western doctors, not by the actors involved. Their linguistic expressions for such actions may be totally different from the ones Western observers use and certainly might mean totally different things to the actors and the significant observers of these actions within their own cultures. Anthropologists and sociologists have decided that one cannot very well understand the kinship system of other peoples except in terms of their own language. How, then, can one conceivably understand something so immensely more complex as 'death' in any terms other those of the actors involved? And, though the differences in meaning might not be as great within one general cultural tradition, still, does it not seem plausible to expect that there are some systematic differences of meaning involved in the uses of the term 'death' between one nation and another or between one subculture and another? It is certainly my contention here that this is the case and that no great advantages can be made in the study of suicide until the researchers determine what these differences in the meaning of death are and how they influence the actions of individuals" (Douglas 1973: 182).
3. For a collection of ethnographic analyses of suicide, see Staples and Widger 2012. On the cultural aspect of suicide, see Maurice Halbwachs, *Les Causes du Suicide* (1930).
4. I think that at that time, Vaqueiros in the area numbered little or no more than 7,000 individuals. Other authors have advanced figures similar to Soto Vazquez's first estimate, e.g., 6,448 Vaqueiros in the census of 1970. Using these figures, the suicide rates double.
5. In the reports I gathered on suicides, 27 were by hanging, 2 by drowning, and 2 by poisoning. Drowning (in a river or the sea) is likely to be fatal because there are no good swimmers in the *brañas*. The two cases of poisoning were atypical and often were cited for this very reason. But, as mentioned, hanging has become synonymous with suicide. The immediate cause–the rope or the cord, frequently in its affectionate diminutive, *el cordelín*–is used to refer to this kind of death ("take to the cord," "catch the *cordelín*," equivalent to the English "stringing oneself up"). The remaining cases, except for two in which I did not learn the method, were by gunshot (3), knife or razor (1, failed), and falling (2).
6. The difference is similar to that between the sexes of suicides for unknown motives.

7. The name has been changed.
8. For such careful preparations with great concern for other people, see Macdonald's *Typus melancholicus* in this collection.
9. "But the house was full of food, how could he have done that? He did what he wanted to, he was the *amo* of all this; nobody told him what he had to eat."

REFERENCES

Bertolote, José. M. and Alexandra Fleischmann. 2009. "A Global Perspective on the Magnitude of Suicide Mortality." In *Oxford Textbook of Suicidology and Suicide Prevention: A Global Perspective*, ed. Danuta Wasserman and Camilla Wasserman. New York: Oxford University Press, pp. 91–98.

Bille-Brahe, Unni. 2000. "Sociology and Suicidal Behaviour." In *The International Handbook of Suicide and Attempted Suicide*, ed. Keith Hawton and Kees Van Heeringen. Chichester: Wiley, pp. 193–207.

Boldt, Menno. 1988. "The Meaning of Suicide: Implications of Research." *Crisis* 9: 93–108.

Cátedra, María. 1989. "La gracia y la desgracia." In Homenaje Andaluz and Julian Pitt-Rivers. *El folklore andaluz* nº 3, 2ª época, pp. 69–78.

——. 1992. *This World, Other Worlds: Sickness, Suicide, Death and Afterlife among the Vaqueiros de Alzada of Spain.* Chicago: The University of Chicago Press.

Colucci, Erminia. 2006. "The Cultural Facet of Suicidal Behavior: Its Importance and Neglect." *Australian e-Journal for the Advancement of Mental Health* 5 (3): 1–13.

Corin, Ellen. 1996. "From a Cultural Stance: Suicide and Aging in a Changing World." In *Suicide and Aging: International Perspectives*, ed. Jane L. Pearson and Yeates Conwell. New York: Springer, pp. 205–224.

Desjarlais, Robert, Leon Eisenberg, Byron Good, and Arthur Kleinman, eds. 1995. *World Mental Health: Problems and Priorities in Low-Income Countries.* New York and Oxford: Oxford University Press.

Douglas, Jack. 1973. *The Social Meanings of Suicide.* Princeton, NJ: Princeton University Press. Durkheim, Emile. 1897. *Le suicide.* Paris: Alcan.

Farberow, Norman L. 1975. *Suicide in Different Cultures.* Baltimore: University Park Press.

Halbwachs, Maurice. 1930. *Les Causes du suicide.* Paris: Alcan.

Hjelmeland, Heidi, E. Kinyanda, B. L. Knizek, V. Owens, H. Nordvik, and K. Svarva. 2006. "A Discussion of the Value of Cross-Cultural Studies in Search of the Meaning(s) of Suicidal Behavior and the Methological Challenges of Such Studies." *Archives of Suicide Research* 10: 15–27.

Honkasalo, Marja-Liisa and Terhi Utriainen. 1993. "Boundaries in Finnish Women's Suicide Notes." *Acta Semiotica Fennica* 2: 229–342.

——. 1996. "Women Writing Their Death and Dying." *Semiotica* 109: 195–220.

Kral, Michael J. 1998. "Suicide and the Internalization of Culture: Three Questions." *Transcultural Psychiatry* 35 (2): 221–233.

La Fontaine, Jean. 1975. "Anthropology." In *A Handbook for the Study of Suicide*, ed. S. Perlin. New York and London: Oxford University Press.

——. 2012. "Explaining Suicide: An Afterword." *Culture, Medicine, Psychiatry* 36 (Special Issue, "Ethnographies of Suicide"): 409–418.

Lester, David. 1997. *Suicide in American Indians*. Commack, NY: Nova Science.

——. 2004. *Thinking about Suicide*. Hauppauge, NY: Nova Science.

——. 2006. "Suicide among Indigenous Peoples: A Cross-Cultural Perspective." *Archives of Suicide Research* 10 (2): 117–24.

Lönnqvist, Jouko. 2009. "Suicide Prevention in Finland." In *Oxford Textbook of Suicidology and Suicide Prevention: A Global Perspective*, ed. D. Wasserman and C. Wasserman. Oxford: Oxford University Press, pp. 793–795.

Macdonald, Charles J.-H. 2003. "Urug: An Anthropological Investigation on Suicide in Palawan, Philipppines." *Southeast Asian Studies* 40 (4): 419–443.

Maris, Ronald. W. 1981. *Pathways to Suicide*. Baltimore: Johns Hopkins University Press.

Moksony, Ferenc. 1990. "Ecological Analysis of Suicide." In *Understanding suicide*, ed. David Lester. Philadelphia: Charles Press, pp. 121–138.

Shneidman, Edwin. S. 1985. *Definition of Suicide*. London: Jason Aronson.

Soto Vázquez, R. 1965. "El suicidio entre los Vaqueiros de Alzada asturianos." *Boletín del IDEA* 54: 167–182 and 55: 69–88.

Stack, S. 2000. "Suicide: A 15-Year Review of the Sociological Literature." *Suicide and Life-Threatening Behavior* 30 (2): 163–176.

Staples, James and Thomas Widger. 2012. "Situating Suicide as an Anthropological Problem: Ethnographic Approaches to Understanding Self-Harm and Self-Inflicted Death." *Culture, Medicine, Psychiatry* 36 (Special Issue, "Ethnographies of Suicide"): 183–203.

Strauss, Claudia 1992. "Motives and Models." In *Human Motives and Cultural Models*, ed. Roy D'Andrade and Claudia Strauss. New York: Cambridge University Press, pp. 1–22.

Taylor, S. 1990. "Suicide, Durkheim and Sociology." In *Understanding Suicide*, ed. David Lester. Philadelphia: Charles Press, pp. 225–236.

Part II

Ancient and Medieval Approaches to Suicide

Chapter 3

"Tell Him to Follow Me as Quickly as Possible"

Plato's *Phaedo* (60c–63c) on Taking One's Own Life

Miira Tuominen

INTRODUCTION

In this essay, I shall scrutinize Plato's *Phaedo* (60c–63c) and its relevance to the conundrum of suicide—not only because the dialogue is one of the few instances in which Plato explicitly considers whether taking one's own life is permissible or justified, but also because it urgently poses the question of the demarcation of the very phenomenon of suicide. Socrates clearly decided[1] to die—he argues at length for compliance with his death sentence in the *Crito*, and the *Phaedo* strengthens the conclusion. He was also causally responsible for his death (he drank the hemlock himself) and seems to have been firmly convinced that this act (drinking the hemlock) would bring about his death. In antiquity, this was a standard manner of execution; thus Socrates' decision, not the drinking of hemlock, is the central factor. The very fact of his decision seems to satisfy the criteria often laid out for self-killing (for these criteria, see, e.g., Cholbi 2009: section 1).

Even though some have argued that Socrates in fact did commit suicide (Frey 1978), many find this conclusion counterintuitive. One reason not to take Socrates' death as a suicide is that it was honorable, noble, or morally praiseworthy, and suicide is not understood in these terms (Cholbi 2009:

section 1). This seems problematic, however. The resort to normative considerations when answering the demarcation problem raises a whole range of questions, for example, about motivation, that make the demarcation problem even more elusive than it already is.[2] To define suicide as a wrongful self-killing would, by definition, rule out justified suicides, and another concept would be needed to discuss the question of whether one can ever justifiably take his or her life.

A somewhat more promising argument against Socrates' death as a suicide is that he acted under compulsion.[3] Even though he was not *physically* coerced, at least not directly, he was, after all, sentenced to death. R. G. Frey in fact argues (1978: 106) that exactly because Socrates was not physically coerced and he drank the hemlock willingly, he committed suicide. This does not seem a very strong argument, however. By contrast, one could argue that Socrates' decision not to try to escape from prison and to willingly put his death sentence into action merely indicates that he accepted an inevitable necessity, and thus did not take his life. But does this mean that Socrates was not the ultimate agent of his own death but merely followed external necessity? This conclusion is clearly quite the opposite of what the bulk of the *Phaedo* tells us: Socrates not only firmly decided to die, but he argued for it solely on the basis of what he found good and seemed entirely free in his decision—which brings us back to the claim that Socrates took his life.

In what follows, I shall argue that the dialogue does not offer a firm answer to either the demarcation problem or the question whether taking one's life is justified. My argument stresses that even though a relatively neutral definition of suicide is desirable, normative issues of good and bad, right and wrong, praise and blame follow on the heels of any discussion of suicide. The idea that Socrates' death was praiseworthy—he followed his own principles and his own style of questioning people, did not try to liberate himself by flattering the judges, and firmly rejected the idea of escaping from the prison—easily colors the conclusions we tend to draw concerning suicide: "Suicide is wrong. Socrates did the right thing. Therefore, Socrates did not kill himself." However, we have some textual evidence (62c6–8)[4] suggesting that Socrates' death is, in the dialogue, understood as a specific case of taking one's life that would be allowed even under an absolute ban on killing oneself. This seems to imply that the *Phaedo* is on a par with the *Laws* book 9 in conceding that one is allowed to take his or her life if compelled by judicial order to do so (873c4–5). Nonetheless, I shall argue that it would underestimate the complexity of the argument in the dialogue (60c–63c) to claim that Socrates took his life (on the basis of 62c7–8) and to identify it as a justified case of killing oneself.[5]

The dialogue clearly presents Socrates' death as morally praiseworthy, but the conclusions concerning taking one's life are far more difficult to establish. As I see it, the dialogue's argument about killing oneself is a kind of a kaleidoscope that problematizes the reader's expectations. From this angle, the point concerning demarcation is rather that *even if* one supposed that (1) Socrates killed himself and that (2) it is wrong *tout court* to take one's own life, one would need to concede that Socrates' case was special because the gods had imposed a compelling necessity on him—in modern terminology, because he acted under coercion. However, this position seems internally incoherent because the concession concerning necessity or coercion contradicts (2). If taking one's life is wrong absolutely and in all cases, why was it not wrong in Socrates' case? Perhaps he did not kill himself, because the gods had imposed a compelling necessity on him and thus he did not depart before the gods had made their decision concerning Socrates' death.[6] And this would imply that Socrates did not take his own life.

My reading differs from previous scholarship on several points. I have just briefly described why I think the view that in the *Phaedo* Plato rejects killing oneself except in Socrates' (kind of) case, defended by Hofmann (2007), is unsatisfactory. Further, even though I agree with Cooper on the general point that the dialogue contains no conclusive argument about the justifiability of taking one's life, Cooper notes this rather briefly (1999: 523) without considering the details of the argument or discussing the demarcation problem. I shall explain the differences between my reading and that of Murray Miles (2001) and some other scholars below, since the divergences hinge on more detailed issues of how the relevant passages should be understood.

It is striking that a discussion of Socrates' death leads to the puzzle of suicide. Alongside Jesus, Socrates can claim perhaps the most notorious death in Western cultural history. What is more, if we follow the arguments about whether or not Socrates killed himself, then we need to ask the same about Jesus. Like Socrates, Jesus was sentenced to death because of his moral teachings. Perhaps like Socrates, Jesus had a chance to get (mighty) help but did not ask for it—except in his very last words, when it was already too late. It is true that whereas Socrates was physically and causally responsible for the act that killed him (drinking the poison), Jesus was only indirectly causally responsible. But is this really the ultimate point differentiating Jesus' death from Socrates'? On the one hand, as mentioned, Socrates' drinking the hemlock was a standard way of carrying out a death sentence. On the other hand, Jesus also seems to have complied with his destiny—perhaps not quite as cheerfully and willingly as Socrates, but he nonetheless did so.

As Miriam Griffin has pointed out (1986: 69), Clemens of Alexandria criticized certain Christians martyrs and argued that they were not martyrs but mere suicides, who, by showing off their principles, provoked the Roman officials to put them to death (*Stromata* 4.4.17.1–3). A possible response to Clemens is to highlight the difference between being engaged in moral or religious teaching *just for the sake of* provoking the officials to issue a death sentence and being engaged in the same teaching *for its own sake* and then complying with the death sentence that may result from it. In the former case, the moral or religious teaching would be a mere instrument for taking one's life, and such a motivation is not ascribable to Jesus or Socrates. As Griffin also notes (69), the question of the borderline between suicide and martyrdom emphasizes the role of motivation or intention in the problem of demarcating suicide—thus challenging Durkheim's conviction that motivation or intention should *not* be included in the definition of suicide.

Socrates' and Jesus' deaths both differ from the kind of case we tend to see as a paradigmatic suicide, a lonesome and desperate act possibly resulting from a long period of depression (for details of such a case, see, e.g., Blauner 2002: 7–8).[7] However, to include such requirements as loneliness, desperation or perhaps even depression in the definition of suicide would result in an unnecessarily narrow conception of the phenomenon. Such a definition would exclude cases that we typically include in the scope of suicide (e.g., rashly committed ones). Further, in depression-related cases that one might expect to categorize as suicide (e.g., those of Finnish men discussed in chapter 7 below), moral issues, especially shame, are surprisingly central. Therefore, it is best not to exclude any deaths in general or Socrates' death in particular from the category of suicide on the grounds that depression did not occur.

An additional peculiar aspect of Socrates' death, also typical of ancient Roman suicides like Cato's, is the person's performance of the decisive act (for Socrates, drinking the hemlock; for Cato, drawing the sword) in a social setting: the rooms in which the two men die are full of other people—people who might try to prevent them from embarking on the fatal act (for the social aspect of Roman suicides, see Griffin 1986: 65–66). This again seems to differentiate them from the kind of solitary decisions typical of our contemporary prototype of suicide.[8] However, to say that Socrates' death was not a suicide just because there were so many other people present does not seem like a good criterion for demarcating suicide either. Even though the presence of other people is not part of the modern prototype, it surely is not decisive in the demarcation problem.

Finally, before briefly considering the *Phaedo*'s background in ancient literature and philosophy, one terminological note needs to be made. "Suicide" is a fairly late neologism—the first reported occurrence in English is from 1643 (Sir Thomas Browne's *Religio Medici*), and *The Oxford English Dictionary* first mentioned in 1651 (see Griffin 1986: 68).[9] Linguistically speaking, it is not a coincidence that *suicidium* did not exist in classical Latin: indeed, it could not have, for classical Latin does not combine nouns and pronouns (*sui*, gen. of *suus*). Therefore, strictly speaking it is anachronistic to apply the term "suicide" to ancient texts; "killing oneself" (e.g., Greek *autothanasia*) or "taking one's life" would be a historically sensitive expression. However, since "suicide" is an established term, I shall not avoid it altogether. The more substantial aspect of this terminological remark is that the ancient expressions used for "killing oneself"[10] (e.g., the Greek *autothanasia* and *auton apokteinunai*, and the Latin *voluntaria mors*) are normatively neutral: they bear no connotations of wrongful killing, as the Latin-based "suicide" perhaps does.[11] On the other hand, in our contemporary society the term "suicide" is often linked to depression and psychiatric, even medical, discussions, a framework that is obviously not applicable to the ancient cases.

BACKGROUND FOR SOCRATES' DEATH IN ANCIENT LITERATURE

Fearlessness

Socrates' serene attitude toward his own death is a touching landmark for not fearing death, but the topic was by no means new at the time of Socrates and Plato. Thales, the first philosopher in Diogenes Laertius' *Lives of Eminent Philosophers* and in Aristotle's *Metaphysics* book 1, is depicted as exemplifying indifference toward death. "Death does not differ from life," Thales says. "Why don't you die, then?" people ask. "Because death does not differ from life," Thales responds. (*Lives of Eminent Philosophers* 1.35; for Anaxagoras, see also ibid. 2.12–13) Similarly, it was told that Pyrrho of Elis—later celebrated as a predecessor of epistemological skepticism—had to be followed by friends on the street because if a wagon approached, Pyrrho would not yield but let the wagon drive over him. He was said not to consider life to be better than death. Why jump away, then?

Of course, not fearing death does not entail that one should kill oneself. Yet philosophical self-inflicted deaths are also well attested in Diogenes Laertius. For example, Zeno, the founder of the Stoic school, was reported to have fallen and broken one of his digits at the honorable age of eighty-two. He took this to be a divine sign that the appropriate moment of death had come and choked himself (*Lives of Eminent Philosophers* 7.28). More strikingly, a later Roman Stoic, Seneca (whose death by his own hand in 65 CE is a well-known Roman suicide, modeled and staged to reflect the death of Socrates),[12] emphasized that one is never compelled to continue living but has an ultimate freedom to end one's life (Seneca, *De Ira* 3.15,14 quoted in chapter 4 of this volume).

This does not imply that ancient philosophers would have been all-inclusive proponents of taking one's life. According to Aristotle, for example, a person killing him- or herself to escape from some evil, such as pain, exemplifies undesirable features of character such as cowardice (*Nicomachean Ethics* 3.7, 1116a10–15). He also suggests that killing oneself be regarded as an injustice against the city-state (*Nicomachean Ethics* 5.11, 1138a11). His argument in the former case concentrates on the way in which someone endures death and judges the flight from evil as base, whereas a courageous and serene approach to one's own death is noble. The latter point about injustice against the city relates to the peculiar context of Aristotle's discussion, namely the question of whether it is possible to be unjust toward oneself—as a possible case of which Aristotle considers taking one's life and then denies that the injustice is directed at oneself; its object is rather the city. By no means, therefore, do Aristotle's remarks amount to a general analysis of the justifiability of killing oneself. Further, whereas the Stoics are in general more admissive, they were not unquestionably proponents of self-inflicted death. They also argue against it when it is done with wrong motives (for Epictetus' arguments, see chapter 4 below).

Taking One's Life as a Moral Decision

Despite the philosophers' differences concerning the permissibility of taking one's life, their arguments hold some important common assumptions. First, most ancient philosophical texts approach suicide as an *ethical* question.[13] From the ethical point of view, the question is whether or under what circumstances a person is entitled or justified in choosing to kill him- or herself rather than to go on living. As is consistent with the general spirit of ancient ethical theories, suicide is seen above all from the perspective of the agent who plans or commits the deed. Much less attention is paid to that agent's close relatives or friends (see, however, Seneca in chapter 4 below and Plato's *Phaedo* in this chapter, at the end of the section "Gods are Our Guardians and We Are Their Property"). Secondly, and consequently, the analysis of killing oneself supposes that one is *responsible* for the choice. The very possibility of ethical evaluation of an act (even if morally condemning it) presupposes that the agent is responsible for the decision to end his or her life. Thus another implication of the same assumption is that taking one's life is primarily seen as a *decision*. Then the question arises whether that decision is or can be correct or justified.

Virgin Suicides, Divine Madness

The philosophical discussion about suicide as a decision subject to moral evaluation differs from both the suicides in the ancient medical literature and the self-inflicted deaths due to divine madness in epic and tragedies (for self-inflicted deaths in tragedies, see also chapter 4 below). Particularly in the suicides caused by divine madness, the agent is not held responsible for the decision to kill him- or herself. The viewpoints of medical science, natural reasons, and divine causes can also be combined in the explanation for killing oneself (see also Plutarch, *Moralia* 249b–d). A striking example of such a case is the Hippocratic treatise *On Diseases of Young Girls* (*Peri partheniôn*) and its explanation of young women or women without children taking their lives.[14] A traditional translation of the name would be *On Diseases of Virgins*, but it has been argued that virginity is not decisive in whether one is a *parthenios* in the Hippocratic sense; even married women belong to this category if they have not given birth (King 2004: 51). The *Peri partheniôn* reports how young girls and women, who have to remain inside at home before they are married, constitute a specific risk group for taking their lives. These "virgin suicides" are explained by a disproportion in the natural fluids or humors in the body. Not having children or having missed menarche destroys the natural circulation of the fluids, and such disturbances cause mental derangement as well (see King 1983: 113–117).[15]

Given that the Hippocratic example involves young women and girls, one might be tempted to suppose that such an analysis only applies to (young) women. However, this initial impression is slightly misleading. It is a common feature of ancient literature that when psychological phenomena are discussed in the medical context, the analysis focuses on explanations through fluids and humors. Doctors typically do not speculate about the contents of people's minds; they explain mental dispositions and human behavior through the natural science of their time.[16] This is because of an implicit rough division of labor between doctors and philosophers: the philosophers and poets talk about the contents of our thoughts and inferences, passions and emotions. Doctors aim at curing imbalance in the physical system. However, this division of labor is not absolute. For example, an epidemic of suicides of young girls reported from Miletus in 277 BCE was not medically cured but came to an end when a naked body of one of the suicides was publicly displayed.[17]

Mythological and epic self-inflicted deaths resulting from divine madness can also be contrasted both to the decisions that philosophers discuss and to such suicides today, which are understood as resulting from a long period of depression. Myths usually portray a short and abrupt attack of folly. In some versions of the story of Heracles, he burns himself to death in a frenzy because of the agony he suffers from Centaur Nessos's tunic (briefly discussed in van Hooff 1990: 98). As in Heracles' case, mythical depictions of madness often explain the attack as occurring through divine or semi-divine intervention: one god or another (or a demigod) has made the hero (or heroine) crazy (a classical discussion of this topic is found in Dodds 1951). The person is out of his or her mind and does not know what he or she is doing. In such cases the action's cause is located outside the agent.

Shame and Guilt

One general type of cases in ancient Greek literature in which taking one's life is supposed to be appropriate includes shameful situations in which the person has lost face, been the object of sexual crimes, or committed horrible crimes. Ajax, for example, is depicted as a heroic man who has to kill himself because he has lost face and is thus disgraced (Achilles' weapons are not given to him in the *Iliad*). He throws himself on his sword. Interestingly, descriptions of Ajax changed over time. In later versions, his anger becomes more violent (he kills a herd of sheep) and after the attack of rage, he comes to his senses and understands that he has acted in a ridiculous manner. Sophocles identifies the realization of ridicule as the decisive cause for Ajax's decision.[18]

Sophocles' *Oedipus*, an archetypal tragedy of shame and guilt, clearly portrays the social expectation that Oedipus should kill himself. According to the chorus, Oedipus would be better off dead (or, literally, "not being" *ouket' ôn*) than living blind (*zôn tuphlos*) (*Oedipus* 1367–68). Oedipus responds by asking, "[B]y which eyes could I have looked at my parents in Hades," "by which eyes could I have looked at my children?" Thus Oedipus' answer, far from denying that his shame would actually merit death, rather considers his crimes greater—so great that even death could not compensate them (1369–74). Death would just transmit him where he would need to face his parents—which he is unable to do because it would be too shameful. To avoid this, he has blinded himself.

TAKING ONE'S LIFE IN PLATO'S *PHAEDO*

"How on Earth Are You Composing Poetry Now When You Are in Prison?"

In Plato's *Phaedo* Socrates sits in prison talking with his friends and arguing, among other things, for the immortality of the soul. At the end of the dialogue he drinks hemlock and dies. As mentioned, there are quite a few people in Socrates' cell but only some of them participate in the narrated discussion. In addition to Phaedo, the narrator, Apollodorus, Critobulus, his father Hermogenes, Epigenes, Aeschines, Antisthenes, Ctesippus, Menexenus, and Crito are mentioned by name; a couple more unnamed Athenians are also said to have been present. Cebes and Simmias, who take a central position in the dialogue, as well as Phaedonides have come from Thebes; Euclid and Terpsion from Megara. Plato is said to have been ill (59b6–10). This is one of the very few references to Plato himself in the dialogues,[19] and one might wonder about the truth of the implication that he was absent.[20] Xanthippe, Socrates' wife, is there at the beginning, but Socrates has her sent home.[21] The friends are let in after the guard has removed Socrates' chains, and the very first exchange between Simmias, Cebes, and Socrates leads to discussion of taking one's life.

Socrates starts rubbing his newly released feet (60b1–2) and exclaims how remarkable a relation pleasure has to its opposite, pain. Even they, being opposites, cannot coincide; one follows the other. Had Aesop composed a fable about this, Socrates adds, he would have a god try to reconcile the opposition between pain and pleasure and, upon being unable to do so, join the two together at their heads (60c1–6). Similarly, the fetters caused pain in Socrates' legs and now that they are gone, pleasure follows.

The mention of Aesop then leads Cebes to bring up Evenus:

> By Zeus, yes, Socrates, you did well to remind me. Evenus asked me the day before yesterday, as others had done before, how on earth are you composing poetry now when you are in prison, you who had never composed any poetry before, putting the fables of Aesop into verse and composing the hymn to Apollo. (60c9–b4, Grube's 1997 translation has been modified; for the rendering, cf. Rowe 1993: 121)

Socrates responds (60d8–61b7) by claiming that he has no intention of rivaling Evenus or his poems but that he has had dreams exhorting him to "practice and cultivate the arts" (60e6–7; tr. Grube 1997). Earlier he had supposed that such dreams encouraged him to practice philosophy, but now, in prison, with the festival of Apollo preventing his execution,[22] he thought that composing poetry was the right way to obey the dreams.

"Tell Him to Follow Me as Quickly as Possible"

Evenus also appears in the *Apology*, in which he is said to teach people to be good citizens for a handsome price, and in the *Phaedrus* (267a2–5), where his rhetorical inventions (covert implication and indirect praise) are ironically applauded in the very formulas whose invention is attributed to him. The reference in the *Apology* (20b7–c1) is of a similar spirit: the man is said to have the expertise, knowledge, or skill Socrates claims to lack in human and political affairs, and to teach it for the price of five minas—a price that is ironically depicted as moderate.

The impression of irony is central to Socrates' greetings to Evenus in the *Phaedo* as well:

> *Socrates*: Tell this [i.e., Socrates' dream] to Evenus, Cebes, wish him well and bid him farewell, and tell him, if he is wise, to follow me as quickly as possible. I am leaving today, it seems, as the Athenians see fit.
>
> *Simmias*: What kind of advice is this you are giving to Evenus, Socrates? I have had many dealings with him, and from my observation he is not at all likely to follow it willingly.
>
> *Socrates*: How so? Is Evenus not a philosopher?
>
> *Simmias*: I think so.
>
> *Socrates*: Then Evenus will be willing, like every man who partakes worthily of philosophy. Yet perhaps he will not take his own life, since, they say, it is not permissible.
>
> As he said this, Socrates put his feet on the ground and remained in this position for the rest of the conversation. (*Phaedo* 61b7–d2; Grube's 1997 translation modified)

Simmias is startled, not so much because of Socrates' insinuation that Evenus should follow him to death but because Simmias finds it surprising that Socrates sends his greetings to Evenus of all people. Why would Socrates pick him out as a true philosopher when it seems clear he is not?

Socrates' addition "perhaps [Evenus] will not take his own life, *since, they say, it is not permissible*" (61c9–10) is of central importance, and I shall soon return to its implications. Before that a literary detail needs to be picked out: when Socrates utters these words, he is said to place his feet back on the ground and to remain seated in the same position for the rest of the conversation. According to instructions, he stands up only after having drunk the cup (117e) in order to walk around and let the hemlock take effect. Socrates' seated position is mentioned again twice later in the dialogue, first in a section in which the discussants have been discouraged by Cebes' and Simmias's objections to Socrates' arguments for the immortality of the soul. Socrates is sitting somewhat higher than Phaedo and takes some of the latter's hair in his hands when consoling his friends (89a9–b5). The second mention (98d5–6) belongs to the famous excursus in which Socrates describes his youthful studies in natural philosophy. He exclaims (98e1–99a4) that if things could be explained in the way of the natural philosophers, his sinews and bones would surely have transmitted him far away from the prison cell. However, he claims, because all explanations require a reference to the good—in this case the fact that Socrates finds it better to stay in prison than to escape—the natural philosophers' model for explanation is untenable.

The reference to Socrates' feet in the description of his position is hardly an accident. Socrates was famous for his bare feet and his worn-out cloak. In *The Clouds* Aristophanes portrays Socrates as barefoot (see also Diogenes Laertius, *Lives of Eminent Philosophers* 2.28; Plato, *Phaedrus* 229a3–4) and, in the *Symposium*—one of Plato's greatest dialogues on Socrates—special reference is made to Socrates having washed his cloak and even wearing sandals, which was rare (174a). The feet are also practically the first thing that is mentioned in the *Phaedo* when the narrator moves to describing Socrates (60b1–2). Besides being a touching literary detail on Socrates as a unique and vulnerable individual, these references also strengthen the connection between the situation, the discussion on taking one's life, and Socrates' firm decision to remain in prison and abide by his death sentence because he finds it better than to escape.

Socrates is thus saying to Evenus that a true philosopher should be willing to follow him to death. However, his addition "perhaps he should not take his own life, since, they say, it is not permissible" qualifies this recommendation with the clause that a philosopher should not rush things by taking his life. Thus the irony of the recommendation seems best described as what Gregory Vlastos (1991: 13–14) calls "complex irony." In a way, Socrates both is and is not recommending that Evenus take his own life. The philosopher's alleged readiness to leave reflects the claim made later in the dialogue according to which true philosophers always practice for death (67e4–5; see also 64a5–6). The core of Socrates' recommendation then seems to be that if Evenus is willing to present himself as a true philosopher and, more importantly, if he wants to *be* one, he should be ready to focus his life on practicing death, and that this practice should be reflected in his readiness to follow Socrates and leave.

"Since, They Say, It Is Not Permissible"

How much, then, is loaded into the clause according to which Evenus should perhaps not kill himself "since, they say, it is not permissible"? First, it could be taken to imply that Socrates is subscribing to the claim that it is not permissible to take one's life. Understood in this way Socrates' statement would be:

> (i) Evenus should be ready and willing to follow Socrates to death but, *because it is not permissible* (as the common opinion also says), he should not take his own life.

The second possibility is that Socrates does *not* subscribe to the common opinion. In this case:

> (ii) Socrates recommends that Evenus follow him to death but because *common opinion does not accept it* (or whoever the precise reference for "they" is) Socrates adds that perhaps Evenus should not be exhorted to take his life.

This second option could also be taken in two ways. The first reading is that (ii.a) a true philosopher *in fact should* be prepared to take his (or her) own life, but Socrates cannot recommend it because the common opinion is so heavily against it. The second alternative is that (ii.b) Socrates himself suspends judgment with respect to the permissibility of killing oneself and *does not claim anything* about whether a true philosopher should be prepared to take his or her life or not. In this case, Socrates is merely saying that a true philosopher should be indifferent about whether he (or she) lives or is dead and should thus not be too attached to life. To this he would then add, without clear commitment to any option, that *perhaps* one should not take one's life, since it is not commonly acceptable.

I find the second version of the second alternative (ii.b) the most likely reading of the relevant lines.[23] I do not think that Socrates can safely be taken to commit himself to any specific view about the permissibility of taking one's life—as the "perhaps" in 61c9 also suggests—but that he is merely referring to a vaguely attributed opinion about the matter ("they say" in 61c10). According to this reading, Socrates' exhortation to Evenus can be taken as a reminder of how demanding a true philosophical life is: philosophy is not something that one can have as a hobby, living by it only when all goes well. Sometimes philosophy leads to hard decisions, even choosing death over life, and this must also be accepted as a part of a philosophical life. Had Socrates chosen escape, it would not have saved his life in the proper sense: despite saving his physical life, it would have destroyed the philosophical one that was most important to Socrates. Socrates' withdrawal, at the moment when practicing for death required facing it, would not only have made him cowardly at one point of his life but would have turned his whole life non-philosophical.

Cebes finds Socrates' statement confusing. On the one hand, Socrates seems to be (1) pointing to a philosopher's willingness to die, while on the other hand he seems to be (2) banning suicide. This confusion, or "apparent contradiction" as Gallop calls it (1975: 80), has been a matter of some controversy. What is more, some scholars, for instance, Miles (2001), have claimed that no contradiction is involved. Miles argues that this is because the first claim about the philosopher's alleged willingness to die operates with a nonmoral notion of goodness, whereas the ban on suicide is a moral claim. This distinction between moral and nonmoral goodness seems somewhat far-fetched in the context and, as I see it, does not take us to the core of the problem that arises with respect to Socrates' own action in the situation. Even though the claim of philosophers' willingness to die does not formally contradict the ban on suicide, Socrates could very well be seen as precipitating his own death, both because he does not agree to escape and because he willingly and firmly complies with his death sentence, that is, chooses death over life.

Cebes asks Socrates to clarify how the two claims relate to each other:

> *Cebes*: How do you mean, Socrates, that it is not right to do oneself violence, and yet that the philosopher will be willing to follow one who is dying?
>
> *Socrates*: Come now, Cebes, have you and Simmias, who keep company with Philolaus, not heard about such things?
>
> *Cebes*: Nothing definite, Socrates.
>
> *Socrates*: Indeed, I too speak about this from hearsay, but I do not mind telling you what I have heard, for it is perhaps most appropriate for one who is about to depart yonder to tell and examine tales about what we believe that journey to be like. What else could one do in the time we have until sunset? (61d3–e4; trans. Grube 1997)

Cebes strengthens his request by referring to Philolaus and some others, who say that it is not permissible to take one's life (61e5–6). Socrates responds:

> It may well astonish you if this subject, alone of all things, is simple, and it is never, as with everything else, better at certain times and for certain people to die than to live. And if this is so, you may well find it astonishing if those for whom it is better to die are wrong to help themselves, and that

> they must wait for someone else to benefit them. "Let Zeus know!" Cebes responded with a chuckle, speaking in his own dialect. (62a2–8; Grube's 1997 translation modified with Rowe's rendering of 62a2–5 and 7–8 in 1993: 126–27)

Scholars have disputed the correct reference of this expression ("this subject, alone of all things," *touto monon tôn allôn hapantôn*, 62a2–3) and the passage in general, which Dorter calls (1982: 11) "one of the most obscure statements in all the dialogues." It can be taken to mean that:

I. It is surprising a. *that* or b. *if* there is no exception to life being better than death, i.e., that/if death is never better than life (as Rowe 1991: 126–27 with reading b. takes it; see also Burnet 1911: 20),
II. It is surprising a. *that* or b. *if* there is no exception to death being better than life (Bluck 1955: 152 with reading a., i.e., claiming that it is surprising but yet a fact that death is always better than life), or
III. It is surprising a. *that* or b. *if* taking one's life is absolutely prohibited (Loriaux 1969: 54–55, Tarán 1966: 334, Gallop 1975: 79–81 and, with some qualifications, Miles 2001: 254).

It is important to note that the first part of the sentence, that is, I or II, is at the end of the passage connected with III in such a way that the whole amounts to a conjunction of either I or II together with III. Therefore, the possible readings multiply according to how we understand the conjunction.[24] However, not all readings are plausible. For example, to say that death is never preferable to life and that one is never allowed to take one's life is not surprising. Both conjuncts are, it seems, in accordance with common opinion, and their conjunction contains no tension; rather, if life is always preferable to death, it is more than expected that one is never allowed to take one's life.

It is also important to note that the astonishment over the latter part of the conjunction (that one is never allowed to take one's life) only makes sense if the first conjunct is either "death is sometimes preferable to life" or "death is always preferable to life." Even though the latter is logically and grammatically possible, I do not think we should decide which reading to follow on the basis of this sentence alone. The whole context concerns the point that in *some* cases (i.e., in the case of philosophers), death is preferable to life.

This point about context also applies to the interpretation of the Greek *thaumaston ei* "it is surprising that" or "it is surprising if" that introduces the object of astonishment. I agree with Dorter (1982: 15)[25] that it would be preferable to choose the same interpretation for *thaumaston ei* throughout the sentence.[26] However, I do not think that the only options are "it is surprising that *p*" in which *p* is taken to be true and "it would be surprising if *p*" in which *p* is taken as false. In addition to these, "surprising if" can be taken to indicate that it would be surprising if *p* were true, but whether or not it is true has not been determined yet (cf. Loriaux's remarks on this in 1969: 49). In fact, I see this as the most plausible reading of *thaumaston ei* in the context. Further, the dialogue later (64a10ff.) offers an argument for the truth of I (that death is sometimes and for some people better than life); hence whether Plato or Socrates is presenting I as true does not depend on the understanding of *thaumaston ei* (surprising that/if) alone.

Therefore, as I see it, the reading that makes best sense in the context is a combination of I and III.[27] It is surprising if I death is sometimes and for some people better than life, but III those for whom death is better are not allowed to let themselves out.[28] One reason to favor this reading, as mentioned, is that the second part of the sentence (III) seems to require that death is at least sometimes and for some people better than life. However, my focus is not so much on the first conjunct but on the claim according to which it is surprising (but uncertain whether it is true) if those for whom death is better than life are not allowed to end their lives. Since, as I shall also argue below in further detail, I do not think that Socrates can safely be regarded as committed to the prohibition of taking one's life, III needs to be understood in the sense that its truth-value is uncertain, at least at this point of the dialogue.[29]

The impression that the focus of the astonishment mainly concerns the latter part of the sentence, that is, that those for whom death is preferable to life are not allowed to let themselves out, is strengthened by the context: it is the prohibition of killing oneself that Cebes asks about in the preceding lines (61e5–9), and Socrates' response (beginning at 62b) concentrates on it as well. Socrates goes on to state (62b1–2) that even though the unconditional ban on suicide might seem implausible, there is a rationale behind it. It is important to note that this does not entail Socrates committing himself to the prohibition, only that he is considering the grounds on which one could reasonably argue for it.

The beginning of Socrates' response in the passage quoted above provokes Cebes to chuckle and to resort to his own Boeotian dialect, which would have been considered rural in Athens. It would be pointless to look for a single interpretation or explanation of this code change, but it might suggest that the unconditional ban on suicide was advocated by Philolaus, who used to be the teacher of Simmias and Cebes in Thebes and thus most probably spoke the same dialect.[30] However, some scholars have rejected the idea that the prohibition was maintained by Philolaus in particular. Christopher Rowe, for example, argues (1993: 124) that Simmias and Cebes' explicit affirmation (61d8) that they had heard "nothing clear" or "nothing definite" about such a ban from Philolaus would be strange indeed had it really been Philolaus's view. Further, Rowe points out that Cebes and Simmias concede having heard the same from some others (61e5–8); thus, even if Philolaus had been a proponent of such a ban, it would not have been a view that was specifically his as opposed to others.

I agree that there is no safe way of attributing the ban to Philolaus in particular, especially if we take this in the sense that no one else argued for it. However, that Simmias and Cebes admit hearing the same from some others and concede having heard nothing definite from Philolaus, does not entirely exclude the possibility that Philolaus maintained some version of the prohibition. Despite the initial statement that what Philolaus said is not definite (in 61d8), Cebes later confirms that he has heard him forbid taking one's life (61e6–7). The addition that some others have said this too and that the claim was somewhat unclear does not constitute conclusive evidence for denying that Philolaus held, in some sense, that one should not take one's life. From my perspective, the opacity of the ascription of the prohibition to Philolaus—or to anyone else for that matter—reflects the general vagueness in the dialogue about who exactly is banning taking one's life and whether we should subscribe to this ban as well.

"Gods Are Our Guardians and We Are Their Property"

Socrates goes on to argue that even though the unconditional nature of the prohibition of taking one's life might seem overstated (i.e., that III seems surprising), it can be reasonably argued for. The argument is, again, not expressed as one of Socrates' own. Rather, he refers to the mysteries, literally the "forbidden [doctrines]":

> Indeed, it does seem unreasonable when put like that, but perhaps there is reason to it. There is the explanation that is put in the language of the mysteries, that we human beings are in a kind of prison, and that one must not free oneself or run away. That seems to me an impressive doctrine and not easy to understand fully. However, Cebes, this seems to me well expressed, that the gods are our guardians and that men are one of their possessions. (62b1–8; Grube's translation slightly modified.)

Again Socrates indicates that what he is going to say might not be true: "*perhaps* there is reason to" the idea that we human beings are in a kind of prison or guard post (*hôs en tini phroura*, 62b3–4). In addition, the very idea about a prison or guard post is expressed vaguely with the indefinite pronoun as "a prison or guard post of a sort," in which "of a sort" can be taken to imply that the place or position of human beings in fact belongs to the general category of prisons or guard posts, or more loosely to indicate that our predicament in some sense resembles being in prison or at a guard post but does not belong to this general category. Moreover, when Socrates goes on to state what exactly he thinks is reasonable, the view is not exactly the same: the claim that concerns him is no longer that we are in prison or that we are at a guard post, but that the gods are our guardians or caretakers and that we are their property (62b7–8). This might seem like a small difference, but I find it important to distinguish between the first claim, that we are in prison or at a guard post of a sort (in either interpretation of "of a sort"), and the claim that we are watched over or taken care of by the gods. This is because the connotations of being in prison seem much more negative than having gods as owners and caretakers or guards—a guardian spirit, for example, surely differs from a prison guard. Further, as becomes clear in the sequel, Socrates takes the gods to be most benevolent owners (see, e.g., 63a6 and 9).

In addition to the ambiguity of "prison or guard post of a sort," discussion has also focused on what the prison or guard post (*phroura*) means in the context: it can be taken as a prison in which we are confined, or a place or position in which we have a task of watching over something (Cooper 1999: 522).[31] Both meanings are possible in Greek, and whereas in a sense the context would seem to suggest the former as more probable, the connotation of us human beings having guardian tasks also gains some credibility from Cebes' subsequent contention (62c1–5) that a slave is not allowed to end his or her life.

This new analogy seems to point to two important aspects in Socrates' contention that there is a reasonable point in the argument for the absolute ban on taking one's life. On the one hand, the human beings' relation to gods can be compared to the relation between slaves and their masters in the sense that the former are the property of the latter in both cases—which entails that neither group is free to leave as they please. On the other hand, it might be that, as slaves, human beings have some tasks allotted to them by the gods. However, because Socrates does not explicitly mention this latter aspect as reasonable, I do not think we should assign much weight to it. The central points are that the gods are our guardians or caretakers and that we are in some sense their property. Consequently, it is not necessary to infer that Socrates places credibility on the idea that we are gods' prisoners. It bears repeating that my analysis of the argument does not imply that Socrates is committed to the truth of the claim that gods are our guardians and we are their property. He merely finds it reasonable, as he says. Therefore, the reasonable argument is that, analogously to the way slaves are not free to escape, human beings are not free to kill themselves because just as slaves are their masters' property, human beings are the property of gods.

The context makes us expect that the argument is for an absolute prohibition of taking one's life, but this expectation is not entirely correct. Even in this argument, there is an exception to the rule: if the gods send a compelling reason, one is allowed to leave. Socrates concludes:

> Perhaps, then, put in this way, it is not unreasonable that one should not kill oneself before a god has indicated some necessity to do so, like the necessity now put upon us (62c6–8; trans. Grube 1997).

The conclusion is important for at least three reasons. First—and not surprisingly—if we suppose that gods are our owners and guardians or caretakers and if they compel us to take our lives, we are of course allowed to do so. How we are supposed to know whether such a compelling reason has been imposed on us is not explained. Secondly, even this conclusion is introduced with a "perhaps" (62c6), as often happens in the context. And this, I find, again indicates Socrates' general noncommittal to any claims about whether one is allowed to take one's life. Thirdly, Socrates' conclusion seems to indicate that he, at least on these lines, takes his own death to be self-inflicted even though compellingly necessitated by the gods and thus justified. However, these lines do not seem to offer a conclusive solution to the demarcation problem because the very compelling reason can be taken as analogous to coercion, which can reasonably be taken to exclude an apparent self-inflicted death from the category.

Cebes presses Socrates further, but not on the demarcation issue. Rather, he returns to the earlier question of how a philosopher can be willing to die and at the same time accept the position of the mysteries according to which we are owned by the gods (62c–e). The focus of Cebes' puzzlement is now the claim that whereas a foolish person might very well be willing to escape from a good master (62d6–9), it is difficult to see how and why a wise person or a philosopher would want to do this (62c9–d7). As mentioned, scholars have discussed whether there is a contradiction between the claims that (1) a philosopher is willing to die and it might be better for him or her to die than to live, and that (2) it is absolutely prohibited to take one's life. We can see now that Cebes' question does not concern this conjunction but the combination of the claim that (1) a philosopher is willing to die and that (3) we are gods' possessions and gods are our good caretakers or masters.[32]

This observation also has implications concerning whether or not Socrates attempts to settle or resolve the tension between (1) and (2). Murray Miles (2001), for example, claims that he does not, and on this general level I agree. However, it is important to note that when Socrates proceeds to respond to Cebes and Simmias, who enters the discussion to confirm that he is puzzled by the same claims that puzzle Cebes (63a4–9), the claims have transformed again. It is not even the combination of (1) and (3) that Socrates finally turns to. His response defends the claim that (4) a man who has spent time doing philosophy is dying bravely and with good hopes that he will attain the greatest goods there where he is going (63e9–64a2). This means that the focus of discussion is moving from problems concerning taking one's life to a new statement, according to which a philosopher should not grieve at death (cf. 63b8–9 and c4; for Socrates' longish defense of the claim, see 64a4–69e5). Puzzling claims about self-inflicted death thereby dissolve into a discussion of a fearless attitude toward death (in 63d–e) that is argued to be proper for philosophers.

It is striking that the transition coincides with an interruption in the discussion between Socrates, Cebes and Simmias. Socrates notes (63d3–4) that Crito has tried to get his attention for quite some time, and when Crito explains why, Socrates is not surprised: the guard wants to point out that perhaps Socrates should not talk but rest, because engaging in an argument might heat him up, which might weaken the effect of the poison and necessitate two or even three doses (63d5e2). Socrates' response (63e3–9) is unsurprising: he is not worried about needing an extra dose of hemlock and will instead continue the discussion with his friends.

This literary detail resonates with the demarcation problem. The presence of the guard and the reference to the poison may be taken to indicate that Socrates acted under coercion: his discussion about taking one's life is interrupted by the official who functions as an instrument of the divine necessity imposed on Socrates to end his life. And yet the character conveying the message is Crito, the man whose eponymous dialogue contains Socrates' argument against escaping from the prison. These details embody the impasse that the demarcation problem leads to: Socrates acted under coercion and yet freely and firmly decided to die. Even though in general the ancient analysis of freedom is not built on an opposition of freedom and necessity, the tension between the death sentence and Socrates' decision is sufficiently clear. Socrates (freely) decided to comply with his death sentence.

I Am Going to Other Wise and Good Gods

When Socrates then responds to Cebes and Simmias on point (4), he concedes he would be vexed by death if he did not expect that he, upon leaving this life, will go to some other gods who are wise and good (63b5–9). He also says he expects to arrive at some departed people who are better than the living ones but is not as certain about this as about the gods. For these reasons he is not upset but hopeful that there is something left for the dead ones—and that this something will be good rather than bad.

The position that Plato makes Socrates sympathize with is thus the following. Socrates sees it as consistent to claim that one is gods' property and that one might consistently *want* to become free from this ownership because one thinks that the gods at whom one arrives after death will be wise and good. The argument goes some way toward responding to Simmias and Cebes, but it adds very little to the question concerning the permissibility of taking one's life. Even if it were so that, after death, we go to some gods that are at least as good as the ones we escaped from, this does not justify the flight itself. We would be like runaway slaves justifying their escape by referring to having arrived at a new master who is at least as good as the previous one—an argument that would hardly convince the previous owner that the escape was justified.

However, it might be significant that the owners are gods: if they know that it really *is* better for philosophers to die than to live, it would be trivial and perhaps also inconsistent of gods to prevent or prohibit philosophers from dying or taking action to end their lives. Further, if the philosopher acts under a compelling necessity that the gods themselves have sent—as Socrates claims they have in his case—they would surely let him act according to that necessity. In any case, the gods would know what is better for philosophers, and petty ownership quarrels would be below their rank.

Let us note one more thing before moving to the concluding section. Up to this point, the discussion of taking one's life in the *Phaedo* has concentrated on relatively abstract concerns about the nature and permissibility of the agent's decision, and little if any reference has been made to other people who are left behind. However, when Simmias jumps in to support Cebes' question concerning philosophers' willingness to die with respect to the ownership issue, he makes clear that the problem is not just of abstract interest and is not only Socrates' individual decision. Rather, he is referring to the way Socrates (63a7–9), from Cebes and Simmias's point of view, seems too eager to go: too ready to leave his friends and too ready to leave the guardian gods. Thus Simmias intervenes, not only to strengthen Cebes' objection but also to insist (63c8–d2) that Socrates should now share his thoughts about why a philosopher can expect something good in the afterlife. Why should a wise man (a practitioner of philosophy and a practitioner of death) see death as a reward rather than a punishment? He goes on to say that, in fact, this thought is common (63d1) and as such not Socrates' private property.[33]

Therefore, Simmias's question seems to entail that here Plato recognizes the pain and sorrow of those who are left behind. Socrates' death and the disappearance of all his thoughts and arguments must have been an enormous personal loss to Plato. At the same time and more generally, this could be taken as recognition of the anguish of the friends of someone who departs voluntarily.

CONCLUSION

Demarcation and Justification of Taking One's Life in the Phaedo

Even though no definite conclusion is reached about the demarcation problem of how to delimit self-inflicted death in general and Socrates' death in particular, the elements of the puzzle are clear and also reflected in the narration of the discussion's end. Socrates decided that it is better for him to comply with his death sentence and to die, but because a (divine) necessity was imposed on him, that is, he in a sense acted under coercion, he thus did not offend the gods. The first component seems to suggest that Socrates took his own life, the second one that he did not.

The key points of the discussion about whether or not one is ever justified in ending one's life are more difficult to detect. First, the theme is introduced with Socrates' ironical exhortation to Evenus to follow him, which leads him to mention the vaguely attributed claim ("they say") of the prohibition of taking one's life. Cebes then connects these two points to a conjunction that puzzles him: (1) a philosopher should be willing and ready to leave but (2) one is not allowed to take one's life. The discussion focuses on the latter point (2). When Socrates articulates the puzzle, the problem turns out to be that it is surprising if those for whom it is better to die are not allowed to let themselves out. As I have argued, the dialogue holds no safe attribution of such a prohibition to Philolaus or anyone else; neither does Socrates commit himself to it. The way in which Socrates proceeds shows that he knows of a reasonable argument for such a prohibition: that gods are our guardians and we are their property, and just as it is reasonable to punish a runaway slave, it would seem reasonable that we are not free to leave.

Cebes makes yet another specification. Whereas he finds it easy to accept that perhaps a foolish person wants to escape from a good owner, the same willingness is difficult to digest when it occurs in a wise person or a philosopher. Cebes' companion Simmias comes in to strengthen the demand that Socrates clear up this difficulty. Cebes and Simmias are thus also baffled by the argument for the prohibition of taking one's life, namely that gods are our guardians and we their property. More specifically, it startles them when it is taken together with the claim of philosophers' willingness to die.

Even though there is no formal contradiction between any of these claims, I do not think the puzzlement needs to amount to a formal contradiction. Rather, the context urges us to consider these claims in the light of what Socrates did and what happened to him. When this observation is made, even the conjunction of philosophers' willingness to die with the prohibition of taking one's life becomes more pressing: (1') philosophers in general and Socrates in particular are willing to die, (2') one is not allowed to kill oneself and (1'') Socrates seems, not only be willing to die but perhaps even to take his life. It is this conundrum that is primary in the context.

Finally, the tension in the demarcation problem highlighted in the dialogue is not merely between coercion and decision. Plato's portrayal of Socrates also seems to imply that he made his decision in complete freedom. Even though in a sense Socrates could not have decided otherwise without compromising everything he took to be good and perhaps even his identity *and* he was sentenced to death, there is no indication that Socrates' decision depended on anything other than his own choice. The whole dialogue together with the *Crito* emphasizes that Socrates was free when deciding what to do. A literary detail indicative of this may be his bare feet on the ground: the decision was made by Socrates, a unique embodied individual, and as he was free to leave this world, he was free to decide to do so.

More General Conclusions

Let us now consider the dialogue's argument from a slightly broader point of view. First, we need to return to the question about Socrates, martyrs, and Jesus. An element of sacrifice is an integral factor in the deaths of both martyrs and Jesus. Martyrs sacrifice themselves for their teachings and their religion; Jesus sacrificed himself (or God sacrificed his son) for all of humankind and its sins. By contrast, even though Socrates died because of his teachings, he hardly seems to have sacrificed himself.

A sacrifice requires that there is a victim: a person or an animal suffers so that some good is produced for some others. Vernant (1991), for example, analyzes the goal of sacrifice as establishing a connection between mortals and immortals. We have seen above, and the *Phaedo* contains ample additional evidence, that Socrates did not think he suffered. Rather, his arguments aim to show that death was good for him (see also 84d8–e2). What is more, Socrates did not understand himself as a victim—quite the contrary; neither did he choose death for the sake of a further cause. Socrates' arguments clearly suggest that he chose death merely on the grounds and because of what he himself thought to be good. Even though posterity might want to see Socrates as a martyr for philosophy, Plato's Socrates makes no move to argue that he died to guarantee that later generations would be able to practice philosophy. Neither do we find any implications that Socrates was bringing into balance something that had gone wrong: the element of redemption is markedly absent from Plato's discussion of why Socrates chose death over life.

In this essay, I have argued for the undecidability of the demarcation problem in Socrates' case, but similar puzzles are still pertinent more generally. A wide variety of social, cultural, and psychological factors are involved in the web of questions and problems discussed under the general heading "suicide," but, as is well known, no such factor alone is a sufficient explanation of whether or why an individual takes his or her life. Further, it seems reasonable to require that for a death to be a suicide, an agent needs to decide–perhaps even freely–to take his or her life. This further accentuates the difficulty of determining conclusively whether a given death is a suicide. An additional problem is that usually this question needs to be studied post hoc by constructing or reconstructing the chain of events or decisions that led to the fatal result, and there is no shortage of borderline cases, such as some car accidents and alcohol-related deaths. All in all, the elusiveness of the argument in the *Phaedo* can be seen to reflect the elusiveness of the phenomenon of suicide.

NOTES

1. In philosophical debates of our time, a similar condition is often formulated as an intention to die; for problems related to the condition, see Cholbi 2009: section 1. Durkheim famously did not consider intentions in his definition of suicide. However, as Griffin too has pointed out (1986: 70), ancient philosophers considered killing oneself as a moral question–a moral decision or act to take one's life–so the question of motives or intentions was relevant to them.
2. A similar point made by Lebacqz and Engelhardt (1980: 701) is that some definitions of suicide are based on prior judgments concerning whether it is justifiable or not. Arguments against Frey about Socrates are also found in Smith (1980).
3. Beauchamp (1992), for example, adds to the general definition of suicide that the agent is not coerced in doing the action that brings about his or her death.
4. Socrates says that the view that was considered earlier, namely that one should not kill oneself (*auton apokteinunai* 62c6–7) *before* the gods send some necessity as they have done in his case (62c7–8), seems reasonable. I shall return to

this point below in the section "Gods Are Our Guardians and We Are Their Property."

5. Therefore, I disagree with Hofmann (2007) on this point.
6. Even Augustine, who represented the firm Christian rejection of taking one's own life (*City of God* 1.20), points out that killing oneself at God's command is not suicide (*City of God* 1.26).
7. Blauner's book describes how she herself survived three suicide attempts, and for those having suicidal thoughts, it also functions as a practical guide on how to avoid acting on them. In each attempt, Blauner observed that even though she was trying to kill herself, she realized upon being resuscitated that she did not want to die.
8. However, in some other cultural settings, for example in the case of a Japanese seppuku, witnesses are needed as well.
9. For the terminology, see also van Hooff 1990: 136–141.
10. Van Hooff translates *autothanasia* as "self-killing," which is also a technical term in suicidology. However, because this connotes a military context for some native speakers who are not suicidologists, I shall avoid this translation.
11. Grisé (1982: 23–28) in fact argues that the Romans did not consider the neologism *suicidium* as a real option precisely because they wanted to avoid a term containing a negative value judgment. I find this claim somewhat overstated but shall not pursue the point in more detail.
12. E.g., Seneca' reported last words were "I offer this liquid as a libation to Jupiter Liberator" (Tacitus *Annals* 15.61–64, translation quoted from Griffin 1986: 65).
13. Miriam Griffin also briefly recognizes this (1986: 70).
14. For the treatise, see, e.g., King 2004: 49–53, Flemming and Hanson 1998, Bonnet-Cadilhac 1993 and van Hooff 1990: 22–23.
15. Jeffrey Eugenides's book *The Virgin Suicides* (1993), filmed by Sofia Coppola under the same title, depicts suicides of young girls in a context somewhat similar to that in the ancient material: unmarried young women are not allowed to go out of the house in which they live. Especially their communication with young men is strictly regulated or even utterly forbidden. The girls find ways to get around the prohibition, but this does not save them.
16. For this tendency, see Marke Ahonen 2008.
17. For the case, see also van Hooff 1990: 98; King 1983: 118.
18. For the different versions of Ajax's story, see, e.g., de Romilly 1976: 9–12.
19. In addition to this passage of the *Phaedo*, Plato is mentioned twice in the *Apology* (34a1 and 38b6). These three occurrences are the only ones outside the spurious letters in which Plato is mentioned as the sender.
20. Rowe (1993: 114) mentions the interesting contrast between Plato's stated or alleged absence from the cell and his continuous presence in the narration as author.
21. Toward the end (116a–b), she returns to bid farewell to Socrates.

22. Athens sent a ship to Delos yearly in honor of Apollo, and no executions were allowed while the ship was on this voyage.
23. Therefore, I agree with Cooper (1999) on this general point. However, as mentioned, he does not consider the details of the argument or make the distinctions just made.
24. For the different possibilities, see Loriaux 1969: 49–59 and Dorter 1982: 12. Rowe (1993: 126) also recognizes both aspects, whereas Miles (2001) is not equally clear on this. Loriaux points out (1969: 49) that the sentence is difficult and that he is not certain which option should be selected.
25. See also Loriaux 1969: 51–52.
26. However, not all scholars agree on this. For example, Burnet's reading (1911: 20) is a combination of Ib and IIIa, thus resulting in the following: it would be surprising if it never were better for someone to die than to live, and it is surprising that (given I) one is never allowed to kill oneself. In a similar vein, Hackforth (1955: 191) also takes the object of astonishment to be a conjunction. According to him, the astonishing claim is that "despite the extreme improbability of death *never* being preferable to life, suicide should always be sinful." Therefore, Hackforth also takes the first part of the conjunct (I) in the sense of "surprising if" (b) but implying, if not clear falsity, at least high improbability, whereas III is understood in sense a, implying that it is surprising but true that self-killing is never allowed.
27. See also Loriaux 1969: 51. Bostock takes the conjunction to be the main object of astonishment as well (1986: 17). However, he takes III in sense a, implying that the absolute prohibition of self-killing is accepted by the discussants. Yet he also grants that this absolute prohibition does not apply to Socrates' case as the gods have sent a compelling necessity on him. In what sense, then, can we take the discussants to agree on the truth of the absolute prohibition?
28. This seems to imply that the prohibition of taking one's life should be taken as the reference of "this alone of all things."
29. See also Rowe (1993: 126–127), who points out that it is unclear whether a Greek speaker would automatically have taken *thaumaston ei* "surprising that/if" in the same sense throughout this thorny sentence.
30. Miles, for example, takes the prohibition as Pythagorean (2001: 244), though not on the grounds of the dialect. However, somewhat surprisingly, later on (p. 256) he identifies as Orphic or Pythagorean, not the prohibition (his no. 2), but the claim of philosophers' willingness to die (no. 1 of the two main claims he focuses on). This might be a slip, in which case his references would be more coherent. However, nothing in my argument depends on how we understand Miles in this respect.
31. Cooper takes it as the most natural reading of the passage that human beings are held captive. Even though I agree that this implication is relevant to the passage, the following reference to caretakers softens the analogy somewhat.
32. It is true that (3) is introduced as an argument for (2) and thus the two claims are closely linked: the impression is that an argument is presented to solve the

tension between (1) and (2), i.e., philosophers' willingness to die and the prohibition of self-killing. However, as I shall argue in the text, the discussion ends inconclusively.

33. It is worth noting that when the Stoic Seneca, whose own death later was staged according to Plato's *Phaedo*, discusses old age in his letter no. 12, he moves to a very positive description of taking one's life. In that context, he perhaps echoes this passage in the *Phaedo* when stating that the truth is no one's private property but common to all: "what is true is mine" and "as all those who swear in words . . . know, the best things are common property" (Seneca, *Letters* 12.11.2–5).

REFERENCES

Ancient Sources

Aristophanes. *Clouds*, ed. K. J. Dover. Oxford: Clarendon Press, 1968, repr. 1970.

Aristotle. *Nicomachean Ethics*: *Aristotelis ethica Nicomachea*, ed. I. Bywater. Oxford: Clarendon Press, 1894, repr. 1962.

——. *Metaphysics*: *Aristotle's* Metaphysics, vol. 1, ed. W. D. Ross. Oxford: Clarendon Press, 1924, repr. 1970 (of corrected 1953 ed.).

Augustine. *City of God*, vol. 1, books 1–3 (Loeb Classical Library), trans. George E. McCracken. Cambridge MA: Harvard University Press, 1957.

Clemens of Alexandria. *Stromata: Clemens Alexandrinus, vol. 2*, ed. O. Stählin, L. Früchtel, and U. Treu. Berlin: Akademie-Verlag, 1960 (Die griechischen christlichen Schriftsteller der ersten Jahrhunderte 52 [Christian Greek Authors of the First Century]).

Diogenes Laertius. *Lives of Eminent Philosophers*: *Diogenes laertii vitae philosophorum*, 2 vols., ed. H. S. Long. Oxford: Clarendon Press, 1964.

Homer. *Iliad*: *Homeri Ilias*, vols. 2–3, ed. T. W. Allen. Oxford: Clarendon Press, 1931.

Plato. *Apology*: *Platonis opera*, vol. 1, ed. J. Burnet. Oxford: Clarendon Press, 1900, repr. 1967.

——. *Crito*: *Platonis opera*, vol. 1, ed. J. Burnet. Oxford: Clarendon Press, 1900, repr. 1967.

——. *Laws*: *Platonis opera*, vol. 5, ed. Burnet, J. Oxford: Clarendon Press, 1907, repr. 1967.

——. *Phaedo*: *Platonis opera*, vol. 1, ed. J. Burnet. Oxford: Clarendon Press, 1900, repr. 1967.

——. *Phaedrus*: *Platonis opera*, vol. 2, ed. J. Burnet. Oxford: Clarendon Press, 1901, repr. 1967.

——. *Symposium*: *Platonis opera*, vol. 2, ed. J. Burnet. Oxford: Clarendon Press, 1901, repr. 1967.

Plutarch. *Moralia*: *Plutarchi moralia*, vol. 2.1, ed. W. Nachstädt, W. Sieveking, and J. B. Titchener. Leipzig: Teubner, 1935, repr. 1971.

Seneca. *De Ira*: *Sénèque. Dialogues*, tome 1, ed. A. Bourgery. Paris: les belles lettres, 1942.
——. *Letters*: *Senecae ad Lucilium Epistulae Morales*, vols. 1–2, ed. L. D. Reynolds. Oxford, 1965.
Sophocles. *Oedipus*: *Sophocle*, vol. 2, ed. A. Dain and P. Mazon. Paris: Les belles Lettres, 1958, repr. and rev. 1968.
Tacitus. *Annals*: *Cornelii Taciti Annalium Ab Excessu Divi Augusti Libri*, ed. C. D. Fisher. Oxford: Clarendon Press, 1906.

Research Literature

Ahonen, Marke. 2008. "Ancient Philosophers on Mental Illness" (Ph.D. diss., University of Helsinki).
Beauchamp, Thomas. 1992. "Suicide." In *Matters of Life and Death: New Introductory Essays in Moral Philosophy*, ed. Tom Regan. New York: McGraw-Hill, pp. 69–120.
Blauner, Susan Rose. 2002. *How I Stayed Alive When My Brain Was Trying to Kill Me: One Person's Guide to Suicide Prevention.* New York: Harper Collins Publishers.
Bluck, R. (trans., introduction and notes). 1955. *Plato's* Phaedo. London: Routledge & Kegan Paul.
Bonnet-Cadilhac, C. 1993. "Translation and Commentary of the Hippocratic Treatise *The Illness of Girls*." *History and Philosophy of Life Sciences* 15: 147–163.
Bostock, David. 1986. *Plato's* Phaedo. Oxford: Clarendon Press.
Burnet, John (ed. with introduction and notes). 1911. *Plato's* Phaedo. Oxford: Clarendon Press.
Cholbi, Michael. 2009. "Suicide." *The Stanford Encyclopedia of Philosophy* (fall edition), ed. Edward N. Zalta. http://plato.stanford.edu/archives/fall2009/entries/suicide/
Cooper, John M. 1999. "Greek Philosophers on Euthanasia and Suicide." In *Reason and Emotion: Essays on Ancient Moral Psychology and Ethical Theory*. Princeton, NJ: Princeton University Press, pp. 515–541.
—— (ed. with D. S. Hutchinson as an associate editor). 1997. *Plato: Complete Works.* Indianapolis: Hackett Publishing Company.
Dodds, E. R. 2004. *The Greeks and the Irrational.* Berkeley: University of California Press. (1st ed. 1951)
Dorter, K. 1982. *Plato's* Phaedo: *An Interpretation.* Toronto: University of Toronto Press.
Eugenides, Jeffrey. 1993. *The Virgin Suicides*. New York: Farrar, Straus and Giroux.
Flemming, Rebecca, and Ann Ellis Hanson. 1998. "Hippocrates' *Peri Partheniôn* (*Diseases of Young Girls*): Text and Translation." *Early Science and Medicine* 3: 241–252.
Frey, R. G. 1978. "Did Socrates Commit Suicide?" *Philosophy* 53: 106–108.
Gallop, David (trans. with notes). 1975. *Plato*: Phaedo. Oxford: Clarendon Press.

Griffin, Miriam. 1986. “Philosophy, Cato, and Roman Suicide: I–II.” *Greece & Rome* 33 (1–2): 64–77, 192–202.

Grisé, Yolande. 1982. *Le suicide dans la Rome antique.* Paris: Les belles lettres.

Grube, G. M. A. (trans.). 1997. *Plato:* Phaedo. In *The Complete Works of Plato*, ed. J. M. Cooper. Indianapolis: Hackett, pp. 49–100.

Hackforth, R. (trans. with introduction and commentary). 1955. *Plato's* Phaedo. Cambridge: Cambridge University Press.

Hofmann, Dagmar. 2007. *Suizid in der Spätantike. Seine Bewertung in der lateinischen Literatur.* Stuttgart: Franz Steiner Verlag.

Hooff, Anton J. L. van. 1990. *From Autothanasia to Suicide: Self-Killing in Classical Antiquity.* London: Routledge.

King, Helen. 1983. “Bound to Bleed: Artemis and Greek Women.” In *Images of Women in Antiquity*, ed. A. Cameron and A. Kurt. London: Croom Helm, pp. 109–127.

——. 2004. *The Disease of Virgins: The Green Sickness, Chlorosis and the Problems of Puberty.* London: Routledge.

Lebacqz, K., and H. T. Engelhardt. 1980. “Suicide.” In *Death, Dying, and Euthanasia*, ed. Dennis J. Horan and David Mall. Frederick, MD: Aletheia.

Loriaux, Robert (commentary and translation). 1969. *Le* Phédon *de Platon*, vol. 1. (Bibliothèque de la faculté de philosophie et lettres de Namur, fasc. 45). Namur: Secrétariat des publications.

Miles, Murray. 2001. “Plato on Suicide (*Phaedo* 60C–63C).” *Phoenix* 55 (3/4): 244–258.

Romilly, Jacqueline de (ed., introduction and commentary). 1976. *Sophocle. Ajax.* Paris: Presses universitaires de France (Érasme 17).

Rowe, Christopher J. 1993. *Plato: Phaedo.* Cambridge Greek and Latin Classics. Cambridge: Cambridge University Press.

Smith, Michael. 1980. “Did Socrates Kill Himself Intentionally?” *Philosophy* 55 (212): 253–254.

Tarán, Leonardo. 1966. “Plato's *Phaedo* 62 A.” *American Journal of Philology* 87 (3): 326–336.

Vernant, Jean-Paul. 1991. “A General Theory of Sacrifice and the Slaying of the Victim in the Greek *Thusia.*” In *Mortals and Immortals: Collected Essays.* Princeton, NJ: Princeton University Press, pp. 290–302.

Vlastos, Gregory. 1991. *Socrates: Ironist and Moral Philosopher.* Cambridge: Cambridge University Press.

Chapter 4

Free Philosophers and Tragic Women

Stoic Perspectives on Suicide

Malin Grahn

INTRODUCTION

Among the ancient thinkers, the Stoics in particular are famous for philosophizing about self-killing and maintaining a tolerant outlook on it. Certain Roman Stoics even presented it as an act of the utmost freedom. The following famous passage from Seneca's *De Ira* exemplifies this kind of attitude:

> In whatever direction you may turn your eyes, there lies the means to end your woes. See that precipice? Down that is the way to liberty. See you that sea, that well? There sits liberty—at the bottom. See you that tree, stunted, blighted, and barren? Yet from its branches hangs liberty. See you that throat of yours, your gullet, your heart? They are ways of escape from servitude. Are the ways of egress I show you too toilsome, do they require too much of courage and strength? Do you ask what is the highway to liberty? Any vein in your body. (Seneca, *De Ira* 3.15,14; trans. van Hooff 1990: 41)

It would be somewhat misleading, however, to conclude that Stoicism is directly positive about suicide, or even glorifies it. Its explicit aim is above all to serve as a philosophy for a happy *life,* and it thus clearly purports to get rid of rather than provoke self-destructive thoughts. However, the ethical dilemma is not whether suicide is justified or acceptable at all. The question is rather discussed in the general framework of Stoic virtue ethics, the purpose of which is to give an account of how to live well and help people to attain happiness. It is true, however, that giving advice on living well also involves a discussion on dying well.

My aim in this chapter is to clarify the reasons why the Stoics held the view that suicide could, in some cases, be a rational and a moral choice, or the choice of liberty, as Seneca formulates it in the above quotation. My first main point is that the Stoics primarily discussed suicide as a choice, in other words the voluntary act of an individual—an act based on a rational decision in the sense that the decision-making process involves the use of reason. The reasoning behind it, however, can be more or less correct, and in terms of moral evaluation it is not the act in itself but the reasoning that motivates it that is decisive.

In justifying this reading I will show that the materialistic and rationalistic framework of Stoic metaphysics undergirds their views that life was not unquestionably to be considered more valuable than death, and thus that the simple maintenance of biological functions was not valuable as such: a life worth living should also fulfill some *normative qualitative criteria*. Moreover, implicit in the framework of Stoic virtue ethics is the idea that a person always has the right to commit suicide because there is no external moral authority such an act could offend.

Stoic scholarship tends to scrutinize suicide on the individual level, discussing its role in the context of moral deliberation.[1] Undoubtedly, this is the level on which the Stoics mostly reflected on the issue. However, not much attention has been paid to the fact that at least some of them also accentuated the role of other people.[2] Another main point this chapter addresses is that a Stoic sage would also have considered the feelings and well-being of others before deciding on self-destruction. Seneca in particular devotes attention to the pain suicide causes loved ones and refers to a person's responsibility, as far as possible, to stay alive for the sake of others. I will show how his concern for the feelings of loved ones fits in with his approval of suicide as expressed in the passage quoted above. Thus in my reading of the Stoic framework, which emphasizes interpersonal relationships, the question whether suicide can be a legitimate choice and, if so, in what circumstances is not the only one to consider. One should also ask, "How should I react when somebody else, say a friend, considers or commits suicide?" and "If I consider committing suicide, how should I take into account other people who will be affected by my death?"

Tragedies portraying suicides strongly emphasize interpersonal relationships and emotional ties with loved ones. The final main task here is to analyze suicide in Seneca's tragedies, particularly *Phaedra*. Tragedies encompass all the ethical and emotional aspects discussed in Stoic philosophical texts: deliberation, lust, grief, and even madness. Yet another powerful aspect of human existence, love, often leads to fatal consequences in tragedies. A further reason I find tragedies particularly interesting in painting a comprehensive picture of suicide in Stoicism, and in Hellenistic and Roman thinking in general, is that they include cases of suicidal women. Stoic philosophical sources are the work of men, the "case examples" are almost exclusively men (e.g., that of Epictetus's suicidal friend, which I discuss below), and when the texts are explicitly addressed to someone, it is usually a man (there are a few exceptions, however, such as Seneca's letters to his mother Helvia and the Roman lady Marcia). However, on the tragic stage we encounter a whole range of female protagonists who often (indeed, much more often than the male protagonists) end up committing suicide. My discussion of Seneca's tragedies highlights one of these tragic suicidal women, namely Phaedra.

THE INSIGNIFICANCE OF DEATH

To understand why the Stoics discussed suicide as the voluntary choice of the agent, and how they motivated this position, it is necessary first to consider their philosophical views on death in general. The Stoic view is that death is nothing more than a natural, materialistic procedure that takes place in accordance with the ordinary laws of nature. Of course, from a first-person perspective my death is something extraordinary for *me*—it will happen to me only once and after it there will be no *me* anymore. However, from the perspective of the whole universe it is just one of the necessary events in the causal order of nature. This view is based on the Stoic materialistic and deterministic metaphysics, which posits that all existing things are of material substance, including the human soul, even though it is a finer form of matter than the human body. Death is nothing more than a natural process in which the material body dissolves together with the material soul. In the face of certain religious explanations, the Stoics claim that the soul receives no punishment or praise after death, but is in much the same state as before birth. Therefore, there are no rational grounds on which to fear death (see, e.g., Seneca, *Letter* 54.1–7; *Letter* 120.18; Cicero, *De Finibus* 1.15).

The idea that a person disappears totally upon death is also thematized in Stoic logic. Chrysippus argues that it must be false to say of Dion (after his death), "This one is dead," for if he is dead there is nothing we can refer to when saying "this"—Dion no longer exists as an object of such references

(Long and Sedley 1987: 38F). Given that Stoic metaphysics does not approve of any kind of dualism between body and soul, there is no need to explain what happens to the soul of a self-killer. In this respect, Stoicism differs markedly from Neo-Platonism and Christianity, for example, both of which address the question of what the soul will suffer after suicide.[3]

Another significant metaphysical doctrine behind the Stoic approach to death and suicide, apart from materialism, is the idea that the whole universe is governed by reason, and that the governing part of the human soul partakes in the universal *logos*. The Stoics argued that human beings, by virtue of their reason, are able to understand their own place in the world and the form of life to which they are naturally best suited. This also supports the Stoic view that when a person dies, nothing bad befalls him or her—death is a natural and, for every living being, inevitable event in the cosmos, which is governed by reason. It is worth pointing out that in Stoicism, nature is considered not only a *descriptive* but also an outstandingly *normative* concept: it expresses the uppermost goal of life.[4] The Stoics maintained that a life worth living should fulfill not only the descriptive definition of being alive but also some of the normative criteria of nature, in other words of the appropriate life for a human being. This signifies use of rational capacities. Seneca points out that a good life for a human cannot consist solely in freedom from pain, as this would not be the kind of life of which only humans are capable—"also a grasshopper and a flea can have that." Not even calmness and the absence of disturbance are sufficient criteria, for "[w]ho is more at leisure than a worm?" Thus, the good life specific to humans must also fulfill some positive criteria, which Seneca identifies with life in accordance with reason, as something unique for humans (*Letter* 87.19).

Seneca emphasizes that life should be evaluated in terms of how it is lived, not how long it is: the main thing thus is quality, not quantity. He also points out that the beauty of a literary work is not measured according to the number of pages. "There are books which contain very few lines, admirable and useful in spite of the size; and there are also the Annals of Tanusius,—you know how bulky the book is, and what men say of it. This is the case with the long life of certain persons,—a state which resembles the Annals of Tanusius!" (*Epistle* 93.12, trans. Gummere). Seneca's comment illustrates an essential aspect of Stoic views on death and suicide: just staying alive, understood in the biological sense as maintaining breathing and other basic bodily functions, would be comparable to an overly long book without positive content or aesthetic value. A life that does not meet any standards of a *good* (that is, ethical) human life would not be valuable in itself, even though it is, obviously, natural in the descriptive sense of the concept. Thus, according to the normative standards of nature, death may sometimes be preferable to life. This formulation, however, raises the problem of how a person can accurately judge his or her own condition so as to be able to decide when life is no longer a worthy human life. It is unclear how the Stoics could solve this problem, insofar as they considered everybody except the sage (an ideal figure exemplifying virtue and happiness) to be fools. I return to this problem below because, as I will show, the solution is closely connected to the Stoic idea of suicide as a voluntary choice that involves moral deliberation (cf. Epictetus, *Discourses* 3.24.100–102; Seneca, *Epistle* 92: 70; to some extent the idea of suicide as a firm decision was common in Rome; see, e.g., Pliny the Younger, *Letter* 1.12.9–10[5]).

It is also worth mention that although the Stoics used the concept of nature in a normative sense, they did not understand nature as a moral authority against which a person who decided to commit suicide would be committing a crime. Thus, the Stoic idea of self-killing does not hold any connotations of murder. This, too, motivates the permissibility of suicide in Stoicism. Stoic virtue ethics takes a similar approach to ethical problems in general: this ethical theory is not intended to give universal rules that a priori would tell people what they should do and what is forbidden, regardless of circumstance. On the contrary, in the Stoic view, a virtuous person is highly sensitive to his or her circumstances and can always make the most virtuous choice available. The preferable option is to make use of one's virtue in the best way possible. Of course, dying is extremely seldom the best way because after death one cannot act virtuously any longer. Sometimes, however, in certain very specific circumstances, it could be: Stoic ethics, which emphasizes that one can always be free and that one never has to suffer, does not categorically preclude any options, including ending one's own life, from the sphere of moral deliberation. Thus, even if it was considered highly unlikely, or even purely hypothetical, that suicide was the best possible choice in some specific circumstances, the Stoics would still see it as a real possibility; therefore their ethical theory must be able to encompass it.

The Stoics' metaphysical view of death also influenced their views on suicide. When it was unavoidable and caused nothing bad for the dying person, the Stoics counted death among the *indifferent things* (*adiaphora*), that is, things outside of one's control that are ethically neither good nor bad but neutral, and do not affect happiness in any way. In other words, they claimed that only virtue and its opposite, vice, were genuinely good or bad, and that everything else fell within the ethically neutral sphere of indifference. It is significant, however, that they did not regard all indifferent things as being on the same level. Some things were indifferent and did not directly influence one's happiness, but were indirectly important in terms of how they were used. Diogenes Laertius mentions wealth, reputation, health, and strength as examples of indifferent things of this kind. Other indifferent matters include things one neither aspires to nor avoids, such as whether there is an odd or even number of hairs on one's head. The Stoics also claimed that some indifferent things were preferable and some were best avoided. Diogenes lists life and health among the preferable, and their opposites, death and sickness, among those to avoid (Diogenes Laertius, *Lives of Eminent Philosophers* 7.104). Thus, even though death is an indifferent thing, it is one that one should (in most cases) avoid.

Even though the Stoics conceived of death as natural and ethically neutral, they were nonetheless aware that people commonly believed that it was something bad, feared dying, and felt pain on account of the death of their loved ones. According to the Stoic theory of emotions, fear is based on the belief that some future event is bad in itself, and distress is an emotion deriving from belief that something in the present is inherently bad. The Stoics claimed that these beliefs are not only false; they also erroneously superimpose ethical worth on things that are in themselves ethically neutral.[6] Accordingly, Stoic philosophy aimed to guide people to get rid of their false conceptions concerning death, together with the accompanying disturbing emotions, and to accept death as a natural and necessary event. According to Epictetus's teaching, we should learn to accept that our loved ones are mortal so as not to be crushed by grief when they die. In a famous passage in *Encheiridion*, he compares a man's devotion to his wife and children to being fond of a jug: one should avoid mental upset (*tarachê*) when one's loved one dies, exactly as one should not get upset when a favorite jug gets broken: "If you are fond of a jug, say 'I am fond of a jug' for when it is broken you will not be disturbed. If you kiss your own child or wife, say to yourself that you are kissing a human being; for when she dies, you will not be disturbed" (*Encheiridion* 3).[7] He thus puts forward the idea that a material object like a jug is, by definition, breakable, and similarly a human being in its material body and material soul is, by definition, mortal. He concludes: "You are a fool, if you wish that your children, your wife and your friends should live forever, for in that case you wish that things which are not under your control should be under your control, and that what is not your own should be your own" (*Encheiridion* 14). Thus, the Stoic philosophy of life teaches us to strive for peace of mind by accepting our own mortality and that of others.

Given that death is indifferent, then, would the Stoics then claim that it is indifferent to kill ourselves, or for our loved ones consider committing suicide? The answer to both questions is negative. In the following sections I will show why.

WHAT SHOULD A PHILOSOPHICAL THERAPIST TELL A SUICIDAL FRIEND? RATIONAL REASONS FOR LIVING AND DYING

Hellenistic and Roman schools of philosophy frequently presented philosophy and medicine as analogical practices: thus, as a medical doctor takes care of physical suffering, the task of the philosopher is to take care of mental suffering. A central goal of Stoic philosophy is to function as a *therapeia*, in other words to help people get rid of their anguish and fears in order to pursue happiness and peace of mind.[8] Fates people would consider tragic and unfortunate are, in fact, ethically neutral outcomes of the causal and rational order of the universe. The aim of philosophical therapy, then, is to correct the wrong ways of thinking that lead people to attach the source of their happiness to indifferent things. According to Epictetus, tragedy arises "when everyday events befall fools" (*Discourses* 2.16). In other words, there is no such thing as tragedy as such; it is rather a question of how things appear to us, in other words how we evaluate the things we encounter in the world and how we act upon them. Epictetus explicitly claims that tragedy emanates from the wrong use of sense-impressions—that is, from how things appear and the meanings we attach to them.

> What, am I any better than Agamemnon or Achilles—are they because of following the impressions of their senses to do and suffer such evils, while I am to be satisfied with the impressions of my sense? And what tragedy has any other source than this? What is the *Atreus* of Euripides? Sense-impression (*to phainomenon*). What is the *Oedipus* of Sophocles? Sense-impression. The *Phoenix*? Sense-impression. The *Hippolytus*? Sense-impression. What kind of a man, then do you think he is who does not take care of his beliefs? How are those men called who follow every impression of their senses?—Madmen (*mainomenoi*).—Are we, then, doing any better? (*Discourses* 2.28.32–33, Oldfather's translation modified.)

Epictetus's comment refers to the well-known Stoic idea that in one sense, human beings are all mad, with the sole exception of sages who, however, very likely do not exist. However, as was common in Greco-Roman thought, the Stoics also distinguished between general madness (from which they thought all common people suffered) and medical madness, which ancient medicine divided into two main types: *mania* and *melancholia* (in Latin usually *insania* and *furor*). Philosophical therapy was meant for fools of the first sort. Those who were mad in the medical sense were usually assumed to be in need of medical treatment and thus were patients of medical doctors rather than philosophers.[9]

I agree with Dagmar Hofmann, who points out that *voluntariness to die* characterizes the Stoic approach to suicide, and since the moral evaluation of suicide depends on how the act is motivated and committed, it was not considered a symptom of a pathological state, as it typically is today (Hofmann 2007: 11, 28–34; *voluntaria mors* was also the standard Latin term). It is indeed interesting to note that despite the medical discourse in antiquity and the references to madness in both its medical and its common meaning in philosophical texts, suicidal thoughts or acts were not treated as symptoms of medical madness. On the contrary, suicide is discussed in Stoic philosophical texts as an ethical problem, under the assumption that the agent is still "within the reach of sound argumentation" and thus mad only in the general, not the medical sense. A. A. Long neatly condenses the goal of Stoic therapy: "Philosophical power and heroism in the service of personal happiness and social concern: It was an extraordinary project—to secure human life, one's own and other people's, from tragedy" (Long 2001: 31).

How, then, would a Stoic therapist attempt to save people from a tragic fate? How would such a therapist treat patients with suicidal thoughts? A story of Epictetus illuminates the answer to these questions. It reports a discussion between the Stoic philosopher himself and a friend who was about to commit suicide by starving himself to death. Epictetus intervened, demanding to know what had motivated his friend's decision. If the reasons for killing himself were indeed rational, Epictetus assured him, Epictetus and other friends would be more than willing to stand by their friend's side during his last moments. However, because the suicidal friend was unable to give any proper reasons for his self-starvation, Epictetus accused him of acting out of plain stubbornness and extravagance. Finally, he talked his friend out of his suicidal thoughts—commenting that luckily the man was reasonable enough to be swayed by sound argumentation. (*Discourses* 2.15)

This story sheds light on Stoic attitudes to self-killing. The Stoic philosopher would not have anything against it as such (and might even be willing to support the person in his or her last moments), but the motivation must be carefully deliberated, and preferably discussed with friends.[10]

The often-repeated Stoic advice is that whenever it is possible to strive for a life in accordance with nature, the deliberate and courageous choice is to go on living. Seneca, too, emphasizes that death is no solution to a bad life when the problem lies in how one leads and thinks about one's own life: "So great is human thoughtlessness, even madness, that certain people are driven to death by the fear of it" (*Letter* 24.23–24). Thus, what the therapist should cure are the person's ways of thinking about death. Death in itself is no cure for a disease of this kind.

Epictetus's story highlights the role of a Stoic philosophical therapist. As a philosopher, this therapist would scrutinize the rationale behind the person's action and evaluate the most reasonable choice to make in this particular case. If the person's own reasoning went astray, the therapist would try to "reach him with sound argumentation" and thus to persuade him to act in accordance with reason, not emotion or some other erroneous motivation such as extravagance. Epictetus's story also exemplifies how a Stoic would deal with the suicidal thoughts of another person. The philosopher friend would act as a guide to living well and recommend choosing death only when it really was the most rational choice.[11] The question remains, then, how a Stoic philosopher can know when suicide is the most rational choice available. In what circumstance would he or she recommend death?

The sources give no evidence of cases in which a Stoic seriously recommended suicide to someone. (Epictetus repeatedly says, "Hang yourself!" to his interlocutors in his *Discourses*, but this should be understood as part of his exaggerated rhetoric, not as an indication that he wanted his interlocutors really to put their heads in the noose.) Nevertheless, the Stoics do discuss the question (either in general or from a first-person perspective) of when suicide is acceptable or even recommendable. Perhaps the most useful guideline they give is that committing suicide is a preferable choice if, for one reason or another, one can no longer make a virtuous choice. Suicide, then, is better than acting against virtue.[12]

When, then, is it no longer possible to pursue a virtuous life? Diogenes Laertius reports that the Stoics would have considered suicide a rational choice if the person was no longer actively able to make moral progress–or, in the case of the sage or the utopian figure exemplifying the Stoic ideals of rationality and virtue, not able to continue acting virtuously–due to severe pain, injury or incurable illness, for example. Diogenes also mentions sacrificing oneself for the sake of one's country or friends as cases in which a Stoic would approve of suicide. Thus, suicide could be a rational choice if one's death would benefit other people, or if one would no longer be capable of ethical action (*Lives of Eminent Philosophers* 7.130). John M. Cooper emphasizes that the moral character of the person considering suicide does not play any role in the moral evaluation of the act. In other words, suicide may be the right choice for a fool or a sage–it depends exclusively on the outer circumstances (the sphere that the Stoics considered ethically neutral, neither good nor bad in itself) and on the options one has. (Cooper 1999: 532)

When Seneca discusses suicide as a rational choice, he describes situations in which the person will die anyway: having been tortured, taken prisoner by enemies, or condemned to death. In such situations, when death is already near, one could choose a more dignified, voluntary departure from life (*Epistle* 70.22–23).[13] Seneca also mentions losing one's rational capacities as a proper reason for committing suicide: it is, after all, the rational capacities that, according to the Stoics, really make a person a *human being* and enable moral progress. Seneca suggests that life will be worth living as long as the commanding part of the human soul still functions properly and thus enables rational deliberation. "I will not abandon my old age if it leaves me all of myself, but that means all of the better part. But if it starts to weaken my intelligence, to dislodge its parts, if what it leaves me is not a *life* but just being alive, then I shall jump clear off a decayed and collapsing building" (*Letter* 58.34–35, trans. and italics Inwood).[14]

In another passage it seems that Seneca even considered leading an unworthy and humiliating life sufficient reason to commit suicide. He cites the case of a Spartan slave boy who "dashed out his brains against the wall" because he did not want to obey an order to fetch a chamber pot. Seneca asks: "So near at hand is freedom, and is anyone still a slave?" (*Epistle* 77.14–15, trans. Gummere; cf. the quotation from *De Ira* at the beginning of this chapter in which Seneca describes suicide as "escaping from servitude"). This case is perplexing, however, because the only form of slavery the Stoics tended to acknowledge as truly ethically bad was the inner form, in which the barrier to freedom from disturbances of the mind is one's own way of living and thinking. It would, indeed, seem consistent with Stoic principles that as far as genuine goals as a human being are concerned, in the final analysis it is not decisive whether one is a toilet cleaner or the emperor of Rome—peace of mind is achievable in either role in that it rests not on outer circumstances but on the internal capacities of the soul that all humans possess in equal measure. (To be sure, we may wonder how plausible it is that someone who is kept as a slave really would have the same possibilities to dedicate his mind to practicing philosophy as a free-born man.)

Interestingly, Epictetus uses exactly the same image of emptying a chamber pot to illustrate a point that directly contradicts Seneca: if you must do something that at first glance seems humiliating, but is so only because of habit and has nothing to do with reason, it is better to do it than not to do it. Thus, if doing an unpleasant job of this kind is necessary *to keep oneself alive*, it is unquestionably what one should do. Epictetus comments: "If, then, you ask me whether you should hold the chamber pot or not, I will tell you that to get food is of greater value than not to get it . . . so that if you measure your interests by these standards, go and hold the chamber pot" (*Discourses* 1.2.10–11, Oldfather's translation modified). Thus, Seneca and Epictetus express two different views on slavery. Epictetus recognizes only inner slavery as something bad and avoidable, and recommends acceptance even of outer slavery if this way one can keep one self alive—that is, he recommends striving for peace of mind based on one's inner freedom even in the extreme circumstances of slavery or imprisonment. Seneca, on the other hand, expresses a stricter view on the normative standards of proper human life in the letter quoted above, even in this case stating, against the Stoic idea that all outer things are ethically insignificant, that the outer conditions of slavery make a human life not worth living.[15] However, in *Letter 47*, in which he argues for the humane treatment of slaves, he points out that people who are born in "freedom" or "slavery" are, as humans, equal, and that the most serious slavery is self-imposed slavery: being the slave of one's own lust (*Letter* 47). I claim that the most serious problem in the Stoic approach is that in accentuating inner freedom so powerfully, it fails to condemn the institution of slavery as such as an ethical and political problem. To argue for a humane treatment of slaves still legitimates the institution of slavery as such, and recognition of the metaphysical equality of all humans is not enough if the social structures of oppression and hierarchy remain.

Yet, what these three positions, of Epictetus and the two different standpoints on slavery in Seneca, have in common is that they emphasize inner liberty, which is universal in humans. Seneca's story of the Spartan slave expresses the Stoic point that nobody can ever force anyone to do anything unworthy. Epictetus and Seneca's *Letter 47* draw attention to the idea of freedom regardless of the outer conditions. Thus the contrasting images of the chamber-pot-changing servant are connected to the same underlying Stoic idea: that our minds can always be free and we never have to be slaves in the internal sense of the term.

What if Epictetus had arrived too late and his friend had already committed suicide? Or if the friend was beyond the reach of reasonable talk and killed himself against all advice? As a Stoic, Epictetus would most probably have reacted to his friend's suicide exactly as though he had passed away in any other circumstances, i.e. considered it as a material process. If Epictetus were a sage (which, indeed, no Stoic claimed to be), he would not have felt pain. Despite his *apatheia*, or lack of emotions, he would not have been as hard as stone, and would probably have shed tears at the funeral. However, he would not have attached his own happiness to this other person because he would have realized at the outset that this person would die anyway. The way a loved one passes away (whether by suicide, rational or irrational, or in another way) is only an accidental characteristic of an event that is insignificant in itself; thus there is no reason for a Stoic to react differently to another person's voluntary or involuntary death.

SUICIDE AND FAMILY: HOW SHOULD THE SUICIDE CANDIDATE TAKE LOVED ONES INTO ACCOUNT?

Above I showed the circumstances under which a Stoic would approve of (or even recommend) suicide, and how he or she would react when a friend or loved one considered or committed suicide. How, then should a Stoic with considered and rational reasons for committing suicide take into account friends and loved ones? If the Stoic sage considers the death of other people indifferent, does it follow that others should be indifferent to his or her own death?

Seneca reflects on the effects of suicide on others, especially close family members, stating that keeping on living is a worthwhile choice because one's death would cause pain to one's loved ones. Moreover, life should be preferred to death because staying alive is simply what a virtuous person does, as long as it is still possible to live a proper human life in the sense defined above, in other words to be capable of using reason and moral deliberation. In *Letter 78* Seneca describes how he suffered from catarrh as a young man, which eventually became so painful that he decided to kill himself. When he thought about his old father, however, he hesitated. His father would probably not have borne his son's death as courageously as Seneca himself, who was prepared to end his life. Having realized this, Seneca gave up his suicidal plans in order not to shock his beloved parent: "So I ordered myself to live–sometimes even to live is an act of courage (*itaque imperavi mihi ut viverem; aliquando enim et vivere fortiter facere est*)." (*Letter* 78.2, transl. Costa) This formulation clearly expresses an attitude different from the Roman heroic conception of suicide. Indeed, Seneca's formulation even sounds like criticism of the latter in that he connects the choice to remain alive to the highly valued virtue of courage.

In *Letter 104* Seneca suggests that a noble man should attempt to stay alive for the sake of others, despite his own troubles and misfortunes. Here, too, relationships with close family members strengthen the argument, and again Seneca takes a personal memory as a case in point. He declares that his wife Paulina's tender feelings toward him had strengthened his own love toward himself and made him take better care of himself. His health was thus not only his own concern but also hers. He writes:

> For we must respect our genuine feelings, and sometimes even against physical pressures our last breath has to be summoned back and kept from passing our lips for the sake of our dear ones, and even at the cost of great pain, since it is the good man's duty to live not as long as he wants but as long as he should. The man who does not value his wife or his friend

> enough to stay alive a little longer, and insists on dying, is self-indulgent. (*Letter* 104.3, trans. Costa)

Both examples—of Seneca's father and wife—show that Seneca placed a high value on relationships and duties toward others. Indeed, even if Stoic virtues are practiced individually, many are practiced in relation to others; it would be paradoxical to assume that a virtuous person was ignorant of others (which, if so, would simply show a lack of virtue).[16]

These stories also serve as excellent counter-examples to the common critique that the Stoic theory of the cognitively fallacious nature of all emotions meant that they would scorn close interpersonal bonds such as love. This critique is insensitive to the Stoics' repeated assertions that the sage, even though emotionless, is not as hard as stone but is also touched by events in the world, and that his or her virtue is specifically expressed in terms of relations to others. Seneca clearly shows his concern not only by attempting to achieve peace of mind, but also by promoting his family's well-being. He does not suggest that his father or Paulina should just reason that they loved a mortal who would die anyway and that death is just a natural material process and nothing to be to shocked about, any more than if their favorite jug got broken. Even if practicing Stoicism himself, he does not expect other people to act or think like Stoics. After all, as stated above, the Stoics did not claim to be sages: they admitted that they were living the lives of ordinary fools, touched by insignificant things. They would reflect carefully on how they influenced the emotions of others, even if they believed that emotions were fallacious and something to get rid of.

Rather, I claim, the Stoic argument that suicide may sometimes be a rational and virtuous choice is meant to support the notion that it is possible to live a life free from suffering without ever having to experience anything truly bad. If one, in some admittedly very rare and extreme circumstances, ended up choosing to die rather than to go on living, such dying is not truly bad. As Epictetus emphasizes, "the door is always open"—when acting as a good human being becomes impossible, we can always opt out.[17] Seneca writes: "'It is grim to live under constraint, but there is no constraint to live under constraint. Why is this so? Because there are on all sides many short and easy roads to freedom. Let us thank god that no one can be forced to stay alive: we can trample down our very constraints" (*Letter* 17.10–11, Costa's translation slightly modified; cf. *De Ira* 3.15). In other words, the Roman Stoic thinkers Epictetus and Seneca emphasize that suicide is a voluntary choice that in itself is ethically neutral—though it may be based on right reasoning, or on wrong motivations such as ignorance, fear, or vanity. The Stoic position is radical, claiming that one is always a free agent, and that even in extreme situations (such as being tortured or enslaved) one's responsibility as a rational being is to choose the most virtuous actions available, even if it dying might appear as one of the possible courses of action one must choose between. However, a virtuous person will always reflect carefully on the circumstances, the available options, and the effects of his or her choice on other people.

SUICIDE AND TRAGEDY: SENECA'S *PHAEDRA*

Seneca was, apart from a Stoic philosopher, a playwright, and suicide is a recurring topic in both his philosophical writing and his tragedies. Of course, as a playwright he leaned on the tradition of Greek tragedy, in which suicidal thoughts and behavior were common. He rewrote stories that already dealt with suicide, such as *Medea*, *Oedipus*, and *Phaedra*, giving new accounts of the motivation behind the decision to commit suicide and of the acts themselves (such as how the character carried it out).[18] One interesting aspect of the tragedies is that they include cases of suicidal women, whereas the philosophical discussion of suicide concentrates almost exclusively on men (on gender in Stoicism, see Grahn 2013). On the stage we encounter a host of heroines who end up taking their own lives, such as Phaedra, Antigone, Medea, and Oedipus' mother Jocasta, whereas very few males do so: Ajax is quite alone with his fate.[19] On the basis of the above discussion on the importance of interpersonal relationships in evaluating whether or not suicide is a preferable choice, one could ask whether the tragic heroines were particularly ignorant about their husbands and children, or whether they had good reasons for their action. In the following I analyze the suicidal theme in Seneca's *Phaedra*. Before making a few philosophical points about this tragedy I will give a short synopsis of the plot.

The story starts with Phaedra bemoaning her misfortune, the source of which is her burning desire for her stepson Hippolytus. From the beginning of the play she yearns for suicide as a release from her incestuous lust, which by her own admission is driving her insane: it is a lust she is neither able to control nor allowed to fulfill. She laments: "A sickness grows in my blood—hotter and thicker than Etna's lava" (*Phaedra* 199). Phaedra is ashamed of desiring the son of her own husband—and yet she cannot help herself. In addition to the fact that Hippolytus is Phaedra's stepson, he seems to be an impossible object of love in that he devotes his life to hunting, isolating himself in the forest and avoiding all contact with the opposite sex (he declares: "I hate and despise all womankind, without exception": 570).[20] With both her honor and her mental health at stake, Phaedra is aware of the impossibility of her situation. In torment she longs to escape from life and wonders whether she should meet death "with noose, or sharp swordpoint" or whether she should "leap headlong from the parapet of the palace" (260). The nurse gives her genuinely Stoic advice: "Noble enough to die is noble enough to contrive a way to live. Restrain that mad passion of yours!" (258). (These words, indeed, seem to echo Seneca's above-quoted words when he decided to live for the sake of his father.)

Phaedra, then, leaves her suicidal thoughts behind and instead confesses her passion to Hippolytus. Outraged, Hippolytus declares her passion unnatural ("the Minotaur wasn't so much a freak as you": 690) and escapes into the woods. Meanwhile Theseus, Phaedra's husband and Hippolytus's father, whom Phaedra had thought dead, returns from his journey to Hades. Phaedra tricks Theseus into believing that Hippolytus had attempted to rape her, and in revenge Theseus puts a lethal curse on his son. After Hippolytus's violent death, Phaedra not only feels ashamed of her improper desire, she also feels guilty for having caused the death of her loved one. With the object of her love gone forever, she sees no reason to go on and longs to find comfort in death, which would finally unite her with Hippolytus. She cries out: "I beg your pardon. I beg everyone's pardon. Perhaps I shall soon see all of you in hell." These are her last words before she throws herself dramatically on Hippolytus' sword (1200).

In Seneca's version of the play, the main motivations for Phaedra's suicide are shame, guilt, and liberation from sorrow. Even though she was literally crazy about her stepson and her passion for Hippolytus is presented as frantic, it is notable that Seneca—in a Stoic fashion, I would add—does not imply that her suicide resulted from madness. On the contrary, she deliberates on her own condition and on the moral nature of her dilemma, and kills herself as a result of these deliberations, taking the death penalty to be the right punishment for her deeds. The play presents her as a courageous figure acting as her own prosecutor, judge, and executioner.

There are certain remarkable differences between Seneca's and Euripides' versions of the plot. In Euripides' *Hippolytus* it is not Phaedra but the nurse who reveals to Hippolytus that his stepmother is madly in love with him.[21] Hippolytus reacts aggressively, swears eternal hatred against all women and declares that he will make Phaedra's wickedness generally known. Afraid that her reputation will be tainted, Phaedra hangs herself and leaves a suicide note in which she accuses Hippolytus of rape. Theseus believes this and curses his son, causing his death without listening to his defense or the contrary evidence given by the chorus.

Whereas Seneca's Phaedra confronts an inner conflict between her emotions and what she recognizes in her introspection as ethically wrong and shameful, Euripides' Phaedra is extremely concerned about her honor and reputation in the eyes of others. As Elise P. Garrison points out in her analysis of suicide in Euripides' plays, the notions of *eukleia*, a good reputation, and its opposite, *dyskleia*, lie behind Phaedra's suicidal motivations. Confronting a conflict between her passions and the moral standards of her society, and she decides to kill herself to ensure that both her own and her children's names will be left untainted after her death. Moreover, Phaedra's suicide note is intended as revenge on Hippolytus, who is going to destroy her reputation. According to Garrison, vengeance usually plays only a secondary role as a motivation for suicide in classic tragedies, so *Hippolytus* is exceptional in this respect (Garrison 1995: 65–71, 78–79). Instead she classifies the typical suicidal motivations as: "to avoid disgrace and preserve an honorable reputation; to avoid further suffering; to end grief; and to sacrifice oneself for a greater good" (2). She analyzes *Hippolytus* with regard to two of these categories: honor and avoidance of further suffering (65–71, 89–93). In Euripides' version Phaedra manages to keep her reputation intact. Although she and other characters condemn her lust as mad, miasmatic, and unnatural at the beginning of the play, at the end she receives comfort and forgiveness. Euripides lets the goddess Artemis speak the following words to Hippolytus on his deathbed:

> You will reap through the long cycle of time, a rich reward in tears.
> And when young girls sing songs, they will not forget you,
> your name will not be left unmentioned,
> nor Phaedra's love for you remain unsung. (*Hippolytus* 1425–30, trans. David Grene)

Seneca, in contrast, does not portray Phaedra's suicide as vengeance, nor is the question of honor central in his play. Even though other characters express concern about the honor of Phaedra's name (the nurse warns her that she will bring disgrace upon her house and stain its honor, *Phaedra* 145), Seneca's Phaedra intends her suicide to clear Hippolytus' name rather than her own. Before killing herself she addresses Hippolytus' corpse: "But now your honor is put together again. I have set that right" (1198) Phaedra's own reputation, however, suffers more in Seneca's version than in Euripides'. At the end of Seneca's play, Theseus condemns Phaedra's name and offers her no forgiveness: "As for her, a hole dug somewhere in dirt that will hide her away deep, where her deadly taint can no longer reach us" (1289) Yet, as I argue below, in the contexts of both tragedy and Stoicism, Theseus's own fate could be considered still worse than Phaedra's.

Van Hooff emphasizes incest victims' shame as a common reason for suicide in ancient material (1990: 25–26, 117–118). It is interesting to note the difference between Phaedra and Oedipus' mother Jocasta, however. Jocasta cannot bear the shame of having been married to her own son (without knowing it, of course)–Phaedra, on the other hand, is not the object but the subject of desire and perfectly aware of the incestuous nature of it. Significantly, when both Phaedra and Jocasta take their own lives, their husbands, Theseus and Oedipus, choose to remain alive–Theseus crushed by guilt, Oedipus in blindness because he is too ashamed to look at his parents and, in Seneca's version, believes that "suicide can't atone for the misdeeds" (Seneca *Oedipus*: 983). Perhaps Theseus, too, decides not to kill himself because of his guilt and considers suffering the right penalty for his deed–one that is even harder to bear than capital punishment.

Seneca emphasizes the ethical nature of Phaedra's dilemma much more than Euripides does. But even if her suicide is deliberate, are the reasons for it sound? She is certainly not a Stoic sage, as she is unable to control her strong emotions. Thus she has faults in her character, and it is these very faults that lead to the tragic events (as the nurse comments–again with a strong Stoic bottom line: "Fate is not the grand auteur of these affairs: they are merely errors of judgments, lapses of taste, and failures of character": 150). Nevertheless, this does not imply that her character as a whole was vicious or mad, or that she was akratic, that is, characterized by weakness of will. Nor could she be considered particularly ignorant of interpersonal relationships when her decision to kill herself is concerned, because all the tragic events have left her no one to live for; certainly the play does not suggest that anyone would be negatively affected by *her* death.

Interestingly, when Epictetus discusses Medea, who killed both her husband and her children, he praises her for her strength of character. He asks his audience to feel pity (*eleos*) for her, rather than to be angry with or condemn her, "as we pity the blind and the lame" (*Discourses* 1.28.7–9, 2.17.19–22). Medea thus appears to be blind in her ethical judgments and decision-making processes.[22] Does this also hold for Phaedra? Should we also feel pity for her, as Epictetus says we should feel for Medea? I think we should. Garrison points out that ancient tragedies tend to treat suicides with sympathy (Garrison 1995: 33). This, it seems to me, is the case with Phaedra: she makes errors (as all ordinary human beings do), but she is not quite beyond the reach of reason. Moreover, her suicide is not presented as a *hamartia*, a tragic error.[23] In Seneca's play it is not Phaedra's suicide that leads to tragic consequences: on the contrary, it is a resolution to a tragedy that has already happened–the death of innocent Hippolytus. The tragic error is rather that Theseus blindly believes that Hippolytus is guilty of attempted rape, and acts too hastily upon this judgment (or also that Phaedra tells her husband this lie in the first place). Moreover, even if Phaedra is a tragic heroine who ends up taking her own life, her suicide, as is typical in ancient tragedies, is not the worst kind of tragic fate. On the contrary, her death is a relief: it puts an end to her suffering and attempts to put things right (to clear her own name in Euripides and Hippolytus' name in Seneca, and to atone for Hippolytus' death). The worst lot is thus that of Theseus, who is left alive, quite alone, a childless widower who has lost hope and given up his expectations for the future, and forever suffers from the guilt of having killed his innocent son. In line with Stoic ideas, the worst fate in the ancient tragedies is not, after all, death, but continuing life in misery.[24] However, neither Phaedra's or Theseus' situation was bad enough to fulfill the Stoic criteria for suicide as a virtuous choice, because nothing was preventing them from practicing virtue. As noted: from a Stoic perspective, tragedies by definition occur among fools, not sages.

CONCLUDING REMARKS

My focus in this chapter has been on how suicide is discussed in Stoic (primarily Roman Stoic) sources, and how it is depicted in Greek and Roman tragedy, particularly in Seneca's *Phaedra*. I aimed to show that the Stoics conceived of suicide fundamentally as an agent's voluntary choice, which always involved moral deliberation and the use of reason. From an ethical perspective, then, the decisive question concerns not whether suicide is permissible, but rather the situations in which a person could be said to have good reasons for preferring death to life. Even though this is left to the individual's own moral deliberation, I emphasize that the Stoic perspective on suicide was neither directly positive nor individualistic in the sense of being ignorant about other people's lives and emotions. A virtuous Stoic would reflect not only upon his or her own condition (such as being ill or imprisoned) but also on that of people who would be affected by his or her death. Careful consideration would be given to social commitments and to how loved ones would survive, and in most cases it would be obvious that the right thing to do was to stay alive for the sake of others.

However, as I have argued, it was important for the Stoics to allow for the possibility that sometimes suicide might be the right course of action. This is attributable, first, to the nature of their virtue ethics, which does not give universal rules of right and wrong. On the other hand, they emphasized the uniqueness and unpredictability of situations we live in as in a state of constant flux, and virtue as a capability or skill in choosing the best possible mode of action in any circumstances. Moreover, the statement that death is a genuine choice that is always available to us is significant in the arguments presented by Epictetus and Seneca in particular, who posit that we can always be free and can never be forced to undergo any suffering or commit any unworthy act against our will. Stoic metaphysics supports the view that death is nothing bad (it is a natural, material process), and that the person ceases to exist when she dies; thus the Stoics could consistently claim that one does not suffer anything bad by choosing death. However, in so doing one could, in some cases, avoid something genuinely bad, such as losing one's virtue.

My analyses of Stoic texts and Ancient tragedies are intended to show that in ancient thinking, suicide in itself does not necessarily involve tragedy. In both Classic Greek and Seneca's tragedies it is portrayed not as *hamartia*, a tragic error, but as the resolution of a tragedy that has already happened. According to Stoic thinking, tragedy occurs in the lives of ordinary people who follow their erroneous judgments and attach the source of their happiness to something outside of themselves. Seneca's *Phaedra* reflects the Stoic view, in that her suicide is depicted as a voluntary act: she makes a deliberate, genuine choice, and thus her death is not presented as determined by tragic events. However, even if she was acting freely in the general sense of making a free choice, in Stoic terms she was still not free in the ideal, ultimate sense in which only the sage is free: she had still enslaved herself to her passion. In the ideal case of the Stoic sage, who knows that the source of happiness lies entirely within oneself, no tragedy would ever occur. The sage makes every effort to live well in any circumstances—but in a very exceptional situation might also decide to die well.

The Stoics considered suicide primarily a matter of choice. It was a choice in which the decisive factor for the ethical evaluation of the act was not the suicide itself, but the entire moral deliberation involved, including the motivations that led to the act. Further, in their belief that everybody who is not suffering from serious medical insanity is within reach of sound argumentation, they appeal even to present-day readers in pointing to the importance of moral deliberation and rational decision-making with regard to the prevention of suicide. On the basis of the Stoic notion of philosophical therapy, one might ask how present-day culture could provide people with sound arguments to fall back on even when faced with hardship and misery. Thinking of suicide solely as a symptom of mental illness easily projects a dangerous image of lost agency. The question remains how a person, even in the midst of personal tragedy, could make use of ethical agency and arguments so as to be convinced that the core meaning of a worthy life is not outside of oneself, and to reflect upon the positive effects one's life can have on other people? Thus, the Stoic emphasis on choice, voluntariness, and ethical deliberation challenges us to consider critically how, even today, suicide candidates could be helped by means of rational, therapeutic and argumentative discussion, and by fostering their feelings of hope, so that self-killing would not appear to be the only way out.

NOTES

1. John M. Cooper (1999) provides a useful philosophical outlook on ancient arguments for and against self-killing. But whereas his remarks on Stoicism concentrate primarily on a paragraph in Cicero's *De Finibus* 3.60–61, I focus mostly on Epictetus's *Discourses* and Seneca's philosophical works, as well as his tragedies.
2. Gretchen Reydams-Schils contributes meaningfully to the discussion on Stoic views on suicide in the all-too-brief subchapter "Suicide and Others" in her work *The Roman Stoic*. She considers Stoic notions particularly from the perspective of the self-other relationship and discusses the (seeming) conflict between permissibility and moral duties toward others (Reydams-Schils 2005: 45–52).
3. For comparison of Stoic, Neo-Platonic, and Christian views on suicide, see Hofmann 2007: 35–64; van Hooff 1990: 181–97.
4. On the conception of nature in antiquity, and the normative standards of nature, see Julia Annas 1993: 135–221.
5. According to Pliny, his friend Corellius Rufus was contemplating taking his life in order to escape the unbearable suffering from gout. When Pliny was going to convince Corellius to change his mind, Iulius Atticus informed him that nothing could change Corellius's mind, so firm he was in his decision (*tam obstinate magis ac magis induruisse*, 1.12.10.3). This left Pliny with admiration as much as grief.
6. On the Stoic theory of emotions, see Nussbaum 1994; Knuuttila 2004; Knuuttila and Sihvola 1998.
7. Here Epictetus seems to be blurring the differences between different kinds of indifferent things, possibly for rhetorical reasons. Surely a Stoic does not have to accept the claim that a jug and a wife are equally irrelevant to one's happiness (just as one's health and the number of hairs on one's head are not indifferent in the same manner).
8. The therapeutic aspects of Stoicism are emphasized especially in Michel Foucault's *Hermeneutics of the Subject* (1981–82, in English 2005), Martha Nussbaum's *Therapy of Desire* (1994), and Pierre Hadot's *Philosophy as a Way of Life* (1995).
9. Mental illness in ancient literature is discussed in Marke Ahonen's doctoral thesis *Ancient Philosophers on Mental Illness* (2008).
10. It may seem to the contemporary reader that the Stoic attitude here is tolerant not only of suicide but also of euthanasia. However, even though the concept of euthanasia stems from Greek, there is no explicit ethical discussion of it in ancient philosophical literature, at least not in the sense in which we understand the term. Literary *eu* + *thnêskô* signify "dying well," but the only derivative of this combination of prefix and word in Liddell and Scott's lexicon is

euthnêsimos, signifying "in or with easy death." On the concept of euthanasia in the context of Greek philosophy, see Cooper 1999. Yet even if the Stoics did not discuss euthanasia as such, their arguments for accepting suicide could be taken to support it. If the reasons in favor of suicide are sound and the decision to commit it is the person's own, the Stoics would surely have seen no reason why another person should not help someone "to step out of the door," as they put it, when he or she is not able to accomplish the act on his or her own. Given that Stoic ethics is based on virtues rather than moral obligations or prohibitions, it would not approve of universal commands such as "killing is wrong." Surely, a Stoic sage would respect his or her fellow human beings and consider them of exactly the same worth as him- or herself. Nevertheless, he or she would always make the best possible choice in each unpredictable circumstance, and I cannot see any reason why there could not be circumstances in which helping someone to die would be the most ethical thing for a sage to do, such as if the person was suffering from a particularly painful, incurable illness and explicitly wished to end his or her sufferings.

11. Miriam Griffin also calls attention to the presence of friends in discussions on suicide from the Roman period. In addition to this "social character," she expressly points out how calm the suicide victims in question are, even if the setting is often described in a rather theatrical way. She writes: "These features make a sharp contrast with what we still think of as the typical suicide of modern civilized countries, i.e. a solitary act expressive of despair and misery" (1986: 66).
12. Cf. Miriam Griffin, who also points out that even if the Stoics are often attributed a reputation for making suicide acceptable, they still did not have "anything more than a severely qualified approval of suicide to offer" (1986: 68).
13. According to Miriam Griffin, "Stoicism, not alone but via the powerful example of Cato, made suicide, not tolerated or acceptable—for it was that already—but fashionable and esteemed" and "helped to provide *the etiquette and style* for suicide" (1986: 197–198).
14. In *De Ira*, Seneca even accepts capital punishment for those who are incurably wicked. He reasons, on the one hand, that some people are so morally corrupt that they are no longer able to act virtuously and thus deserve this treatment, just as a doctor amputates a limb that cannot be saved. Yet his arguments also refer to the benefit of the whole human community and claim that just as the amputation of a diseased limb might be needed to maintain a human life, execution might be necessary to benefit the rest of the community (*De Ira* 1.15–16, 2.31). Thus, despite the Stoic arguments promoting cosmopolitanism and the equal ethical worth of all humans, in some texts Stoic thinkers accept a striking amount of cruelty and oppression, as in Seneca's discussions of tough punishments in *De Ira*, and his tolerance of slavery in his letters.
15. Martha Nussbaum points out that as long as there are acts we can do for others, taking Seneca's advice literally and escaping oppression by killing oneself appears at worst as "egocentric." She writes: "For the person who reacts to tyranny by leaping into a well does not do anything for others; and he protects

his gentle involvement with humanity with the price of a selfish sort of non-involvement" (1994: 436). According to my reading, however, the Stoic's point is not to promote non-involvement but rather to leave open the possibility that no one can ever be forced to suffer a tragic fate—or to turn other people's lives into a tragedy. As I will argue in detail below, more often than not this would signify exactly staying alive for the sake of others, even if it means facing hardship. I take Nussbaum to agree with my conclusion, too, as she pays attention to the last lines of Seneca's *De Ira*: "Let us cultivate humanity" (438).

16. For an illuminating discussion on the ethical importance of other people in Stoic ethics, see Annas 1993: 223–328, Grahn 2013: 321–360, and Reydams-Schils 2005: 59–82.
17. In addition to the frequently mentioned image of "stepping out of the door," Epictetus and Seneca use the simile of an actor leaving the scene. Both thinkers seem to assume, somewhat implausibly, that one would be able to kill oneself at any time. In support of this point Seneca describes suicides committed in prison or other extreme situations when suitable instruments are not immediately at hand thus: "If you do not lack the courage, you will not lack the cleverness to die" (*Epistle* 70.24–25; cf. *Epistle* 77.14–15).
18. Suicidal thoughts and acts were common in classic Greek plays. According to Elise P. Garrison, in thirteen out of thirty-two extant Attic tragedies, "suicide or self-sacrifice figures prominently whether actual, threatened or contemplated." Suicide also plays an incidental role in ten other scripts, and some plays there are several such deaths (Garrison 1995: 1). On the role of suicide in ancient myths, see Garrison 2000.
19. Oedipus also considers suicide a resolution to his misery, but decides to blind himself instead. In Seneca's version of the play, the messenger reveals that Oedipus considered suicide insufficient punishment for his misdeeds (Seneca *Oedipus*, 950–1000), reflecting Sophocles' play in this respect; see chapter 3 above.
20. Seneca's Hippolytus resembles a caricature that some critiques of Stoicism might draw of a Stoic sage: connecting life *kata phusin* to withdrawal into the woods, and *apatheia* to a person who scorns love and human relations. Of course, as noted, this was not what Seneca meant by the nature or proper role of emotions in human life.
21. In an earlier version of the play, Euripides included a direct confrontation between Phaedra and Hippolytus, but he apparently had to revise this and change the plot so that the nurse functions as a mediator between the main characters (see David Grene's preface to his translation of *Hippolytus*, 1955).
22. In his discussion of Medea, Epictetus calls her decision to kill herself and her children an "outburst of a soul of great force" (*psychês megala*). For Medea had "a proper conception of what it means for anyone's wishes not to come true," and thus she decided to take her revenge on her husband Jason (*Discourses* 2.17.19–21) This, of course, does not alter the fact that she had faults in her character, or that she (like Phaedra) erred in her judgment and acted irrationally in killing herself and her children. Epictetus emphasizes that had she just given up her

husband, she could have lived undisturbed. He does not blame her for wanting something beyond her own power and attaching the source of her happiness to another person, however: "What else has she (Medea) to follow but that which appears to her to be true? Nothing" (*Discourses* 1.28.8–9). As mentioned earlier, a central goal of Stoic philosophical therapy was to help people avoid tragedies by persuading them not to see things as intolerable misfortunes and not to be carried away by erroneous conceptions of what is ethically good and bad. Consequently, had Medea not followed her instincts, and had she stopped wanting to get her husband back, her story would not have become a tragedy.

23. I take it as a general feature of Greek tragedies that they do not present suicide as *hamartia*. Here is a clear difference from plots such as that of Shakespeare's *Romeo and Juliet*, in which the tragic error expressly occurs when Romeo takes poison in the false belief that Juliet is dead. On *hamartia* in Aristotle's *Poetics* and Greek drama, see Stephen Halliwell (1998: 146, 212ff.).
24. Similarly, in Seneca's version of *Oedipus*, Oedipus wants to condemn himself to continuous misery in reincarnation, and wishes to be reborn to new suffering after suffering. "Let me live a brand new life, then die, only to be reborn to misery, a never-ending cycle" (Seneca *Oedipus*, 988–990).

REFERENCES

Ancient Sources

C. Plinius Caecilius Secundus (Pliny the Younger). *Epistulae*, ed. Roger A. B. Mynors. Oxford: Oxford University Press, 1966.

Diogenes Laertius. *Lives of Eminent Philosophers*, trans. R. D. Hicks. Cambridge and London: Harvard University Press, 1995.

Epictetus. *Discourses*, books 1–4, trans. W. A. Oldfather. Cambridge and London: Harvard University Press, 2000.

Euripides. *Hippolytus*. In *Four Tragedies*, trans. David Grene. Chicago: University of Chicago Press, 1955.

Lucius Annaeus Seneca. *Epistles*, vols. 1–6, trans. Richard M. Gummere. Cambridge, MA: Harvard University Press, 1917–25.

——. *On Anger* (*De Ira*). In *Moral Essays*, vol. 1, trans. John W. Basore. Cambridge, MA: Harvard University Press, 1928.

——. *17 Letters*, trans. C. D. N. Costa. Aris and Phillips, 1988.

——. *Phaedra*, in *The Tragedies*, vol. 1, ed. and trans. David R. Slavitt. Baltimore and London: The Johns Hopkins University Press, 1992.

——. *Selected Philosophical Letters*, trans. Brad Inwood. Oxford: Oxford University Press, 2007.

Marcus Tullius Cicero. *De Finibus bonorum et malorum*, trans. H. Rackham. Cambridge and London: Harvard University Press, 1951.

Research Literature

Ahonen, Marke. 2008. "Ancient Philosophers on Mental Illness" (Ph.D. diss., University of Helsinki).
Annas, Julia. 1993. *The Morality of Happiness*. Oxford: Oxford University Press.
Cooper, John M. 1999. "Greek Philosophers on Euthanasia and Suicide." In *Reason and Emotion: Essays on Ancient Moral Psychology and Ethical Theory*. Princeton, NJ: Princeton University Press.
Foucault, Michel. 2005. *The Hermeneutics of the Subject*, trans. Graham Burchell. New York: Palgrave Macmillan.
Garrison, Elise P. 1995. *Groaning Tears: Ethical and Dramatic Aspects of Suicide in Greek Tragedy*. Leiden: Brill.
——. 2000. "Suicide in Classical Mythology: An Essay." Available at www.stoa.org/diotima.
Grahn, Malin. 2013. Gender and Sexuality in Ancient Stoic Philosophy. *Philosophical Studies from the University of Helsinki*, vol. 41.
Griffin, Miriam. 1986. "Philosophy, Cato, and Roman Suicide I–II." *Greece & Rome* (N.S.) 33(1): 64–77; 192–202.
Hadot, Pierre. 1995. *Philosophy as a Way of Life: Spiritual Exercises from Socrates to Foucault*. Oxford and Malden, MA: Blackwell.
Halliwell, Stephen. 1998. *Aristotle's* Poetics. Chicago: The University of Chicago Press.
Hofmann, Dagmar. 2007. *Suizid in der Spätantike: Seine Bewertung in der lateinischen Literatur*. Stuttgart: Franz Steiner Verlag.
Hooff, Anton J. L. van. 1990. *From Autothanasia to Suicide: Self-Killing in Classical Antiquity*. London and New York: Routledge.
Knuuttila, Simo. 2004. *Emotions in Ancient and Medieval Philosophy*. Oxford: Clarendon Press.
Knuuttila, Simo, and Juha Sihvola. 1998. "How the Philosophical Analysis of Emotions Was Introduced." In *The Emotions in Hellenistic Philosophy*, ed. Juha Sihvola and Troels Engberg-Pedersen. Dordrecht, Boston and London: Kluwer Academic Publishers.
Long, A. A. 2001. "Ancient Philosophy's Hardest Question: What to Make of Oneself?" *Representations* 74, 19–36. Berkeley, Los Angeles, and London: The University of California Press.
Long, A. A., and D. N. Sedley, eds. 1987. *The Hellenistic Philosophers*. Cambridge: Cambridge University Press.
Nussbaum, Martha. 1994. *Therapy of Desire*. Princeton, NJ: Princeton University Press.
Reydams-Schils, Gretchen. 2005. *The Roman Stoic: Self, Responsibility, and Affection*. Chicago and London: The University of Chicago Press.

Chapter 5

Moral Philosophical Arguments against Suicide in the Middle Ages

Virpi Mäkinen

INTRODUCTION

The advent of institutional Christianity was perhaps the most important event in the philosophical history of suicide. Christian doctrine held that suicide was morally wrong, even though Scripture contains no unequivocal condemnation of suicide.[1] For medieval scholars, the main doctrinal source was the Bible, and the biblical suicides (especially those of Samson and Judas) gave rise to discussion. The fifth commandment, "Thou shalt not kill," was the most frequent single text cited in medieval questions and commentaries on suicide. Some nonnarrative biblical passages could also prompt discussion, for example, Paul's words "I long to be dissolved and to be with Christ."

The most used classical sources were Macrobius's commentary on Cicero and Aristotle's *Nichomachean Ethics* (Murray 2000: 241). Especially Aristotle's idea that wasting one's substance or property was "a certain kind of self-destruction" raised arguments against suicide (*Nichomachean Ethics* 4.1, 1120a2–3). Plato and the Platonist and Stoic traditions were also used, especially within the Franciscan school. Medieval scholars knew of classical suicides (e.g., Cato, Lucretius, Diogenes and Epicurus) and discussed these cases as well.

The main ancient Christian source on suicide was Augustine. The most familiar Augustinian suicide text for medieval scholars was chapters 16–27 of book 1 of *De civitate Dei* (*The City of God*). However, Augustine mentioned suicide also in book 19 of the same work, as well as in his other writings, especially *De libero arbitrio* (*On Free Will*), *On Patience*, and *Contra gaudentius* (*Against*

Gaudentius).[2] Augustine's writings tackled suicide, among other moral topics, and condemned it categorically, mostly on biblical grounds. He also knew the Neo-Platonic philosophy, which took a very negative attitude toward suicide. Augustine was first to articulate that the fifth commandment prohibits even suicide. In his *De civitate Dei*, Augustine stated: "The words 'Thou shalt not kill' refer to the killing of a man—not another man; therefore, not even thyself. For he who kills himself, kills nothing else than a man" (liber I, c. 20). According to Augustine, the commandment applies to suicide because it does not specify whom or what one may not kill. However, Augustine recognized exceptions to the fifth commandment, such as killing nonrational creatures (i.e., plants and animals) and killing in war and for justice.

In his *Contra gaudentius*, Augustine also discussed suicide in the psychological sense. He described suicide as "mad"—as an expression of *furor* or *dementia*.[3] For him, suicidal *furor* was literally diabolical; only Satan urged a human being to commit suicide. Therefore, Augustine stated, suicides went immediately to Hell. It is notable that in this text, Augustine's sources are mostly non-Christian. However, the pseudo-Clement too had stated that the punishment for suicide was 'Hades' (Amundsen 1989: 117–119).

This chapter will offer an overview of the different kinds of moral philosophical arguments on the prohibition of suicide in medieval sources. My main aim is thus to provide a synopsis of the dominant arguments rather than to analyze them thoroughly.[4] This essay shows that scholastics discussed the prohibition of suicide as both a morally normative and a naturalistic argument. They also developed interesting psychological ideas about the prohibition, for instance, when speaking about the idea of natural right and duty to preserve human life. These latter formulations interestingly resemble the early modern discourse on the subject among seventeenth-century theorists of natural law.

"NATURALISTIC" ARGUMENTS ON THE SANCTITY OF LIFE

In the 1320s, Pope John XXII summarized the scholastic discussion on suicide as follows:

> But according to divine law a suicide is punished by eternal pain, for by killing himself he acts against natural law, against charity, and against the Lord's commandment. Hence he is in mortal sin and dies in it, as did Judas, who was damned because he despaired of pardon and hanged himself, *et cetera*. (Cited in Murray 2000: 239)

In the above quotation, the pope listed the most often stated theological arguments against suicide: it was against natural law, charity and the fifth commandment, "Thou shalt not kill."

Although the commandment not to kill mainly concerned homicide, suicide was seen as a synonym, understood as homicide of oneself.[5] Thomas Aquinas, for example, argued that "murder is a sin, not only because it is contrary to justice, but also because it is opposed to charity which a man should have towards himself; in this respect suicide is a sin in relation to oneself" (Thomas Aquinas, *Summa theologiae* 2a 2ae q. 64, a. 5, obj. 1). However, some suicides were not treated as real sin, an example being suicide committed in a fit of madness (for more on this see Huot 2003). Intention was an important criterion in defining whether a suicide was a mortal sin in the late Middle Ages. We will come back to this theme later.

Referring to Augustine, medieval scholars often stated that suicide violates the order of love (*ordo caritatis*) and is, therefore, opposed to *caritas*. The commandment of love claims that one should love first God and then one's neighbor as oneself. For medieval scholars, the latter part of the commandment required that we should first love ourselves in order to love our neighbors. Therefore, self-love was not a defect of fallen nature but an exemplification of the virtue of charity (*Summa theologiae* 2a 2ae, q. 64, a. 5, 610; see also Knebel 1991).

One should also note here that medieval scholars treated charity as a certain attitude (*modus agendi*) that supervenes actions and confers on them their moral value (Knebel 2005: 122). Charity was incorporated into the tradition of natural law (*lex naturalis*), which God created to govern the world and human existence, and these scholars spoke of man's natural inclination toward God. For medieval authors, natural law also included the natural instinct toward self-preservation, which was the first duty to be deduced from the virtue of charity. Natural inclination toward self-preservation was treated as a rational inclination, one in harmony with charity.[6] Self-preservation was also morally imperative, and therefore suicide was seen as opposed to this natural inclination toward self-preservation. Aquinas, for example, argued that suicide was against natural inclination of everyone to love him- or herself and to remain in existence.[7]

The *ordo caritatis* and its obligation toward God and oneself, especially toward self-preservation, was an important factor even in late scholastic discussion on human life, and therefore on suicide as well. Even though Spanish scholastics and Jesuit theologians did not agree in all aspects; they were all certain that sacrificing one's own life ran contrary to natural inclination. I will discuss this theme further below.

ARGUMENTS OF THE RIGHT TO SELF-PRESERVATION AND SELF-OWNERSHIP

In the late thirteenth and early fourteenth centuries, new, voluntarist ideas on the human being as an active and rights-bearing individual had important consequences in moral philosophy. Individual and inalienable rights, such as the rights to self-preservation, self-ownership, and liberty, have their earliest roots in late medieval and early modern discourse on rights. Did these ideas of individual rights have any influence on the discussion of suicide? Are there any conditions under which suicide is morally permissible or psychologically understandable, and if so, what are they?

Authors of late medieval voluntarist moral philosophy stated two basic grounds for human autonomy and freedom. First, they created a new formulation of natural rights. Natural law or right (these terms were taken as synonyms) was understood as "what is permitted and approved but not commanded by any law." With this definition the scholars began to carve out, within the framework of natural law ethics, an area of human autonomy where the law did not command or forbid, but left humans free to choose their own courses of action. From then onward, the idea of permissive natural law as a basis of natural rights had a continuous history up to the eighteenth century—persisting even in the work of Immanuel Kant (Tierney 2006).

Toward the end of the thirteenth century, the idea of self-preservation also came to be an important factor in the natural rights tradition. Some medieval theologians, such as Henry of Ghent and Godfrey of Fontaines, spoke about a natural right to subsistence, which they derived from the duty of self-preservation (for more on this, see Mäkinen 2001, 2006). In question eleven of his *Quodlibet VIII*, Godfrey of Fontaines argued that "by natural right each person is obliged to maintain his or her life, which is not possible without using external goods, [and] therefore, by the law of nature each person has dominion and a certain right in the common exterior goods of this world, which right they cannot lawfully renounce" (*Quodlibet* VIII, q. 11, 105). According to Francisco Vitoria, natural self-love could imply a corresponding right to defend one's own life (Francisco Vitoria, *De homicidio*, 244).

The claims of self-preservation in traditional scholastic ethics seem to have been so powerful that hardly anything could weaken them. As Doyle has stated,

> even in relation to Jesuit authors, the issue of the prehistory of human rights is often addressed in dominion over them, in terms of the recognition of a natural right to life and of a right to self-defence—in short, in terms of the expansion of individual self-assertion. (Doyle 2001: 117)[8]

One historically prominent analogy, and perhaps the most interesting one for our subject, is that human beings are God's property, and therefore suicide is a wrong to God akin to theft or destruction of property.[9] Medieval authors saw our control over our body as limited only to *usus* (some use the notion of possession), whereas God retained *dominium* (in the sense of dominion, ownership, authority). According to the argument of ownership, suicide nullified a human being's relationship to God (as suggested by, e.g., Thomas Aquinas and John Locke).

Thomas Aquinas, in his *Summa theologiae*, question 64, discussed the objection that maintains that it is lawful for a human being to suffer spontaneously a lesser danger in order to avoid a greater, and thus it is lawful, for instance, to cut off a decayed limb even from oneself, in order to save the rest of one's body; likewise, sometimes a man, by killing himself, avoids a greater evil, for example an unhappy life, or the shame of sin, and therefore, a man may kill himself.

Aquinas's reply to the objection pointed to the free will of a human being as follows:

> Man is made master of himself through his free will: wherefore he can lawfully dispose of himself as to those matters which pertain to this life which is ruled by man's free will. But the passage from this life to another and happier one is subject not to man's free will but to the power of God. Hence it is not lawful for man to take his own life that he may pass to a happier life, nor that he may escape any unhappiness whatsoever of the present life, because the ultimate and most fearsome evil of this is death, as the Philosopher states [*Nicomachean Ethics* 3.6, 1115a26]. Therefore to bring death upon oneself in order to escape the other afflictions of this life, is to adopt a greater evil in order to avoid a lesser. (*Summa theologiae*, 2a 2ae, q. 64, a. 5, obj. 3)

Here Aquinas referred not so much to God's ownership as to God's power over the human mind and body. John of Wales, a Franciscan friar who worked in Oxford and Paris from 1258 until his death in 1285, explicated the ownership argument in his *Communiloquium* (A General Discourse) on the same subject, c. 1265–70, as follows:[10]

> We are God's possessions, and his servants, and should obey his commands like servants. Like prisoners, we should remain in our bonds. Like faithful followers, we should guard the treasure entrusted to us, and not reject the divine gift of life. For if it is insulting to reject human gifts, how much more should we converse those gifts bestowed on us by our God. (*Communiloquium*, pars 7, dist. I, chap. 6h [fol. 134v]. References and trans. in Murray 2000: 212)

The other ground of human autonomy was the idea of self-dominion, also called self-ownership or self-mastery. The theologian Henry of Ghent was one of the earliest scholars to state the explicit idea of the right of self-dominion. In his *Quodlibet IX*, question twenty-six (probably written in 1289), he posed the question "[w]hether one condemned to death can licitly flee?" In his response, Henry elaborated different kinds of rights that the judge and the condemned person possessed in the body of the criminal: the judge had the power to capture, hold, and execute the condemned person, whereas the criminal had the power of using his body to preserve his life, so long as he did not injure another. Furthermore, Henry described the power of the criminal over his body as being equitable, licit, right, and necessary because natural law permitted it (*Quodlibet* IX, q. 26, 307–309; see also chapter 3 in this volume, where Miira Tuominen elaborates Socrates' arguments against escape from prison).

Henry concluded that the criminal could licitly flee, for two reasons. First, the condemned's right to preserve his or her life and acquire the necessities of life overrode the judge's right to imprison and kill the condemned. The individual's right to preservation of life was greater than the judge's right to condemn because everyone was compelled by necessity. In this particular question, Henry stated that self-preservation was a natural right. There were, however, certain limits to such a right. First, although everyone had the right to self-preservation in the case of extreme necessity, one should always act in accordance with the law. And second, the criminal also had a property right (*proprietas*) over his own body, whereas the judge had only the right to use (*ius utendi*) the criminal's body. Moreover, Henry maintained, one was obliged to use the right over one's body to preserve one's life, though without injuring anyone. Henry's whole argument concerning the moral rights and duties of a condemned criminal was based on elucidation of the individual rights of each party (*Quodlibet* IX, q. 26, 309). In that same question 26, Henry also referred to the question of suicide in the case of extreme necessity as follows:

> The right of the condemned person was greater because the judge was not compelled by such necessity to hold and kill the criminal as he [the criminal] was to preserve his own life. If he were left unbound, with the door of his goal open, he ought to escape; not to do so would be equivalent to suicide. (308–309)

Perhaps the most detailed treatment of self-ownership was elaborated by the German theologian Conrad Summenhart. In his treatise *De contractibus*, he equated the terms right (*ius*) and ownership (*dominium*), and this equivalence had important consequences for the development of the dominion of self. For Summenhart, the dominion of human actions–that is, the power of free choice, which had usually been understood as a psychological attribute of humans–was now treated as a right to liberty (*De contractibus*, tract. 1, q. 1, 1; see also Brett 1997; Varkemaa 1999). Summenhart had various definitions for the concept of *dominium*. For him, *dominium* did not always apply only to external things; it was also possible to say that the soul had *dominium* of itself or that the will had *dominium* of itself in moving from not acting to acting (*De contractibus*, tract.1, q.1, 4). Having come to regard self-dominion as the freedom of choice, Summenhart identified this freedom as a right to liberty understood in a juridical sense:

> Similarly liberty is a species of right and a free man has that right in himself, namely of doing what he pleases. Whence the right (of liberty) is defined in the Institutes (1.3.1) as a natural faculty to do what one pleases unless prohibited by force or law. (*De contractibus*, tract. 1, q. 1, 1; trans. in Tierney 2006: 183)

For Summenhart, the human right of free choice extended even to the possibility of voluntary self-enslavement (*De contractibus*, tract., q. 74, 337; see also Tierney 2006: 184); a free man was *sui iuris*, belonging to himself or existing in his own right. However, self-dominion did not include the idea that one owned one's members and could cut them off or otherwise abuse them (*De contractibus*, tract., q. 74). When discussing suicide, Summenhart stated that our bodies did indeed belong to God, but not every use or commitment of them required a direct divine authorization; rather, God had left to man a wide range of free choice:

> Although man by virtue of his creation is obliged to God in everything he can do, still God does not demand so much from man but rather leaves him his liberty provided only that he keeps the commands of the Decalogue . . . free man has the faculty of doing whatever he pleases unless prohibited by force or law. (*De contractibus*, tract. 1, q. 1, 1)

In Summenhart's work, the freedom of choice inherent in man's dominion of himself was understood as a right to liberty, and the exercise of the right extended only to choices that were not explicitly prohibited by the Ten Commandments. Therefore, an intentional act of suicide was a sin. Summenhart also briefly mentioned the question whether one has a right to sacrifice one's life for good purposes; in other words, if there are enough grave arguments, is it right to cut off one's members or act so that the consequences are one's own death? However, he did not deal further with the question.

Summenhart's treatise was widely quoted by Spanish neo-scholastics of the sixteenth century, whose works offer another important source for the development of self-dominion. In his *De relectio homicidio*, Francisco de Vitoria asked whether, if a man's life belongs to God, he ever choose to bring about his own death. He responded by explaining, more explicitly than Locke, the correlation between divine ownership of the self and an individual's self-ownership:

> Although man is not the master of his body or his life as he is of other things, nevertheless he does have something of ownership and right in his life so that if someone harms his body he injures not only God, who is the supreme lord of life, but also the individual man himself. Therefore he can laudably set aside this right that he has in his own body, even though he has a right of defending himself, and so patiently suffer death. (*Relectione de homicidio*, 1118)

Vitoria went on to discuss various circumstances in which a man might choose to give up his own life, approving of the act in some cases but not in others. For instance, a man who had just enough bread to keep himself alive while others were starving had a right to keep the bread, but he could relinquish his right and give the bread to another to save the other's life. Likewise, a shipwrecked sailor could abandon the plank he clung to in order to save the life of another[11] (1112).

Vitoria argued further that, if two men were in a state of extreme need, one could give up his bread to save the life of the other; indeed, a man could even sacrifice his life to save an enemy. A person attacked by a robber could certainly kill his assailant in self-defense, but he would act more perfectly if he yielded his own life rather than send the thief to eternal damnation. So Vitoria maintained that in many cases, a man could licitly preserve his life and yet was not bound to do so. Here again a right, including the right of self-defense, conferred a certain freedom of choice on the right holder. Vitoria's basic point was that a man could not lawfully say "I want to kill myself," but he could sometimes choose a course of action that would bring about his own death (1128).

The right of a man in himself was understood as a zone of human autonomy, an area of licit behavior where one could act as one chose. Although a right of self-defense always existed and could not be alienated, one might choose not to exercise the right one possessed in his or her own life. One could not deliberately kill oneself, for that would be an injustice to God, but it was sometimes permissible and even laudable to set aside one's own right in life and accept death for the sake of another. Vitoria presented this as a controversial doctrine, for many held that a private individual could not relinquish the duty to preserve his own life. Vitoria nonetheless thought the opposite view more probable.

THE ARGUMENT OF INTENTIONALITY

In his *Relectione de homicidia*, Francisco de Vitoria stated that no one can kill him- or herself with full knowledge and intention. This metaphysical argument was based on Thomistic theology. The reasoning is that because the will always wants some good, no one can want evil which come of his or her existence. Hence, no one can kill oneself with full volition. Vitoria also discussed the objection to this proof: the thought that to kill oneself, or simply not to exist, can be thought to be good; thus someone may kill him- or herself with knowledge and volition. Vitoria's reply was that such a person is then making a mistake and thinks it to be good for him- or herself.

Vitoria's treatment of suicide in his *Relectio de homicidia* strongly emphasized intentionality. In this, he differed from Thomas Aquinas, to whose *Commentary on the Sentences* he referred. This difference is evident, for example, in Vitoria's discussion of the question of suicide in the context of extreme necessity. According to Vitoria, "it is lawful to give to another bread which I need in order to avoid death." This accorded with the idea of self-preservation, as well as man's duty to God. Vitoria continued: "But I deny that this is killing oneself, for such a one is not killing himself intentionally, but by accident through helping a neighbor. Hence, whatever may follow is lawful, since he is not intentionally killing himself. Indeed, it pains him greatly to die and be unable to survive" (*Relectione de homicidio*, c. 6, 177). Here Vitoria was emphasizing the difference between an intentional act and an accident.

Vitoria also used the difference between the terms active and passive in the context of killing oneself to emphasize the importance of human will in, for example, the question whether it was lawful for a man condemned to death to anticipate his executioners by taking poison, if that was the kind of death to which he was condemned. Vitoria replied to the posed question more explicitly as follows:

> . . . it would first be necessary to see whether those laws about giving poison are just; and if they are, it is certain that it would be lawful to drink it. Since, therefore, that law existed not among barbarians, but within a well-ordered republic, we can say it was lawful for him to drink poison when he was condemned to death.–But the opposite seems true: because such a person is actively killing himself.–I answer that, especially in a moral matter,

> it is necessary to look for equity and to resort to sophisms. Therefore, I say that it makes no difference whether he is active or passive, for he would be as much a killer whether he is passive or active. (*Relectione de homicidio*, 177)

Vitoria gave yet another example of a man who, if he were to await a falling millstone, would be working toward his death just as if he were to take the stone upon himself and kill himself. Vitoria showed that when the law is just, it did not matter whether a condemned man drank poison by his own hand or someone else poured it into his mouth.

In secular and canon law, lawyers also took note of intentionality when discussing the punishment for an attempted suicide or the completed act. The Toledo law (693) stated that the punishment for attempting suicide was two months' excommunication, implying ostracism and denial of sacraments. However, canon law collections contained very few laws considering attempted suicide. A similar silence prevailed in penitential books from the eighth to tenth centuries. The Celtic books, for example, which emphasized intention in general, did not differentiate between attempted and completed murder or suicide. Later penitentials, notably the eleventh-century *Corrector of Burchard of Worms*, show an awareness of intention, and therefore of the significance of attempted wrongs, but the penitential books did not, as a rule, extend this attitude to suicide. Nevertheless, there is one exception: *Poenitentiale vigilanum* (early or mid ninth century), which stated, "Whoever tries to kill himself by hanging or by any means whatever, and God does not abandon him to be killed, for which cause he does five years' penance" (Clause 37). It should be noted that a man who failed to kill himself might nevertheless injure himself. A few medieval laws concerned self-injury, but none of them considered it as a suicidal act (references from Murray 2000: 401).[12]

Attempted suicide in secular law was different than in canon law. Roman law held three mentions of attempted suicide. First, a slave who had attempted suicide was blemished and as such fetched a lower market price. Second, a soldier who attempted suicide was put to death, unless the suicide was attempted for one of an approved list of Stoic motives. Third, the law (Digest 9.48) stated an unspecified punishment for attempted suicide on the grounds that it was the act of a desperado (Murray 2000: 411).

Lawyers in medieval civil law also discussed attempted suicide, but they did not always assign a punishment to an act. A whole succession of jurists recommended capital punishment of attempted suicide from the thirteenth century onward, but in practice lawyers were more humane and tended to soften cruel punishments (Murray 2000: 412–414). This was evident also regarding the most important and influential developments in thirteenth-century criminal law, which concerned the individual's criminal intent and responsibility. Before this change, criminal responsibility was mainly based on the consequences of a crime. Then canon lawyers began to distinguish different modes of subjective responsibility. In the law of criminal evidence, the individual shifted as well, from the margins to the center of attention. This development of criminal law and criminal procedure in the thirteenth and fourteenth centuries can be understood in the context of the simultaneous trend toward individualization that took place in moral philosophy and theology as well as in canon law (see Mäkinen and Pihlajamäki 2005).

ARGUMENTS OF THE POSSIBILITY OF REPENTANCE

Medieval civil law sources provided a certain amount of legal information relevant to completed suicide. Roman legal texts, which the medieval lawyers used and commented on, stated that the act of suicide was innocent. Suicide was called *delictum*, 'offense,' in Roman law. In the *Codex*, Roman ancient authorities saw suicide as inherently guiltless. Another Roman law principle in the *Novellae* stated that a suicide entailed confiscation if it could be construed as a confession to a certain class of crime. It was not criminal, however. (Murray 2000: 278–279).

These kinds of texts were certainly difficult for medieval lawyers, who were influenced by Christian doctrine as early as the sixth century. Cino of Pistoia (d. 1336) commented on the suicide texts in the *Codex* (c. 1310) to distinguish suicide from an offense against the state or another authority as a *delictum in se commissum*, 'an offence committed against oneself.' This shows that Pistoia still makes suicide a *delictum* not favored in the Christian thought (Cino of Pistoia, *Commentaria in Codicem*, book 6, ch. 22, §7; cited in Murray 2000: 279). When commenting on the *Novellae*, Jacques de Révigny had accidentally read into this Roman law text the idea–foreign to it–that suicide is intrinsically criminal (Murray 2000: 281). However, again there was a gap between law and practice. In relation to suicide, expressions like "despite what the written law says, lay judges . . . [i.e., do the opposite]," or "whatever the law says, the whole world nevertheless agrees in upholding [the opposite principle]" were common (Murray 2000: 284).

Medieval scholars also discussed whether a suicide could repent for this sin. Referring to Aristotle's claim in *Nichomachean Ethics* that no man can do an injustice to himself, one could argue that no man sins by killing himself. In response to this, Thomas Aquinas stated that by committing suicide, one deprives oneself of the time needed for repentance (*Summa theologiae*, 2a 2ae, q. 64, a. 5, obj. 3). A Franciscan theologian, William of Ockham, discussed suicide when speaking about the nature of voluntary acts. Ockham, using as his example a man who voluntarily jumps from a cliff, stated that the act (jumping) was an intentional act (i.e., suicide). Yet according to Ockham, that man remained able to make conversion during the descent if he (meritoriously) wished not to fall, for the sake of God. This kind of wish was possible because, having jumped, the man could no longer control the progress of descent[13] (William of Ockham, *Quodlibeta septem* III, q. 14).

Commentators like Bartolus of Sassoferrato (d. 1357) also discussed the possibility of a confession. Commenting in the *Digest* (28.3.6.), Bartolus posed the question "[w]hether suicide counts as a confession if committed during an appeal." His reply quotes Ulpian, who drew a distinction between the motives behind the act of suicide and those that excuse it: weariness of life or impatience with bodily weakness as in the case of some philosophers, this latter motive being from Accursius's *Glossa ordinaria.* This shows how the medieval lawyers interpreted Roman legal texts through their Christian views. Bartolus went on to explain the idea of ostentation, declaring that "[s]ince death is the most fearful of all things the philosophers, by killing themselves, sought to prove themselves courageous and fearful of nothing." Aristotle had linked death and courage in his *Nicomachean Ethics*, which seems to have been Bartolus's source as well. For Bartolus, suicide was not a virtue, since courage, in order to be a virtue, must tend to a proper goal, which death is not. Therefore, his final answer to the whole question was that suicide committed during a juridical appeal cannot be waved aside; the sentence must stand. Using an Aristotelian principle with Christian theology, Bartolus pushed Roman law a significant distance toward the end of the sliding scale that was unfavorable to suicide (Murray 2000: 282).

THE ARGUMENT OF *RESPUBLICA*

Like Aristotle, medieval scholars viewed human beings as political by nature: as they saw it, human beings were naturally inclined to life in a republic, and this natural inclination came from God. Therefore, suicide injured the community of which the individual was a part and a member. Suicide injured the community because a part derived its being from membership in a whole (Murray 2000: 230–239). It followed that everyone was part of community and humanity. Therefore, by killing oneself, one did injury to the community (*Nichomachean Ethics*, 5.11, 1138a11; *Summa theologiae* 2a2ae, q. 64, a. 5, resp., 316).[14] Thomas Aquinas, for his part, explained the argument as follows:

> Whatever we obtain in one part of a whole must in that measure obtain in the whole. Since every man is part of a community, what happens to him must affect the community, with the consequence that to kill oneself is to do an injury to that community. This is clear from the Philosopher. (*Summa theologiae*, 2a 2ae, q. 64, a. 5, resp., 316; cf. Aristotle, *Nichomachean Ethics*, 5.11, 1138a11.)

Aquinas also asserted that the suicide did injustice and injury to his or her city as well, which was why the city was punished this act by confiscating of the suicide's goods and dishonoring the corpse. His words were straight from Aristotle's *Nichomachean Ethics*, book 5, with the addition of confiscation (*publicatio bonorum*).

Referring to Thomas Aquinas's *Summa theologiae*, Francisco de Vitoria also maintained that the suicide harmed the commonwealth. Commenting on the question whether it was licit to kill a man who was harmful to the state, he answered positively, arguing that a single member could be cut off for the good of the rest of body. Returning to his argument on suicide, Vitoria concluded that a person who killed himself injured the commonwealth as well as God: "One who kills himself takes away from the commonwealth what is its own." It should be noted here that the good of the part was not its own but belonged to the whole. Accordingly, the part as such could not be injured in the sense of being deprived of some good belonging to it (Doyle 1997: 227, n. 198).

In Vitoria's *De homicidio*, the argument for a community's power over its members was accompanied by a particularly careful and nuanced treatment of the individual right of self-defense. Vitoria was quite clear about the existence of this right. He argued that a man could even kill himself in self-defense, and if he did so, he was exercising an authority derived from God through natural law (*Relectio de homicidio*, 179–180).

Vitoria's treatment is interesting for our subject because it shows that in his time, suicidal behavior was mainly seen from a psychological viewpoint. He addressed the objection that one who commits suicide does no injury to anyone—neither to himself, because he is willing to end his life, nor to society, for indeed some societies granted legal permission for suicide—by stating that "man, whom God has made part of the commonwealth, is inclined by nature more to the common good than the private."

ARGUMENTS OF PLATONIST INFLUENCE

For medieval scholars, Aristotle and Augustine were perhaps the main ancient sources concerning suicide, but Plato and the Neo-Platonist tradition were also influential in those discussions. The Neo-Platonist tradition in particular took a very negative stance toward suicide. Plotinus gave two reasons against taking one's life in his treatise: suicide was evidently a violent, emotional act that would scar the soul; moreover, the soul was bound to the body by God and was not permitted to dissolve these bonds on its own initiative. (Murray 2000: 142–144)

The Franciscan theologian Alexander of Hales took some ideas against suicide from Plato's *Phaedo* and other Platonist works. He argued that when the soul was violently separated from the body, their bond was broken but not untied, since the rupture involved a measure of passion that held the soul to the material world. Another reason Alexander brought against suicide was that people were put on earth to grow toward perfection, and while life lasted there was a chance for greater perfection. Sinners could not raise themselves to life when they were dead and should therefore do so before dying. He also stated that whoever committed suicide in the hope of beatitude was caught in the toils of passion, because hope, like fear, is a passion. Alexander himself took these principles from Macrobius and attributed them to Plotinus, but they were most probably from Porphyry (Alexander of Hales, *Summa theologiae fratris Alexandri*, 128; reference from Murray 2000: 222, n. 8).

CONCLUSIONS

A German Dominican, Johannes Nider (d. 1438), discussed suicide in his widely copied and cited commentary on the Ten Commandments called *Praeceptorum, sive orthodox et accurate decalogi explicatio.* Nider's text is a good summary, as it includes several arguments against suicide laid out in medieval moral philosophical texts:

> Whoever raises a hand against himself, by killing himself of his own free will, sins mortally, unless this is done by special and certain revelation of God, as Augustine said of Samson in *The City of God*, Bk. I [Ch. 21]. In any other case, the self-killer sins mortally, and all the more gravely in that he acts against his natural inclination, by which each of us is bound by reason to love himself, and naturally does love himself. Thus he sins against natural inclination, that is, against charity towards himself, and against the common justice of which he is a member, and he robs himself, too, of any time to repent. (Johannes Nider, *Praeceptorum*, praeceptio 5, ch. 15, §7, 347)

Nider also describes forms of alleged suicide, for instance, self-mutilation and overzealous ascetic practices, which shorten a man's lifespan. When harmful, vigils and fasting violated the fifth commandment, as William Saint-Amour and Gerard of Abbeville had already professed when criticizing the Franciscan habit of poverty in the mid-1250s (see Mäkinen 2001). But for Nider, these kinds of suicide were simple suicides (Murray 2000: 241).

An interesting general theme that seems to rise from medieval arguments against suicide is that the prohibition of suicide was seen as both morally normative and "naturalistic." On the one hand, the scholastics maintained that suicide violated natural inclination to self-preservation and *ordo caritatis*, which both were based on natural law stated by God. On the other hand, they pointed out that suicide went against the natural inclination to self-preservation, which was also seen as an individual and inalienable right to life.

Turning from the medieval to an early modern discussion of suicide, the deontological arguments seem to have moved slightly toward pre-libertarian arguments in which an individual's freedom, liberty (autonomy), and inalienable rights played a certain but not yet dominant role. Although an individual was seen to have an inalienable right to self-dominion and self-ownership, even to self-preservation, the ultimate dominion over one's body and soul still belonged to God. Even John Locke, who asserted the doctrine of self-ownership ("every Man has a *Property* in his own *Person*"), thought that human beings ultimately belonged to God and were bound by God's laws. Locke also taught that human beings had inalienable rights. As Gary D. Glenn (1984: 80) argues, "this inalienable rights teaching is contained in his argument that suicide is absolutely forbidden by nature."

NOTES

1. There are seven suicides in the Scriptures, most notably that of Judas Iscariot (Matt. 27:3).
2. For Augustine's teaching on suicide, see Murray 2000: 101–110; Amundsen 1989: 123–141.
3. Augustine, *Contra gaudentium*, book 1, chap. 27, §30 (PL 43, 724A) on *dementia*; chap. 30, §34 (PL 727A) on *furor* and *amentia*.
4. I am grateful for the helpful comments on earlier versions of this essay from Prof. Simo Knuuttila, Dr. Miira Tuominen, and this collection's anonymous reviewers, whose contributions substantially improved my argumentation.
5. See, e.g., Petrus Abelardus, *Sic et non*, chaps. 155–156; Robert Grosseteste, *De decem mandatis*, 61, 27: " . . . [all suicide] contra naturam universalem videtur facere."
6. See, e.g., Thomas Aquinas, *Summa theologiae* 2a 2ae, q. 26, a. 4: "Homo ex charitate debet magis seipsum diligere, quam proximum"; Godfrey of Fontaines,

Quodlibet XII, q. 5, 132–134: " . . . propter amorem naturalem quem habet unusquisque ad seipsum, cui etiam amor caritatis non repugnat, tenetur quilibet se conservare in esse quantum potest sine iniuria alterius."

7. See, e.g., Thomas Aquinas, *Summa theologiae*, 2a 2ae, q. 64, a. 5. These natural law arguments were common in medieval discussion until Hume and others critiqued them, arguing that the natural law arguments cannot be disentangled from a highly speculative theistic metaphysics, that these claims are not confirmed by observations of human nature (e.g., the existence of self-destructive human behavior casts doubt on the claim that we 'naturally' preserve ourselves), and that other acts (e.g., religious martyrdom) that God is assumed not to condemn also violate these natural laws, making prohibitions on suicide appear arbitrary. See David Hume's unpublished essay "On Suicide" (1783).
8. Cf. Knebel (2005: 121): "I object to this view: it is part of the story, but not the whole story. The whole story must include the late scholastic endeavour to overcome the ethics of self-assertion."
9. See also Miira Tuominen's discussion of Plato's arguments on self-killing in the *Phaedo* in chapter 3 of this volume.
10. For more on this topic, see Swanson 1989.
11. Vitoria's example of a shipwrecked sailor is from Cicero's *De officiis*.
12. See also Constable (1982), who discussed a broader subject, namely religious ascetism.
13. I thank Prof. Reijo Työrinoja for this example.
14. In his *De civitate Dei*, Augustine also argued against suicide with respect to *respublica*. As private citizens, all people were forbidden to kill even a malefactor, let alone an innocent person, he maintained with reference to the case of Lucretia.

REFERENCES

Ancient, Medieval, and Early Modern Sources

Alexander of Hales. *Summa theologiae fratris Alexandri*, ed. Quaracchi, 4 vols. Roma 1930–48.

Aristotle. *Nichomachean Ethics*, trans. and ed. H. Rackham. Cambridge, MA: Harvard University Press, 1929.

Augustine. *De Civitate Dei*. Available at The Latin Library, http://www.thelatinlibrary.com/augustine/civ1.shtml.

Conrad Summenhart. *De contractibus licitis et illicitis*. Venice, 1580.

Francisco de Vitoria

——. *Relectione de homicidio (On homicide & Commentary on Summa theologiae II^{a}–II^{ae} Q. 64 (Thomas Aquinas)*, trans., intro. and notes John P. Doyle. Milwaukee: Marquette University Press, 1997.

Godfrey of Fontaines. *Quodlibet XII*. In *Les Philosophes Belges*, V, 1–2, ed. J. Hoffmans. Louvain: Institut supérius de philosophie de l'Université, 1932.
Henry of Ghent. "Quodlibet IX." In *Henrici de Gandavo opera omnia*, ed. R. Macken. Leuven, 1983, pp. 307–309.
Petrus Abelardus. *Sic et non*, ed. B. B. Boyer and R. McKeon. Chicago and London: University of Chicago Press, 1976–77.
Robert Grosseteste. *De decem mandatis* (Auctores Britannici Medii Aevi 10), ed. R. C. Dales and E. B. King. Oxford: Oxford University Press, 1987.
Thomas Aquinas. *Summa theologiae*, ed. P. Caramell, 3 vols. Turin, 1952–76.
William of Ockham. *Quodlibeta septem*, ed. Joseph C. Wey. (Opera Theologica 9). St. Bonaventure, NY: St. Bonaventure University, 1980.

Research Literature

Amundsen, D. 1989. "Suicide and Early Christian Values." In *Suicide and Euthanasia: Historical and Contemporary Themes*, ed. B. Brody. Dordrecht: Kluwer.
Brett, Annabel. 1997. *Liberty, Right and Nature: The Language of Individual Rights in Later Scholastic Thought*. Cambridge: Cambridge University Press.
Constable, G. 1982. *Attitudes toward Self-Inflicted Suffering in the Middle Ages*. Brookline, MA: Hellenic College Press.
Doyle, John P. 2001. "Francisco Suárez, S. J. on Human Rights." In *Menschenrechte: Rechte und Pflichten in Ost und West*, ed. K. Wegmann, W. Ommerborn, and H. Roetz. Münster: Lit Verlag, pp. 105–132.
Glenn, Gary D. 1984. "Inalienable Rights and Locke's Argument for Limited Government: Political Implications of a Right to Suicide." *Journal of Politics* 46 (1): 80–105.
Huot, Sylvia. 2003. *Madness in Medieval French Literature: Identities Found and Lost*. Oxford and New York: Oxford University Press.
Knebel, Sven. 1991. "Naturrecht, Folter, Selbstverzicht: Spees *Cautio Criminalis* vor dem Hintergrund der spätscholastischen Moralphilosophie." In *Die politische Theologie Friedrich von Spees*, ed. D. Brockmann and P. Eicher. Munich: W. Fink Verlag, pp. 155–189.
——. 2005. "Casuistry and The Early Modern Paradigm Shift." In *Moral Philosophy on the Threshold of Modernity* (The New Synthese Historical Library 57), ed. J. Kraye and R. Saarinen. Dordrecht; Springer, pp. 115–139.
Mäkinen, Virpi. 2001. *Property Rights in the Late Medieval Discussion on Franciscan Poverty* (Recherches de Théologie et Philosophie médiévales, Bibliotheca 3). Leuven: Peeters.
——. 2006. "Rights and Duties in Late Scholastic Discussion on Extreme Necessity." In *Transformations in Late Medieval and Early-Modern Rights Discourse* (The New Synthese Historical Library 59), ed. V. Mäkinen and P. Korkman. Dordrecht: Springer, pp. 37–62.

Mäkinen, Virpi and Heikki Pihlajamäki. 2005. "The Individualization of Crime and Medieval Canon Law." *Journal of History of Ideas* 65 (4): 525–542.
Murray, A. 1998. *Suicide in the Middle Ages, vol. I: The Violent against Themselves*. Oxford and New York: Oxford University Press.
——. 2000. *Suicide in the Middle Ages, vol. II: The Curse on Self-Murder*. Oxford and New York: Oxford University Press.
Swanson, J. 1989. *John of Wales: A Study of the Works and Ideas of a Thirteenth-Century Friar* (Studies in Medieval Life and Thought 10). Cambridge: Cambridge University Press.
Tierney, Brian. 2006. "Dominion of Self and Natural Rights Before Locke and After." In *Transformations in Late Medieval and Early-Modern Rights Discourse*, ed. V. Mäkinen and P. Korkman. Dordrecht: Springer, pp. 173–203.
Varkemaa, Jussi. 1999. "*Utrum homo sit dominus personae suae?* The Question of Individual Liberty as An Example of The Confrontation of Canon Law and Moral Theology in Summenhart's *Opus septipartitum*." In *Nordic Perspectives on Medieval Canon Law*, ed. Mia Korpiola. Saarijärvi: Matthias Calonius Society, pp. 51–61.

Part III

Morality, Politics, and Violence

Suicide in Contemporary Societies

Chapter 6

"She Kissed Death with a Smile"

The Politics and Moralities of the Female Suicide Bomber

Susanne Dahlgren

INTRODUCTION

Suicide bombing is a phenomenon that hovers at the margins of suicide studies. More commonly, it is studied within the framework of "terrorism studies," a burgeoning field of political science with its own journals and book series. A "theory of suicide terrorism" has emerged with links to theorization on ethnic conflicts and asymmetric warfare (Bloom 2005a: 76). There is good reason to ask whether the deeds of suicide bombers have anything to do with actual suicides. When the purpose is to kill as many bystanders as possible (and to give one's life in doing so), homicide might sound like a more appropriate framework. In situations of war, *kamikaze* is perhaps the most well known category of these acts. Still, the word "suicide" is an essential part of the English-language[1] terminology for people who, with their own bodies, instigate destruction around themselves. This contrasts with the Arabic term *shahīd* (*shahīda* fem.), meaning "martyr," which contains no hint of suicide.[2] In this chapter, my aim is to examine the phenomenon of suicide bombers to see what types of representations arise and to ask what suicide has to do with it all.

Sacrificing one's own life on a mission is a phenomenon rooted in antiquity. All societies engaged in armed struggle honor those who die as a part of it. Durkheim (1951: 283) discussed the phenomenon as altruistic suicide in the context of sacrifice, which is offered by the suicide as a duty "at the command of his conscience." The current Western media, however, mesmerized in particular by "Islamic suicide terrorists," has largely failed to present the acts in their historical and cultural contexts. This mesmerizing image is depicted so intensively that the false assumption of a link between Islam and suicide terrorism has gained traction side by side with the trumped-up image of only Muslims engaging in such activities, prompting a reminder that the suicide explosive belt—the vest that carries the explosives around the waist—was in fact invented by Tamil Tigers, and that a sizable number of suicide missions in the last decades were carried out as part of the internecine conflict in Sri Lanka.[3]

Between 1985 and 2006, 225 women carried out successful suicide bombings, about half of them for the Tamil Tigers in Sri Lanka. Since the mid 2000s, the number of female suicide bombers has been on the rise as new conflicts emerge and old ones intensify. In December 2010, the first woman suicide bomber in Pakistan detonated her vest. More cases arose in Iraq and Pakistan especially, giving rise to the new term "Burqa Bomber." Alongside these two movements, female suicide bombings have taken place in Palestine in relation to two waves of *intifada*. The prominence of the discourse derives in part from connections to the alleged "clash of civilizations" between "Islam" and "the West." In most media reports, the personality of the suicide bomber remains unrecognized and thus dehumanized, leaving the background of these fatal deeds incomprehensible to a Western audience. The Islamic suicide terrorist emerges as an emblem of evil, or at least a fool recruited to engage in the fatal act with the help of (empty) religious promises.

In this chapter, I will examine Western media[4] to reveal how they represent suicide bombing in Middle Eastern conflicts and female suicide bombers in particular. Even though suicide acts are, to start with, a difficult topic for any media to relate to, the picture is even blurrier when it comes to the woman suicide bomber. Just as female felons raise dubious thoughts, women suicide bombers draw additional speculation about the perpetrators' motivations and morality. My interest in women linked to Middle Eastern conflicts comes from my background as a Middle East anthropologist specializing in law and morality (Dahlgren 2010). As I have not carried out ethnographic fieldwork on terrorism as such, this essay does not provide firsthand material on the cases in question. As an anthropologist, I see suicide bombing as a complex matter calling for not only political but also cultural contextualization. From an anthropological perspective, an act of suicide martyrdom (*istishhād*) in Arab cultures can be seen as part of a complex political web in which such actions take place without seeming irrational or demonic in nature. By this I mean that it is fruitless to dismiss women *kamikaze* by contextualizing their acts simply against the background of an individual woman's life circumstances.

There is something unusual about the way the media, Western and Arab alike, discuss Muslim women as bombers. A particular kind of mysticism attaches to a female body carrying out a deadly mission, rendering women's bodies a degree more problematic than male bodies in the same context. In the West, suicide bombers are often depicted as "crazed cowards bent on senseless destruction who thrive in poverty and ignorance," as Scott Atran describes a large part of Western reporting (Atran 2003: 1534), so any attempt to uncover the political background of the perpetrators tends to be labeled as sympathy for the devil. Understanding that suicide attacks are part of a military tactic used in warfare (McCloud and Simpkins 2008: 1), I will look at some cases of female suicide bombers in the Israeli-Palestinian conflict in an attempt to highlight the differences in the treatment of male and the female bodies in media commentary on suicide terrorism. To analyze these peculiarities, I will also examine what Islam, the religion of Muslims, says about suicides and suicide bombers, and how current Islamic scholars and laypeople in Arab countries have discussed the attacks. Bearing in mind that not all suicide bombers within Middle Eastern conflicts have a religious motivation, I will discuss both religiously motivated cases and those that lack a religious rationalization. With reference to the facts that different Western newspapers and news sites[5] present about these women, I will outline different stereotypes of female suicide bombers and ask how much the image is actually linked to suicide as such, and what other contextualizations emerge. Drawing together these elaborations, finally, I will reflect on what this phenomenon is and how it is best culturally contextualized.

"THE ISLAMIC SUICIDE TERRORIST"

The first stereotype that emerges in media reports is the religiously devoted woman who has been sent on a fatal mission by an Islamist organization. The case of the 22-year-old Reem al-Riyashi from Gaza City is illustrative. In 2004, during the second Intifada, she became the eighth Palestinian female suicide bomber to detonate her body at a border crossing from Israel to Gaza, killing four Israelis as part of the resistance to Israeli occupation of Palestinian territories. She left behind two children and pictures of herself dressed in a combat suit, with an automatic rifle on her lap. She was not the first Palestinian woman to use her body in an explosion, but she was the first woman in Hamas, or the Islamic Resistance Movement, whose leadership had theretofore objected to women engaging in suicide bombings.[6] After her attack, Shaykh Yassin, the late spiritual leader of Hamas, called upon more women to volunteer, saying that Mrs. Riyashi had "opened the door for women to die in the fight against Israel" (McGreal 2004).

Reem a-Riyashi's act caused uproar among Palestinians, even among the supporters of Hamas. Newspapers both in and outside Palestine were full of speculation as to her motives, and the organization that had sent her on her mission faced considerable criticism (McGreal 2004). Hani Almasri, a writer for the Palestinian newspaper *Al-Ayyam*, commented that Hamas's release of pictures of Reem al-Riyashi and her small child, both holding firearms, only damaged the Palestinian cause (McGreal 2004). In Israeli media, as in many European newspapers, Israeli intelligence officials' explanations captured headlines by asserting that Reem al-Riyashi had suffered from depression for years and had earlier tried to commit suicide (McGreal 2004).

Much less attention was devoted to Reem's own words, recorded in a videotape released after her death. There she relates how, since the age of thirteen, she had dreamed of turning her "body into deadly shrapnel against the Zionists." She continues:

> I always wanted to be the first woman to carry out a martyrdom operation, where parts of my body can fly all over . . . God has given me two children. I love them [with] a kind of love that only God knows, but my love to meet God is stronger still. ("Women Demand" 2008)

With these words, Reem expresses something profoundly ritualistic in her act: she imagines her body parts flying through the air in all directions, like a visual carnival or fireworks, while also describing how they will become like shrapnel, killing and wounding the enemy. She is willing, even eager, to make the ultimate sacrifice, which leaves nothing terrestrial behind in the fight against the enemy, because she believes it also allows her to join God. This idealistic vision thus joins two glorifying moments: that of sacrificing oneself in a worthy battle, and that of joining God.

However, in Reem's case, the visual material (photos and videos) grabbed the spotlight and preempted her own message to the world. Consciously presenting herself as a combatant in battle, Reem gives the impression of a woman engaged in something abnormal for a mother. This image is further enhanced by the fact that her two-year-old daughter appears in the photo with her. Not only is the young child depicted together with a heavily armed mother, but the child herself is allowed to hold a weapon. These photos shocked Palestinian audiences and the wider world as well.

"HER FAITH TURNED RADICAL"

The case of 36-year-old Muriel Degauqe, a Belgian woman who converted to Islam and accepted a "martyrdom plan," made headlines in 2005. Stereotypes of a woman lured into a deadly mission and discourses of deep religious commitment permeated media reports on Degauqe, whose background as an ordinary European young woman piqued the European and American media's interest in her life story. One newspaper article explained her background thus: "The first female European Muslim convert to commit a suicide bombing in Iraq was a former bakery worker from a middle-class Belgian family, who joined her husband in an extremist network that sent them to fight and die, authorities said" (Rotella 2005).

The reader gets the image of a working-class woman lured by a Muslim husband to join an extremist network. The title of the article has already made the link to religion: "Before 'Martyrdom' Plan, Belgian Woman's Faith Turned Radical." Further highlighting the image, the report tells how Muriel "had drug problems in her youth, married a Muslim and converted to Islam in her early 20s. . . . She plunged into fundamentalism several years ago with her second husband, a Moroccan-born extremist." To complement the image, the newspaper quotes an "anonymous top Belgian law enforcement official" who reaffirms: "This was not a very young woman, but she was fragile psychologically." The level of Muriel's "extremism" is further attested by her mother, who is reported to have said that "her daughter had been obsessively religious, pressuring relatives to shun television, cigarettes and alcohol . . ." (Rotella 2005).

The way the above article portrays Muriel Degauqe's case brings several speculative motivations to the fore. The report paints a picture of a woman who left her earlier, not-so-decent life behind and, in an act of reprimanding herself, became something irreversibly different. Here the shift from a wild youth into a religiously pious life is used to explain her "psychological fragility." It is as if the people she killed in her mission became victims of her personal problems. The newspaper articles make no note of her political views, and her "extremism" is depicted only in religious terms, according to her mother's understanding of what constitutes extreme Islam. Also absent is any mention of political engagement on the part of her Moroccan husband, who joined her mission to Iraq and was later killed in a firefight. To quote a "specialist," the newspaper interviewed a forensic psychologist and former CIA officer, Marc Sageman, who describes female converts as representing "an explosive convergence of Western and fundamentalist culture." To explain why women have increasingly become involved in suicide operations, Sageman asserts that it is because "militant fundamentalists" have started to provide religious justification for women's combat roles. The reader of the news article is left with the idea that a woman's foolishness and a highly manipulative religiously extremist organization form the background to Muriel Degauqe's suicide mission.

"SHE WANTED TO REPENT PAST SINS"

The discourse of compromised morals that the subject wants to amend is present in reports on several Palestinian female suicide bombers. Hanadi Jaradat, a 29-year-old lawyer from Jenin, West Bank, blew herself up in the crowded Maxim restaurant in the Israeli town of Haifa in 2003. The attack left 20 Israeli civilians dead and 48 wounded. Whereas her story involves traumatic personal experiences at the hands of Israeli security forces who broke into her house and executed her brother and cousin in front of her, there is also speculation about an intimate relationship she allegedly had with her fiancé, a Palestinian Islamic Jihad operative who was killed in a clash with Israeli IDF troops. Intimate relationships prior to marriage are normally condemned in the current Palestinian society framed by religious and customary discourses of "women's modesty," even though in the difficult circumstances of many militants living in hiding from authorities, such illicit affairs might also be condoned. The third reason given for Hanadi's action was her alleged wish to avenge the death of her fiancé. As Bloom reports, similar ideas of "moral corruption" have been suggested in the cases of all Palestinian female bombers (Bloom 2005b).

The claim that these women are, for various morally compromising reasons, outcasts in their own society has been endorsed by author and journalist Barbara Victor.[7] According to this rationalization, the first four female Palestinian suicide bombers found themselves in situations where the act of martyrdom was seen as their final chance to reclaim the "family honor" that had been lost due to their own actions or those of other family members (Victor 2003). Bloom also claims that the first female Hamas suicide bomber, Reem al-Riyashi, was rumored to have been coerced by both her husband and her lover as a way of saving face after an extramarital affair. Official Israeli government reports have suggested a shared characteristic among Palestinian female bombers: that they were all outcasts–young women who found themselves, for various reasons, in "acute emotional distress due to social stigmatization"(Israel Ministry of Foreign Affairs 2002; see also Bloom 2005a: 163).

Most suicide terrorism studies do not base their findings on first-hand material collected among perpetrators, but on materials collected by someone else. Thus interviews and studies carried out directly among failed suicide bombers, or among people who knew those who carried out the acts, have been circulated and recirculated in analytic texts, too. One source of such material is a reporter and host of the *National Geographic Explorer* TV show, Lisa Ling, who has collected interviews with families of female suicide bombers in Palestine, among other places (*National Geographic Explorer*, 13 December 2004). She elaborates:

> What we found in talking to the [bombers'] families and people in the community—and I want to limit this to the women whose stories we looked into—all of them had very traumatic personal stories and issues. Those things, combined with the horrors of living under occupation, could have provoked them to act. (National Geographic Channel, 13 December 2004)

When asked the nature of the personal problems, she answers:

> One [terrorist], for example, was the first female suicide bomber in the Palestinian/Israeli conflict, Wafa Idris. She was married off at a very young age and could not have kids. In that society a woman, a wife, who can't have kids is considered worthless. The husband [divorced Wafa and] married someone else and had kids with her. (National Geographic Channel, 13 December 2004)

About Wafa's emotional state, Ling suggests: "Wafa also worked with a humanitarian organization on the West Bank where she saw a lot of carnage [from the Israeli-Palestinian conflict]. You might say that she was a very depressed person" (National Geographic Channel, 13 December 2004).

In these accounts, speculation about the culprit's emotional and mental state is represented alongside suggestions of feelings of shame. Even though Ling actually spoke with people who knew Wafa Idris, the conclusions she draws about her mental state are only her opinions. The opinions of this TV show host, then, have started to set the tone of suicide terrorism studies. In a society like the Occupied Palestinian Territories, where more or less everybody is emotionally hit by daily violence, emotional reasons are hardly enough to explain martyrdom operations. Thus the need arises to speculate on compromising personal stories that could have motivated the female bombers.

"RECRUITED TO MEND HER HONOR"

An Israeli security report from 2002, quoted on many news sites, characterizes women as liable to "personal, emotional or social vulnerabilities." The report attempts to prove how such "vulnerabilities" make these women easy prey for recruiters:

> Women whose social standing is problematic, including women who have acquired a 'bad name' due to assumed promiscuity or extra-marital relationships, have often been convinced to take part in terrorist operations as a means of rehabilitating their status and character in Palestinian society. Included among these operations are suicide bombings.

The report continues:

> The strength of this type of persuasion can best be understood in the relevant cultural framework—a society where women are often considered to embody the honor of the family. Any hint of impropriety, no matter how minor, can have serious consequences for the woman involved, even prompting male family members to murder her in a so-called 'honor' killing. (Israel Ministry of Foreign Affairs 2002)

Here the report applies the discourse of women as victims of a patriarchal culture who lack wills of their own.[8] The agency of individual women is entirely dismissed, and the image of women passively drifting or forced into deadly operations emerges. The ultimate victims of the "violent culture" are the people who die in suicide attacks.

The idea that women can be lured into becoming suicide bombers if they are morally corrupt has become widespread in world media, so much so that hints of the idea's use as a recruitment method, too, were easy to present in a case linked to the Iraq War. In January 2009, a 50-year-old Iraqi woman called Samira Ahmad Jassim was reported to have acknowledged "she was part of a plot in which young women were raped and then sent to her for 'matronly advice.'" She was said to have told how she tried to persuade these victims to become suicide bombers by emphasizing that it was their only escape from the shame and a chance to reclaim their honor. The woman, nicknamed Umm al-muminīn, Mother of the Believers, reportedly had recruited eighty such women for the militant Islamist organization Ansar al-sunna, which is suspected of having ties with the Iraqi al-Qa'ida and participating in missions against the local Shi'a. In a testimony given to the Associated Press agency after her arrest by Iraqi security forces, the woman claimed that she herself had been a victim pressured by Ansar al-sunna, whose representatives had threatened to bomb her house if she did not cooperate (Abdul-Zahra and Murphy 2009). Verifying the details of the story is difficult, but it certainly fits well with the stereotype of female suicide bombers as morally damaged, passive victims of extremist organizations that has become so widespread in the global media.

"DEDICATING HER BODY TO THE NATION"

For Palestinians and other Arabs, the arrival of women suicide bombers was no easy thing to swallow, at first. But since the confusion and shock in the wake of the first Palestinian female suicide bombers, women martyrs have slowly found acceptance among Arab political and religious leaders. This narrative sees female bombers as having sacrificed their lives in the unbalanced struggle against an enemy equipped with F-16 warplanes. But religious discourse has not been the only framework in Palestinian society where this sacrifice is discussed and given meaning. An equally powerful narrative designates these women's sacrifice as serving another higher cause, that of the nation.[9] In the Arab world at large, the *shahīda* (female martyr) has been interpreted as donating her body to the struggle for an independent Palestinian state (Hasso 2005: 35). As Hasso summarizes, the woman martyr's actions are seen as resistance to settler-colonial domination of Israel and its Zionist policies of downgrading, humiliating, and liquidating the Palestinians (43). Still, she is not treated the same way as the male *fidāʾī*, combatant, the celebrated hero of the resistance. Yet women martyrs want to make a similar contribution, as illustrated in the words of Andalib Takatkeh, a 20-year-old woman from Bethlehem who blew herself up at a bus stop in 2002, killing several bystanders: "I have chosen to say with my body what Arab leaders have failed to say. . . . My body is a barrel of gunpowder that burns the enemy . . ." ("Palestinians Shocked" 2002).

Despite this political message in the video recording that Andalib Takatkeh left behind, news reports mainly depicted her as a "school drop-out" who supported her poor family by working in a textile factory in the nearby town of Beit Jala, often sealed off by Israeli army roadblocks. According to Associated Press, which spoke to her father after her death, "Andaleeb's parents, her sisters, best friend and close relatives painted a picture of a small, soft-spoken woman who had not given any of them the slightest hint of her intentions" ("Palestinians Shocked" 2002).

A similar story is told about Wafa Idris, a 27-year-old paramedic who worked for the Palestinian Red Crescent Society before her suicide mission in 2002. Her work was to go by ambulance to sites where people had been victims of violence, often in the form of Israeli attacks. Wafa was not active in any political organization during her lifetime, though her brothers were members of a secular organization, the PLO-based Fatah. Still, Western rumors have it that she became the first female Palestinian human bomb by accident, when explosives detonated in a bag of explosives she was allegedly carrying to hand off. Despite that narrative, her example encouraged other women to make the deliberate decision to join the deadly missions. Reflecting on her daughter's sacrifice, Wafa's mother Wasfiyeh commented: "Maybe it was because of all the wounded people she saw in the ambulances. She wanted to help her people. She was a daughter of Palestine" ("Female Bomber's Mother" 2002).

In her mother's words, upon her act Wafa became the emblem of the entire nation of Palestine. Other reports, too, linked her act to the nationalist discourse. An editorial in the Egyptian newspaper *al-Sha'ab* entitled "It's a Woman!" proclaimed:

> It is a woman who has shocked the enemy with her thin, meager, and weak body. . . . It is a woman who blew herself up, and with her exploded all the myths about women's weakness, submissiveness, and enslavement. . . . It is a woman who has now proven that the meaning of [women's] liberation is the liberation of the body from the trials and tribulations of this world . . . and the acceptance of death with a powerful, courageous embrace. (*Al-Sha'ab*, 1 February 2002, quoted in Bloom 2005:148)

In the same Egyptian newspaper, the notion of liberation is engraved onto the idea of the hereafter as the liberation of the body from worldly hardships. Thus the exploding body is purified of any profane misdeeds. Wafa's sacrifice is discussed with reference to her body and the gendered qualities of the body being blown up. Ayaat al-Akhras, aged eighteen when she died, remains the youngest Palestinian woman to have carried out a suicide mission. She too was praised on the basis of her feminine qualities and attributes, which then were linked to religious rhetoric. Ghazi al-Gosaibi, Saudi ambassador to the UK, wrote a poem in praise of Ayaat that was published in the London-based Arabic newspaper *al-Hayat* on 13 April 2002:

> Tell Ayaat, O bride of the Heavens!
> All beauty stands ransom for your eyes
> When paragons, the cream of my people, are castrated
> A beautiful [woman] stands up to the criminal
> She kisses death with a smile
> While leaders flee away from death
> (extract from "You Are the Martyrs," al-Gosaibi 2002)

In this poem, eyes and smile denote the feminine qualities of the blown-up body. Her smile overcomes worldly evil and elevates her to an extraterrestrial sphere, making her like an angel. Western media strongly denounced the poem, and accusations of praising suicide terrorism were raised. The publication of the poem cost al-Gosaibi his career as the ambassador in London and he had to resign.

SUICIDE AND RELIGION

As Robert Pape suggests, Islamic religion and even Islamic fundamentalism have little to do with suicide attacks. Reasons lie instead in foreign occupations, particularly, in the case of Afghanistan and Iraq, in U.S. warfare (Pape 2010). Still, Muslims in the Near East are widely engaged in public discussion of whether martyrdom attacks should be accepted in the first place, and if so, should be equated with suicides. In religiously condoning suicide bombing, Hamas spiritual leader Shaykh Ahmad Yassin has been joined by, among others, the Lebanese Hizbollah's spiritual leader Muhammad Husayn Fadlallah, and Egyptian cleric Shaykh Yusif al-Qaradawi, a global media personality who hosts a popular TV show on the currently Qatari al-Jazeera TV channel. In commentary he is reported to have issued at a conference in Stockholm in 2003, Qaradawi provides several reasons why martyrdom operations are allowed in religion. In commenting on classical jurists' opinions[10] concerning the question of breaching an unequivocal prohibition in the Qur'an, he elaborated,

> . . . there are two types of Fatwas [Islamic jurists' religious opinions]: Fatwas concerning a situation of calm and choice, and Fatwas concerning a situation of distress and necessity. It is permissible for a Muslim, when in a situation of extreme necessity, to do what is prohibited to him [in circumstances allowing] choice. . . . Thus, one of the clerics has espoused the rule: "Necessities permit prohibitions." Our brothers in Palestine are, without a doubt, in a situation of extreme necessity to carry out martyrdom operations in order to unsettle their enemies and the plunderers of their land and to sow horror in their hearts so that they will leave, and return to the places from whence they came . . . (MEMRI 2004)[11]

In contrast to the above scholars, the grand shaykh of Al-Azhar University, the leading religious institution of Sunni Islam, and longtime grand mufti of Egypt, Shaykh Muhammad Sayyid Tantawi (1928–2010) condemned suicide missions, characterizing groups that carry out suicide bombings as enemies of Islam. "Extremism is the enemy of Islam," he proclaimed in 2003. About suicide bombings, he said, "If it is against . . . women, children and old men, then it is not resistance but infidelity" (Mostin 2010). Other Muslim leaders have expressed similar opinions. In a later move in London in 2010, Muhammad Tahir-ul-Qadri, a Pakistani cleric and head of the Minhaj ul-Quran religious and educational organization, issued a 600-page fatwa against suicide killings. In his religious opinion, suicide bombers are destined for hell (Tahir-ul-Qadri 2011).

Much has been said and written about Islam and suicide bombings. Both camps – those who provide a religious apology for acts of self-destruction as part of struggle, and those who see Islam as forbidding the taking of one's own life outright—base their arguments on the Qur'an and Prophetic Sunna. The Qur'an does not mention the Arabic word for suicide, *intihār*, at all. Relevant verses include 2:195, "Give generously for the cause of God and do not with your own hands cast yourselves into destruction," and 4:29–30, "Do not destroy yourselves, God is merciful to you, but he that does that through wickedness and injustice shall be burned in fire" (*The Koran* 1993). The exegesis by those who condone suicide missions is constructed by linking human bombs with martyrdom rather than suicide. Suicide operations are construed as a legitimate jihad (i.e., struggle) against a mighty enemy, as the Arab media commonly frame the Palestinian resistance to Israeli occupation (Allen 2002).

Still, in both the Islamic religion and present-day societies where Muslims live, suicide is extremely rare[12] and remains a contested issue. Nadia Taysir Dabbagh, a Palestinian-born ethnographer, has studied suicides that occurred in the Occupied Palestinian Territories from 1997 to 1999. According to her, quite similar attitudes toward suicide prevail between Muslim and Christian Arabs. For Muslims, suicide is haram, that is, forbidden in the strongest sense of any prescribed limits set for mankind. The Eastern Orthodox Church, the biggest Christian congregation in Palestine, echoes Islamic views in condemning suicides. In the West Bank town of Ramallah, Dabbagh encountered the possibility of the community not even saying prayers for a suicide (Dabbagh 2005: 39–40).

In her ethnography, Dabbagh draws a clear line between suicides on the one hand, and suicide bombings as acts of martyrdom, *amaliyyat intihariya*, on the other. Indeed, they are seen as polar opposites (Dabbagh 2012: 292). Suicide is a private, individual act that invites condemnation by society and religion, whereas the very public act of martyrdom (as in suicide bombing) engages a whole group of actors whose role is to be glorified and exalted by society and religion, even outside the immediate community where it is performed (Dabbagh 2005: 52).

THE MENTAL CASE AND THE MONSTER

Feminist studies on women as perpetrators of homicide and murder have found a difference in media reporting based on the sex of the offender (Berrington and Honkatukia 2002; Nikunen 2005; Brennan and Vandenberg 2009). A clear stereotyping emerges in the categorization of female culprits. Women who have committed serious crimes are either described with understanding (e.g., "a depressed mother killing her child") or rendered monstrous. On this basis, Berrington and Honkatukia outline two types of female offenders, the "mad" and the "bad." The latter type comprises female offenders who have committed felonies in ways not typical of their gender. Extreme use of violence, mass killing, and use of firearms or explosives are features framed as typical of male but not female offenders. Thus women's violent behavior is depicted as a threat more horrifying to the public order than is men's. In outlining the concept of public order in these frameworks, these authors highlight patriarchy, particularly the aspect of society's gendered expectations of women (Berrington and Honkatukia 2002: 59).

Following this approach, female suicide bombers could be seen as linked to similar public stereotypes of male and female expectations that hold violence to be typical of men and preservation of life typical of women. The presentation of women suicide bombers in the Western media bears some resemblance to the way Finnish media present men who first kill their family and then themselves. In such "extended suicides," as they are called in Finland, the executors are mainly men (see Nikunen 2011 and chapter 7 below). Even though both acts—first the intentional killing of several other people, and then the perpetrator's killing of him- or herself—contain a dimension of violent crime, media reports tend to present the killer/self-killer in these cases as a victim. This seems to suggest that, unlike a responsible decision that can be morally (and judicially) condemned, the deeds of these people are not fully seen as responsible actions. The perpetrators are instead deprived of their moral and political agency and viewed as subject to external manipulation and necessity. As Minna Nikunen has shown, courts in Finland tend to apply the leniency principle in cases of women who kill their own children (Nikunen 2005: 301).

Still, there is more to the case of the female suicide bomber. Another aspect that induces fear of female suicide bombers is that even as speculation about the perpetrators' weaknesses is common, the media seldom attempt to explain these women's political motivations. The fact that suicide bombing uses the body as a weapon adds a further gendered element to the reporting. Media representations often focus on the female body in the public space—asking whether it is "too" naked or "too" covered, or in the "wrong place" (such as in a rape)—and the feminine/non-feminine qualities it displays.[13] In addition, suicide attackers need media attention to spread their political message, which influences the way their acts are reported in the media. Alongside that, preoccupation with Islam as a "religion of evil" has seized the focus ever since terrorist attacks carried out in the name of Islam became widely known.[14] Rarely is coverage of suicide attacks juxtaposed with reports on the atrocities faced daily by people living under siege in Gaza or war in Iraq. Contextualizations of the violent circumstances that ultimately spur dramatic responses, such as women's attempts to inflict major damage by voluntarily exploding their bodies, are often absent.

"ROOT CAUSES" OF FEMALE HUMAN BOMBS

As is evident in the case studies of female suicide bombers discussed above, these women's morality and personal motivations come into question. This does not happen in the same way it does in cases of, say, female murderers. Since the initial confusion, local discussions have mostly honored female suicide bombers as heroines and paid tribute to them in poetry. In Western media, however, they constitute an enigma. How can a woman set out on a mission that has no escape plan? How can a mother make such a final sacrifice? All Western media reporting on suicide missions is negative, but male culprits escape the moralizing that women are subjected to. The bomber's sex makes the headlines only when she is a woman, thus reinforcing gendered images of violence.

The media stereotype seems to have transferred to some academic studies, too. In an essay on women suicide bombers entitled "Feminism, Rape and War," Mia Bloom claims that "[w]hen men conduct suicide missions, they are motivated by religious or nationalist fanaticism, whereas women appear more often motivated by very personal reasons" (Bloom 2005a: 145). This is certainly true of, for instance, kamikaze pilots (Ohnuki-Tierney 2002), none of whom was ever accused of suicide bombing as Muslim women have been. Frequent classificatory stereotypes pertaining to female suicide bombings are as follows: (1) extremism on the part of the organization that uses suicide missions; (2) religious indoctrination and recruitment that targeted the bomber; (3) a personal vendetta following the arrest or killing of the bomber's family member; (4) depression, personality disorder, or other mental problems; (5) personal misdeeds that the bomber wants to make amends for in her community and to herself; (6) traumatic personal experiences of violence, or those of a family member; (7) shameful personal experiences, such as an illicit relationship or rape, that the candidate wants to compensate for by mending the "family honor"; and (8) the naïveté of a mission candidate tricked into an operation she does not fully comprehend (see, e.g., Alvanou 2007).[15] Whereas the first five or six motivations can appear as reasons for male suicide bombings as well, the last ones represent causes attributed to women only.

SUICIDE BOMBING AS A MORALITY DISCOURSE

In Western media, female suicide bombers are discussed first and foremost as women. Their reasons for participating in suicide missions are sought in their gendered personal history. These accounts discuss the female bomber bodily in terms of both her mental state, as in narratives of despair and suffering or guilt and shame, and her physical attributes, such as smiles, eyes, and exploding body parts. In Arab media, this discourse of (female) weakness, alongside images of motherhood, is rhetorically transformed into strength, thus allowing a sense of altruism.[16] In Western media, in contrast, the feminine quality creates an image of foolishness or evil. In local media the female body tends to be the starting point, but the focus then shifts to larger religious and political concerns, thus sidestepping the perplexing question of the difference between acceptance of the female body and that of the male body in acts of combat and armed resistance.[17]

Organizations that recruit suicide bombers present the body as a gift to the cause, and communities surrounding the bombers honor the body as a sacrifice. In Western media, such sympathizing prompts accusations of support for terrorism. Terrorism is narratively constructed as part of the "War on Terror" and made comprehensible in the narrow context of militant Islamism. This narrative does not regard state terrorism as terrorism when, for example, Israeli forces kill civilians and demolish houses, confiscate land, and carry out targeted killings of Palestinian leaders. U.S. war crimes in Iraq are not discussed as terrorism but as mistakes in legitimate warfare. However, Islamic jihad, Hamas, and al-Aqsa Martyrs Brigade, which use suicide missions, motivate these acts as a reply to F-16s and Apache helicopters that the Palestinian combatants does not possess. In this kind of asymmetric warfare, instead of high-tech weapons, they are left with only a human body loaded with explosives to send in reply, as the narrative has it.

In her book *Dying to Kill*, Mia Bloom observes that female insurgents of the Tamil Tigers are not stigmatized due to their gender the way Palestinian women are (Bloom 2005a: 158). Though she acknowledges the multiple contexts in the overall media coverage of female Palestinian suicide bombers, Bloom nonetheless comes to quite questionable conclusions about the phenomenon. She contends, for example, that Palestinian women differ from Tamil women in that education has given them choice in their lives. Yet, according to her, they still chose to die as martyrs. Palestinian women's participation in suicide missions poses the challenge of understanding why educated women react in this fashion, Bloom concludes.[18] Interestingly, the kamikaze pilots of the Second World War were also highly educated university students or academic scholars (Ohnuki-Tierney 2002).

As Hasso reminds us, Palestinian female suicide bombers themselves want to promote a narrative with their actions by raising the question of Palestinian women's assumption of a role alongside the male *shahīd* (martyr) in deploying human bombs to sow destruction and fear among the enemy. Their actions are also a message to weak Arab leaders, castigating their failure to find a way out of the Palestinians' suffering. Thus these women take up a role alongside their brothers to protect the "honor" of the community—a role conventionally reserved for Arab men (Hasso 2005: 30).

Bloom also analyzes female suicide bombers within the paradigm of gender equality, asking why these women engage in suicide missions if they do not enhance women's equality. She disregards the fact that Palestinian women are surrounded by patriarchal discourses that limit a woman's role in resistance to simply a mother giving birth to as many new (male) fighters as possible (Peteet 2001: 144).[19] As I pointed out above, Palestinian public debates frequently discuss the female body within the morality discourses of religion and nationalism (see also Alvanou 2007). A woman's bodily sacrifice is made comprehensible within those discursive repertoires. Western media, however, render her sacrifice as beyond comprehension by leaving out the social and political context in which these women live and these narratives of sacrifice are produced. Instead the narrative of Palestinian women as victims competes for space in Western coverage, as in the following excerpt from an Israeli study:

> In such cases, Palestinian women, both those who are said to be devoted to Islam and those who conduct more secular or free lifestyles, eventually become willing (or unwilling?) tools (victims), i.e., deadly human bombs exploited for the sake of the ongoing Palestinian-Israeli confrontation. This aspect of the confrontation reflects the still rather inferior status of Palestinian women, especially those pushed to the fringes of Palestinian society, who are forced to perpetrate (or be involved in) such deadly attacks against Israel. This way, however, such women atone for their sins by becoming martyrs, thus also attaining glory and eternal life in paradise. (Intelligence and Terrorism Information Center 2004)

It has been suggested that martyrdom should figure more prominently in suicide discussions (Leenaars 2004: 5). From this perspective, suicide bombings bear some resemblance to Durkheim's description of altruism, where "the ego is not its own property, where it is blended with something not itself, where the goal of conduct is exterior to itself, that is, in one of the groups in which it participates" (Durkheim 1951: 221). In other contexts, such as philosophical discussions of altruistic suicide, it is normally assumed that an altruistic suicide is one in which others are rescued by killing oneself, a supposition that does not seem to hold in the case of suicide bombers, who kill rather than save others. An additional and politically thorny complication in the case of Palestinian suicide bombers is their status as civilians living in an area of (implicit) warfare (Allen 2002). What would be a legitimate way for them to respond to attacks on their fellow civilians?

CONCLUSIONS

Women's participation in combat missions with no escape plan, called suicide bombing or martyrdom, has met with ambiguous reactions, both in their own communities and outside the conflict zones in the Middle East. In the 1960s and 1970s women participated in combat operations alongside men, but in recent decades women have mainly played supporting roles, carrying messages or ammunition to men and participating on the "home front" by bearing children to outnumber the enemy. Thus the agency of a female suicide bomber has called for particular, gendered explanations. Even though dying for others has been regarded as a major sacrifice and greatly respected and admired in the Near Eastern war context (Dabbagh 2005: 44), for women, such a sacrifice has remained controversial and ambiguous.

Several current studies on suicide terrorism in the West have emphasized that suicide bombers cannot be categorized solely as mad or evil. The same holds for the stereotypical media depiction of them as politically abused, emotionally dependent beauties. A perspective on the individual is generally considered insufficient. Blaming extremist religion as a principal cause has been discarded, too. Suicide bombing is merely a coordinated community response suited to contexts of violence, aggression, and retaliation in Middle Eastern conflicts (Asad 2007). Against this background, suicide bombing appears as a genuine hybrid: though it is suicide, it is also a violent act directed at the general other, be it in everyday life in the area of conflict, or in the international media. Recent discussions on suicide bombing highlight social structural problems and violence as both origin and sustenance of the acts (e.g., Rajan 2012; Singh 2010). A comprehensive view on the problem requires ethnographic research to allow the women's own voices to be heard.[20] It is astonishing that this kind of research is still lacking.

NOTES

1. The word "suicide" also appears in other European languages in reference to this phenomenon: terrorista suicida, attentatore suicida, zelfmoordterrorist, självmordsbombare, itsemurhaterroristi, selbsmordattentäter, un terroriste suicide.
2. As is pointed out in chapter 3 above, even discussions of martyrdom normally suppose that only the person who sacrifices him- or herself is killed; thus the notion of martyrdom also applies in a somewhat non-standard way in these cases.
3. The Tamil Tigers or the Liberation Tigers of Tamil Eelam, inspired by leftist political ideologies, aim to establish an independent Tamil state in Sri Lanka. Most Tamils are Hindus by religion. According to Sri Lankan official sources, 274 male and 104 female suicide bombers died in operations carried out by Black Tigers from 1987 to 2008 (Sri Lanka Ministry of Defense 2011).
4. I focus on newspapers and news sites available on the Internet. Often the same story is published in several newspapers and Internet sites.
5. I will also make use of some local media that are available to the English-speaking audience in the West. However, Palestinian newspapers have not been studied here.
6. In an interview in the newspaper *al-Sharq al-Awsat*, the late Hamas spiritual leader Shaykh Ahmad Yassin declared that Hamas objects to the inclusion of women in warfare for reasons of modesty. A woman must be accompanied by a male chaperone if she is to take part in an overnight operation (Bloom 2005a: 150).
7. Victor has written books on famous politicians and media personalities such as Lionel Jospin and Madonna.
8. As Minna Nikunen has suggested, a similar discourse of victimization is present in Finnish public discussions on women who kill their family members. See Nikunen 2005: 301.
9. For a detailed analysis of local reactions to female suicide bombers/martyrs, see Hasso 2005: 23–51.
10. Extreme necessity is also presented as implying exceptions to the prohibition on self-killing at one stage of Socrates' argument in the *Phaedo*, and even Augustine allows self-killing if it is commanded by God (see chapters 3 and 5 above).
11. This is the Middle East Media Research Institute's report on an earlier article in the newspaper *al-Sharq al-Awsat*.
12. Few Muslim-majority countries appear in World Health Organization global suicide statistics (2011). Among Arab countries, Bahrain ranks the highest with

4.0 suicides per 100,000 men and 3.5 per 100,000 women. Egypt and Jordan report only 0.1–0.2 for men and 0.0 for women, indicating that suicides are not actually reported in national health statistics. By comparison, the same rates are 61.3 and 10.4 in Lithuania, and 53.9 and 9.5 in Russia, two of the countries that top the WHO suicide statistics for 2011. Dabbagh asserts that no in-depth study of suicidal behaviour has been carried out in the Arab world (Dabbagh 2005: 3).

13. This is evident in relation to female criminal offenders in general.
14. A special issue on suicide attacks in the *Journal of Islamic Law and Culture* 10 (1) discusses this phenomenon from various perspectives of Islamic law.
15. Some of these categories come up in Bloom (2005a) and Huma Yusuf's article in the *Christian Science Monitor*, 8 July 2008.
16. Israeli researchers have commented on a phenomenon reported in the Israeli newspaper *Haaretz*: "[since the suicide mission of Wafa Idris] scarcely a day goes by without five to 10 articles being published in praise of her act. Arab pundits compare her to Joan of Arc" (Nir 2002). As late as 2009, a library in a Yemeni provincial hospital was named after Wafa Idris (as reported at www.yemenportal.net and restored in MEMRI 2009).
17. For instance, an *al-Sharq al-Awsat* report on the suicide mission of Wafa Idris ("Report" 2002) points out that she was "eloquently dressed" and always "smiled," and then goes on to explain the violence in the everyday practice of Palestinian paramedics like Wafa who were sent to collect body parts of victims of Israeli attacks.
18. A similar concern is raised in the report, "Female Suicide Bombers: Dying for Equality?" (Schweitzer 2006).
19. On giving birth as ideology, see Kanaaneh 2002.
20. Such research can be carried out among women who have survived failed suicide operations; it can also consider materials that women bombers have left behind.

REFERENCES

Abdul-Zahra, Qassim, and Brian Murphy. 2009. "Iraq Arrests Female Suicide Bomber Recruiter." *Huffington Post*, 3 February. http://www.huffingtonpost.com/ 2009/02/03/iraq-arrests-female-suici_n_163505.html.

al-Gosaibi, Ghazi. 2002. "You Are the Martyrs." Translation and reprint available at http://www.islamonline.net/English/Views/2002/04/article17.shtml.

Allen, Lori. 2002. "There Are Many Reasons Why: Suicide Bombers and Martyrs in Palestine." *Middle East Report* 223: 34–37.

Alvanou, Maria. 2007. *Palestinian Women as Suicide Bombers: The Interplaying Effects of Islam, Nationalism and Honor Culture.* Strategic Research and Policy Center, National Defense College, IDF (Working Paper Series 3). Tel Aviv: Hameiri Press.

Asad, Talal. 2007. *On Suicide Bombing*. New York: Columbia University Press.

Atran, Scott. 2003. "Genesis of Suicide Terrorism." *Science* 299 (5612): 1534–1539.

Berrington, Eileen, and Päivi Honkatukia. 2002. "An Evil Monster and a Poor Thing: Female Violence in the Media." *Journal of Scandinavian Studies in Criminology and Crime Prevention* 3 (1): 50–72.

Bloom, Mia. 2005a. *Dying to Kill: The Allure of Suicide Terror*. New York: Columbia University Press.

——. 2005b. "Mother, Daughter. Sister, Bomber." *Bulletin of the Atomic Scientist* 61 (6): 54-62. Also available at http://www.icst.psu.edu/publications/bloom.mother-daughter-sister-bomber.6JUL09.pdf.

Brennan, Pauline K., and Abby L. Vandenberg. 2009. "Depictions of Female Offenders in Front-Page Newspaper Stories: The Importance of Race/Ethnicity." *International Journal of Social Inquiry* 2 (2): 141–175.

Dabbagh, Nadia Taysir. 2005. *Suicide in Palestine: Narratives of Despair*. Northampton, MA: Olive Branch Press.

——. 2012. "Behind the Statistics: The Ethnography of Suicide in Palestine." *Culture, Medicine, and Psychiatry* 36 (2): 286–305.

Dahlgren, Susanne. 2010. *Contesting Realities: The Public Sphere and Morality in Southern Yemen*. Syracuse, NY: Syracuse University Press.

Durkheim, Emile. 1951. *Suicide: A Study in Sociology*. New York: The Free Press.

"Female Bomber's Mother Speaks Out." 2002. *BBC News*, 30 January. http://news.bbc.co.uk/2/hi/1791800.stm

Hasso, Frances S. 2005. "Discursive and Political Deployments by/of the 2002 Palestinian Women Suicide Bombers/Martyrs." *Feminist Review* 81: 23–51.

Intelligence and Terrorism Information Center. 2004. Special Information Bulletin of the Center for Special Studies (March). http://www.terrorism-info.org.il/Data/pdf/PDF1/women_784048710.pdf.

Israel Ministry of Foreign Affairs. 2002. "Blackmailing Young Women into Suicide Terrorism." *Israel Government Portal*, 12 February. http://www.mfa.gov.il/MFA/Government/Communiques/2003/Blackmailing percent20Young percent20Women percent20into percent20Suicide percent20Terrorism percent20-.

Kanaaneh, Rhoda Ann. 2002. *Birthing the Nation: Palestinian Women in Israel*. Berkeley: University of California Press.

The Koran. 1993. Trans. and notes by N. J. Dawood, with parallel Arabic text. London: Penguin Books.

Leenaars, Anton A. 2004. "Altruistic Suicide: A Few Reflections." *Archives of Suicide Research* 8 (1): 1–7.

McCloud, Aminah, and Na'eem Simpkins. 2008. "Editorial." *Journal of Islamic Law and Culture* 10 (1): 1–4.

McGreal, Chris. 2004. "Palestinians Shocked at Use of Suicide Mother." *The Guardian*, 27 January. http://www.guardian.co.uk/world/2004/jan/27/israel.

MEMRI (Middle East Media Research Institute). 2004. "Fatwa of Sheikh Yousef Al-Qaradhawi. Al-Qaradhawi Speaks On The Legitimacy Of Martyrdom Operations," trans. MEMRI. Originally published in *Al-Sharq Al-Awsat*, 24 July 2003.

http://web.archive.org/web/20041009222904/abdulhaqq.jeeran.com/fatwa_sheikh_qaradhawi.html.

——. 2009. "Library Named After Palestinian Suicide Bomber Wafa Idris Inaugurated at a Yemen Children's Hospital." http://www.memri.org/report/en/0/0/0/0/0/0/3296.htm.

Mostin, Trevor. 2010. "Sheikh Mohammed Tantawi Obituary." *The Guardian*, 10 March. http://www.guardian.co.uk/world/2010/mar/10/sheikh-mohammed-tantawi-obituary.

National Geographic Explorer (documentary television series). 2004. Season 19, episode 1: "Female Suicide Bombers: Dying to Kill." 13 December.

National Geographic Channel. 2004. "Female Suicide Bombers: Dying to Kill." Brian Handwerk's interview with Lisa Ling. *National Geographic News*, 13 December. http://news.nationalgeographic.com/news/2004/12/1213_041213_tv_suicide_bombers.html.

Nikunen, Minna. 2005. *Surman jälkeen itsemurha. Kulttuurilliset luokitukset rikosuutisissa.* [Murder-Suicide: Cultural Categorization in Crime News]. *Acta Electronica Universitatis Tamperensis* 422. http://acta.uta.fi/teos.php?id=10735.

——. 2011. "Murder-Suicide in the News: Doing Routine and the Drama." *European Journal of Cultural Studies* 14 (1): 81–101.

Nir, Ori. 2002. "The Palestinians See a 'Joan of Arc'." *Haaretz*, 10 February. http://www.haaretz.com/print-edition/news/the-palestinians-see-a-joan-of-arc-1.53335.

Ohnuki-Tierney, Emiko. 2002. *Kamikaze, Cherry Blossoms, and Nationalisms: The Militarization of Aesthetics in Japanese History.* Chicago: University of Chicago Press.

"Palestinians Shocked by Daughter's Bomb Death." 2002. *Houston Chronicle*, 14 April. http://www.chron.com/CDA/archives/archive.mpl/2002_3536126/palestinians-shocked-by-daughter-s-bomb-death.html.

Pape, Robert A. 2010. "It's the Occupation, Stupid! Extensive Research into the Causes of Suicide Terrorism Proves Islam Isn't to Blame—the Root of the Problem Is Foreign Military Occupations." *Foreign Policy*, 18 October. http://www.foreignpolicy.com/articles/2010/10/18/it_s_the_occupation_stupid?print=yes&hidecomments=yes&page=full.

Peteet, Juliet. 2001. "Women and the Palestinian Movement: No Going Back?" In *Women and Power in the Middle East*, ed. Joseph Suad and Susan Slyomovics. Philadelphia: University of Pennsylvania Press, pp. 135–149.

Rajan, V. G. Julie. 2012. *Women Suicide Bombers: Narratives of Violence.* London: Routledge.

"Report on the Suicide Mission of Wafa Idris." 2002. *Al-Sharq Al-Awsat*, 2 February. http://www.aawsat.com/details.asp?issueno=8435&article=86037.

Rotella, Sebastian. 2005. "Before 'Martyrdom' Plan, Belgian Woman's Faith Turned Radical." *Los Angeles Times*, 2 December. http://articles.latimes.com/2005/dec/02/world/fg-suicide2.

Schweitzer, Yoram, ed. 2006. "Female Suicide Bombers: Dying for Equality?" Memorandum No. 84 (August). Tel Aviv, IL: Jaffee Center for Strategic Studies, Tel Aviv University.

Singh, Rashmi. 2010. *Hamas and Suicide Terrorism: Multi-causal and Multi-level Approaches*. London: Routledge.
Sri Lanka Ministry of Defence. 2011. "Humanitarian Operations: Factual Analysis July 2006–May 2009." http://slembassyusa.org/wp-content/uploads/2011/08/Sri-Lankan-Humanitarian-Operation-Factual-Analysis.pdf
Tahir-ul-Qadri, Muhammed. 2011. *Fatwa on Terrorism & Suicide Bombings*. London: Minhaj-ul-Quran.
Victor, Barbara. 2003. *Army of Roses: Inside the World of Palestinian Suicide Bombers*. New York: Rodale Press.
"Women Demand Equal Opportunities—To Blow Themselves to Smithereens." 2008. *Scotsman*, 1 June. http://news.scotsman.com/latestnews/Women-demand-equal-opportunities-.4140387.jp.
World Health Organization. 2011. "Suicide Rates per 100,000 by Country, Year and Sex, 2011." http://www.who.int/mental_health/prevention/suicide_rates/en/.
Yusuf, Huma. 2008. "Female Suicide Bombings in Iraq: Why the Recent Surge?" *Christian Science Monitor*, 8 July. http://www.csmonitor.com/ 2008/0708/p99s01-duts.html.

Chapter 7

"When We Stop Living, We Also Stop Dying"

Men, Suicide, and Moral Agency

Marja-Liisa Honkasalo

> Dear Anne. Here we are. I didn't want it to be this way but having pondered my problems since February, I couldn't find any other solution. There are several reasons but remember, you are not one of them. This is what I want to repeat. After so many challenges, I feel I don't succeed at anything. I am far from where I would like to be and then this problem with the firm . . . I was so alone with it, there were new guys leaving, again. I am disappointed with myself and my life. I am really a pitiful man. This is one reason why I think it would be better for you to live without me . . . Don't blame others for this, everything that took place is my fault. Pekka[1]
> (A suicide note by a Finnish man)

How is moral agency negotiated and enacted at the social edge of human life? In this chapter, I will portray this question as it appears in death letters written by men who have committed suicide. Pekka, the writer of the above message, is one of almost three hundred Finnish men who wrote a suicide note before committing suicide in 1987. Referring to men's death letters as my research material,[2] I ask how Finnish men write about the limits of livable lives and how they make their evaluations and judgments on death in a country where cultural values such as autonomy, independence, and individualism are deeply rooted in the country's rural past (Abrahams 1991). Hence, considering agency, I will use the voices of the men themselves.

At a general level, moral agency is regarded as the capacity to distinguish between right and wrong and the will to act according to one's own judgment. Charles Taylor (1989) sees human agency as constituted by moral affirmations that arise given in the process of evaluation by others and by oneself. This agency is moral in the sense that it is conceived as what we ought to will, with regard to what a good life amounts to. Moral agency relates to two issues: a person's capacity to make moral judgments and take action in accordance with such judgments, and the concept of the subject as a being in relationships with other subjects.[3] The latter point is crucial to this article. I shall argue that the suicide notes in my research material contain ample evidence that the men who wrote them evaluated their life as a whole and themselves in moral terms.

Anthropological discussions of moral agency emphasize the social and cultural context, taking into account everyday life, social hierarchies, and inequalities, all of which condition moral agency and its relationality (Kleinman 1995: 44–45). Moral agents are embodied and embedded in interaction with one another, both personally and on the macro-scale of social and cultural relationships (Mahmood 2005). The interaction has the power to shape the agency and cultural sedimentation of previous experience that form the content and limits of responsibility.[4] Instead of the concept of an abstract, solely rational agency that is widely employed in the social sciences, I will follow the above views on agency as being embedded. Suicide as a human act opens up a window for analyzing the varieties of agency, its limits, and vulnerability, which are heightened in the context of suffering and death. Contemporary societies respond to such vulnerabilities with an urge to cure them. In contrast, I will study moral agency, which in real-life situations renders people more or less vulnerable and more or less able to live their life.

In the abundant existing research, suicide has been studied from two main perspectives.[5] First, contemporary psychiatric research categorizes suicide as an individual phenomenon and as a more or less causal consequence of mental disturbance, notably depression. This research tradition allows only a small conceptual space to the suicide's agency or the cultural context in which he or she acts. Second, sociological and epidemiological research portrays suicide as a macro-level phenomenon that is largely determined by a variety of demographic facts. In this chapter, by contrast, I focus precisely on the social and cultural actor as he describes himself in the suicide notes. Hence, I will refer to Michel Foucault's (2003: 7) idea of subjugated knowledge, by which he means knowledge "from below" that has been written out of history. Subjugated knowledge includes a whole set of knowledge forms that are either hidden behind more dominant knowledge—in my case, psychiatry or science more generally—or insufficiently elaborated, such as "naïve," commonsense knowledge, which ranks low in the scientific hierarchy. Hence, subjugated knowledge is of crucial importance in critical research on culture.

I will make a twofold argument. First, the actor who commits suicide is a moral person who, despite possible mental suffering or possible psychiatric diagnosis, is able and willing to reflect on and evaluate his life, death, and suicide. Second, this person's judgment is not totally free but constrained by the cultural script of the Finnish cultural ethos of "coping no matter what" or solitary self-control, *pärjääminen*[6] (Kortteinen 1994), which provides rather rude rules for managing his life.

This essay concentrates on men because their ways of committing suicide are distinct from Finnish women's in terms of bodily violence, lethality, and argumentation for ending their lives. A comparison by gender would not have allowed me to portray the abundance of detail in the men's letters or the differences between the men themselves. According to my previous study on suicide (Utriainen and Honkasalo 1996), women's suicide notes differ from men's in the ways they address the other and their use of bodily metaphors.[7] The ratio of completed to attempted suicides differs by gender in most countries (for a comprehensive review, see Wasserman and

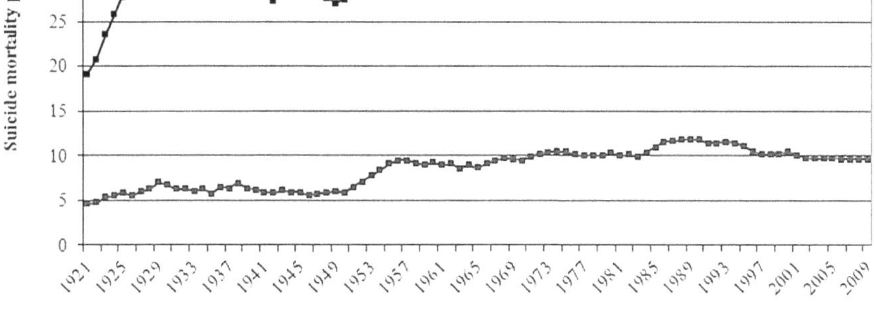

Figure 7.1. Suicide Mortality among Men and Women in Finland, 1921–2009. *Source*: Statistics Finland, various annual volumes of population statistics, Official Statistics of Finland in Mäki 2010

Wasserman 2009). Also, gender difference in the incidence of suicide has always been great; male suicides constitute about 80 percent of suicides in Finland (see figure 7.1). The same gender difference holds for lethal violence more generally (Lehti 2011). What struck me most, in reading more than two hundred suicide notes written by Finnish men, is the multiplicity of moral themes and emotions, notably guilt, but also—and even more frequently—shame. Thus I will focus specifically on these themes and the men who addressed them.

SOCIAL CONTEXT

Finland

Finland is a Nordic country with a population of 5.5 million. The welfare state and the political system are quite similar to those of Sweden and other Scandinavian countries. However, compared to Sweden, Finland's social and structural change from a rural to an industrialized country was both extremely rapid and late, beginning after the Second World War. Finland stands out among the other Nordic welfare states—and always has—as a nation with a relatively high rate of lethal violence, considering both homicide and suicide (Kivivuori 2001). The cross-national literature on violence is dominated by theories that focus on structural and institutional factors as the source of variation in lethal violence. In international comparison, Finland is associated with consistently low rates of poverty, income inequality, and corruption, although its unemployment rate tends to be higher than other Nordic countries' (Kangas 2000; Moreno 2002). As a nation with minimal levels of structural disadvantage together with stable institutions, high levels of social trust, educational achievement (Simola 2005), and generous policies of collective social protection, Finland indeed presents a puzzle to the criminological paradigm (Savolainen et al. 2008).

In this chapter, I ask whether cultural context would contribute meaningfully to attempts to understand the problem of Finnish violence. A culture may be understood in a Bourdieuian[8] way as embodied practices or a co-entanglement of (hi)stories, as Macdonald and Naudin write in this volume. In my analysis, the central concept of a cultural ethos of coping no matter what, or solitary self-control (*pärjääminen*), is close to their way of thinking about culture; however, *pärjääminen* as an ethos is also something that is constructed and practiced. Co-entanglement of histories and shared social practices reconcile the intractable puzzle of individual cases, in their highly idiosyncratic and unique complexity, with the uniform, compact body of cultural values and structural norms. Entanglement of histories, including the sheer multiplicity of narratives, makes a web too intricate to be deciphered from the outside without intimate knowledge of each person's history, connections, and disposition. This is crucial to understanding suicide as a cultural and simultaneously personal phenomenon.

Two Finnish sociologists have used the cultural ethos of coping no matter what, or solitary self-control, as an important explanatory factor. As early as the 1930s, the sociologist Veli Verkko (1951) highlighted the robust (masculine) Finnish drinking habits, that is, the heavy use of alcohol, as a background factor in violence. He understood the heavy use of alcohol and violence as a counterpart or negation of the Finnish *sisu*, endurance or perseverance, or again, solitary self-control. According to Verkko, drunkenness changes "the proportion between irritation and reaction, which are the most prominent characteristics leading to violent crime" (Verkko 1951: 22). Solitary self-control entails autonomy (defined in individualistic terms), independence, and surviving overwhelming odds, which all feature as central themes in cultural narratives within Finnish society. Another sociologist, Kortteinen (1994), posits these themes as constituting the cultural form that provides a frame for shaping and affirming certain central moral values. This cultural form is present in Finnish narratives that cut across generations, among men moving away from rural areas and skilled factory workers moving within major cities. The roots of *pärjääminen* lie deep in history, originating in a variety of ecological, religious, and political contexts (Abrahams 1991). One source is likely to concern the country's distinctive colonial history of agriculture and forestry in remote areas with challenging climatic conditions. The organization of work in rural communities tends to take place around individual households that are geographically dispersed at a considerable distance from one another. Community life is of an extremely private nature, and a persistent conflict between personal autonomy and communal responsibility tends to be writ large in cultural representations of Finnish village life (Roberts 1989). Considering the need for privacy and the strict ideal of autonomy, Finnish village life contrasts with the Vaquieros' way of living, described by María Cátedra in this volume. The cultural factor of Lutheranism is entangled with rural moral discourses and has contributed to a strong work ethic and an emphasis on individual responsibility. This is true, more or less, in the history of all the other Nordic countries as well.

Another important factor is the frequent experience of wars between Russia and Sweden throughout the centuries, with Finland on one side or the other. Since 1917, this experience of conflict has shaped the cultural image of "real Finns" as an independent nation daring to stand up for itself in the face of a great enemy. Hence, with respect to its history of warfare, Finland differs profoundly from the other Nordic countries.[9] "Through a granite stone" is a popular saying that captures some of the cultural ways in which things need to be done in order to take pride in them. It expresses an ethos with a tripartite structure: life is hard, one has to cope with it alone, and if one has survived, one can be proud. If not, then one should bring an end to what is interpreted culturally as a failure. Suicide is seen as one important alternative among the ends.

SUICIDE MORTALITY IN THE CONTEXT OF FINNISH VIOLENCE

Ever since reliable mortality statistics from different countries became accessible, suicide mortality in Finland has been one of the highest in Europe. During the 1970s and 1980s, the rate among men fluctuated around 60 deaths per 100,000 persons in age groups 25–64 and over. Despite their similar social structures, Finland's suicide rate among men tops that of other Nordic countries; indeed, only in the Baltic countries and Hungary is that rate higher (Eurostat 2011). The gender ratio of suicide in Finland hovers around 4:1, but the female suicide rate is not higher than in other Nordic countries (Cantor 2002)—on the contrary, the average female suicide rate in Finland is lower than in Denmark, for example (see figure 7.1.).

In almost all societies, suicide is *gendered* in the sense that men commit more suicides than women. The situation is the reverse in some South Asian countries, for example China, India, Thailand, and Sri Lanka, where women commit suicide more often than men. In Finland, suicide among working-aged men and women was the fourth most common cause of death in 2006, meaning that every eleventh male and every fifteenth female death in persons of working age was a suicide (Official Statistics of Finland 2007; also see figure 7.1). Socioeconomic differences relative to suicide rates are also large. From 1971 to 2000, suicide incidence was highest in the low-income groups among men (Mäki and Martikainen 2007; see also figure 7.2).

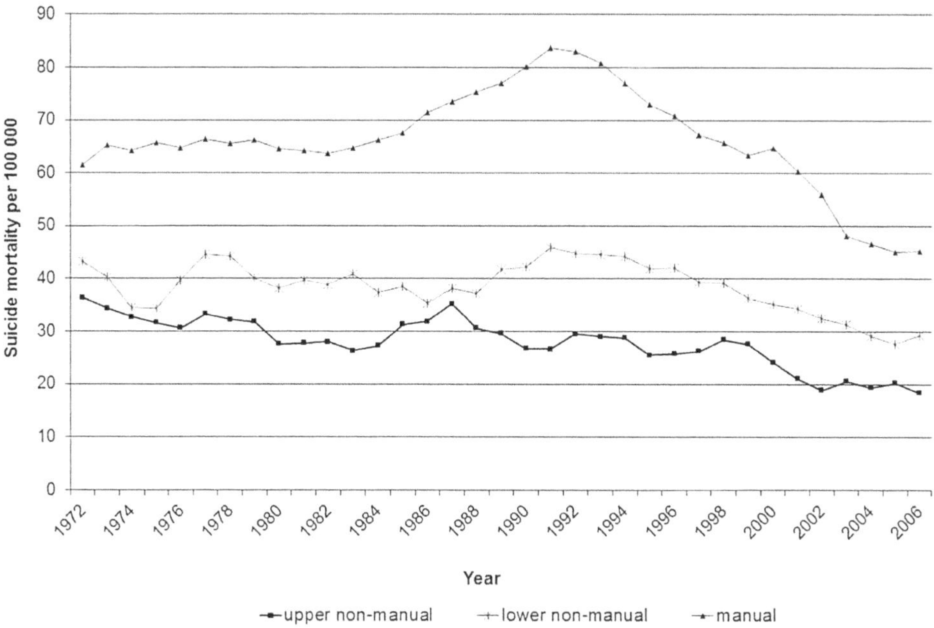

Figure 7.2. Socioeconomic Trends in Suicide Mortality among Men Aged 25–64 and Older in Finland, 1971–2007 (three-year moving averages adjusted for age and marital status). *Source*: Mäki 2010

Homicide

As mentioned, in addition to the high frequency of suicide and the sharp gender difference in the statistics, Finland is a special case also considering *lethal violence* more generally. Compared with other Nordic countries, the (male) homicide rate in Finland is more than twice as high. Finland differs from most other countries, where criminological studies have demonstrated an inverse relationship between suicide mortality and homicides–the more homicide, the less suicide. Counted in numbers of violent acts per 100,000 persons, Finland is the most violent country in Western Europe–and, according to available historical statistics, has "always" been so (Savolainen et al. 2008). This includes both homicide and domestic violence committed by men. The vast majority of the victims are also men (Kivivuori and Lehti 2006 ; see also Granath et al. 2011; Lehti and Kivivuori 2012).

The proportion of women among homicide offenders in Finland stands at 6–7 percent, and women make up between 25 and 30 percent of

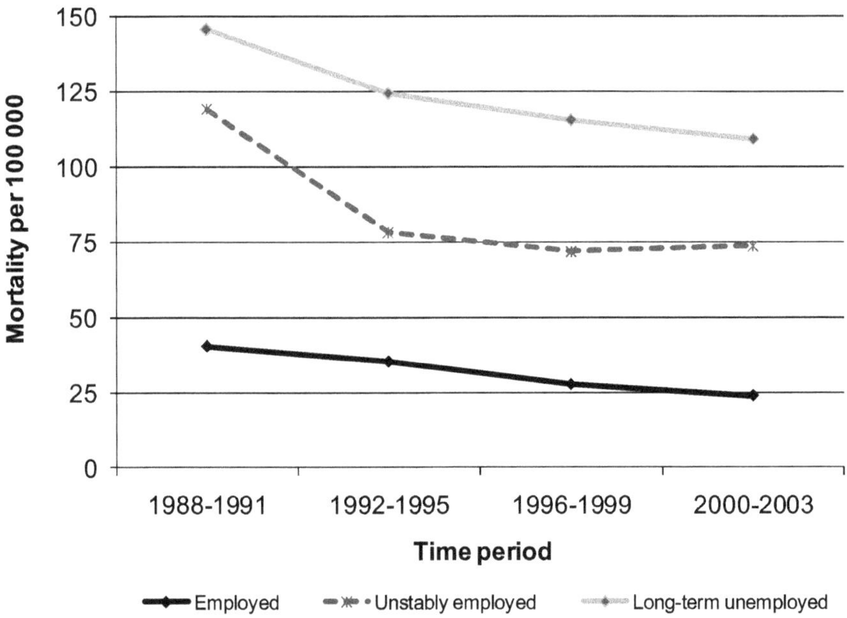

Figure 7.3. Age-Adjusted Suicide Mortality among Men aged 25–64 by Employment Status in Finland, 1988–2003. *Source*: Mäki 2010

all victims. A persistent gender-based trend was observed quite early on in homicide, according to which the higher the homicide rate, the lower the percentage of female victims and offenders (Verkko 1951).

Murder-Suicide

A recently increasing social phenomenon in Finland is "murder-suicide," which the Finnish media frequently refer to as "extended suicide." This refers to a category of acts in which a person first murders his or her family or schoolmates and follows these homicides with suicide. This category comprises school shootings[10] but most frequently the cases are classed as domestic violence. Eight murder-suicides were committed in Finland in the year 2011 alone, and a total of fifteen have been reported since 2008 (Piispa et al. 2012). Men are the perpetrators in more than 90 percent of cases. Most victims of this kind of lethal violence are women (Lehti 2009a, 2009b), a fact that led the Finnish social psychologist Minna Nikunen (2005, 2011) to apply the notion *femicide*. Developed by Radford and Russel (1992), this notion contextualizes violence against women as a gender issue on a vast

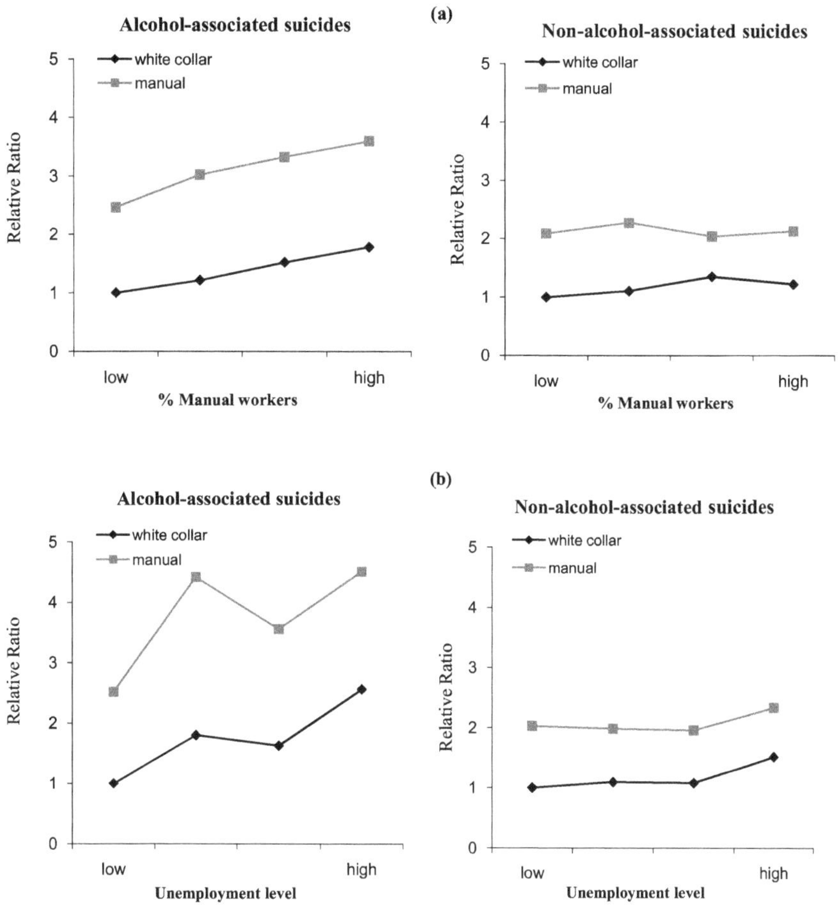

Figure 7.4. Age-Adjusted Relative Ratios of Alcohol- and Non-alcohol-associated Suicide among Finnish Men Aged 15–64 by Individual Socioeconomic Status by Area Proportion (%) of Manual Workers (panel a) and by Unemployment Level (panel b), 1991–2001. *Source*: Mäki 2010

continuum of sexual violence (about the continuum, see Piispa et al. 2006). In Finnish public discourse, lethal violence against women is discussed mostly in gender-neutral terms. However, murder-suicide in intimate relationships is actually, in addition to femicide, also filicide because in most cases the perpetrator first kills the couple's children before killing the partner. From 2005 to 2010, a total of 135 women were killed in intimate relationships and over 50 children died in murder-suicide incidents (Piispa et al., 2012). A Finnish study (Kivivuori and Lehti 2006) found that the most common motive among perpetrators is fear of losing the partner by divorce, a common motive in Finnish suicides too. In a recent study of filicide followed by suicide, Kauppi (2012) followed a sample of seventy-five filicide-suicides in Finland between 1970 and 1995. Mothers were more often perpetrators of neonaticide, the killing of newborn children, whereas the perpetrators in the rest of the cases were predominantly fathers. Murder-homicide has provoked extensive public discussion about causes and consequences–and, notably, possibilities for prevention. Another discussion concerns the content of the category of this hybrid kind of violence. The public discussion tends mostly to use the term "extended suicide," emphasizing a willingness to understand the perpetrator's motives or life situation as a committer of suicide, not a murderer (Nikunen 2011). One important reason for the urge to understand lies certainly in the last decade's vast public discourse about suicide as a psychiatric problem linked to depression. The gendered dimension, whereby the women constitute a majority of the victims, has only rarely been present (Nikunen 2011).

"Finnish Violence": Concluding Remarks

Considering geographical differences, the differences between the numbers for suicide versus other violent acts become even sharper. Areas with declining population, such as the northern and eastern parts of the country, show higher figures for incidence of violence than do the more affluent areas in the south. Several studies have indicated a significant association between socioeconomic status and suicide mortality among men, a relation that applies also to external causes of death, such as accidents, violence, and alcohol intoxication. Altogether, the lowest socioeconomic groups account for more than three times as many violent acts as do groups with higher socioeconomic status, and in 2008, only 17 percent of homicide offenders were employed (Savolainen et al. 2008: 73, see also Mäki 2010: 52).

When all the data are considered together, the sociocultural pattern of "Finnish violence" becomes obvious. Male gender, together with low socioeconomic position and a geographically isolated living area, correlate with increased likelihood of lethally violent acts, including domestic violence, suicide, and homicide, in the last case both as actor and victim. Heavy use of alcohol is associated with these figures (Lehti and Kivivuori 2005). The research of Verkko (1951) emphasized "the Finnish national character" as the main factor behind the high rate of lethal violence. However, careful analysis considering social class and economic status demonstrates that "the nature of the Finnish man" does not seem to explain male violence exhaustively, as socioeconomic differences in violent behavior among men are large. An exhaustive study of Finnish violence thus requires inclusion of cultural and sociological analytical counterparts.

FINNISH WAYS OF MAKING SENSE OF SUICIDE

In this chapter, I am seeking the suicide's own ways of making suicide morally meaningful to himself and his addressees (see also chapter 6, above). For all the research on persons who have attempted suicide, this perspective is generally lacking. Several prevalent garden-variety theories of "Finnish suicide" consider suicide *endemic* (see also Cátedra in this volume). In everyday discussions, Finns often regard suicide as something culturally or even genetically inherited, part of the "folk character" that may also include melancholy and heavy use of alcohol. Suicide has always "been there," that is to say, it goes as far back as the stories in the national epos, the Kalevala, where the protagonist (together with his loved one) commits suicide, as do some other prominent figures. Suicide also occurs frequently in other mythological sources, such as folk poems (e.g., Achté and Pentikäinen 1989).

The other chief way of making suicide meaningful is communicated by the notion of a "culture-bound syndrome." By this term anthropologists generally mean a culturally communicated pattern of behavior whose etiology is widely shared among the population. Culture-bound syndromes are considered channels or common idioms through which people express discomfort and distress (e.g., Nichter 1981; Farmer 1988; cf. Honkasalo 2009). Shared suffering is often expressed through one's body. In fact, culture-bound syndromes include a range of (quite powerful) symbolic meanings with moral and social dimensions. According to these criteria, suicide and the heavy use of alcohol in Finnish contexts would also be included in the category.

Suicide as endemic or inherent and suicide as a culture-bound syndrome—these ideas have some interesting features in common. Both phenomena have implications for recognition, interpretation, and communication of suicide in Finnish social settings. That suicide is endemic means that—somehow, and in idiosyncratic ways—people think it is "natural." In this sense, it is neutral and thus accepted, at least to some extent. The acceptance is ambivalent because suicide is also judged morally as an avoidable act that causes suffering and often brings shame on those who are left behind. However, a look at suicide statistics reveals the notion of "culture-bound syndrome" as something dubious in this case. What culture, or whose culture, is being talked about? First of all, the category does not take into account women's ways of acting and expressing their distress. The incidence of men's suicide, its social determinants, and its methods, as well as the ratio of suicides to attempted suicides, differ from those of women (Mäki 2010, Lönnqvist et al. 1993). Given the backdrop of the general level of violence in the country, one might ask: whose culture is it, anyway? Second, the different rates of suicide and general violence according to socioeconomic position show that suicide and violence are also gendered phenomena bound to social class. Hence, if suicide is a "culture-bound syndrome," it is neither gender- nor social class–neutral. But questions still arise, for instance about a "masculine culture." The statistics delineate a picture of a specific masculinity: quite marginalized, unemployed, low-income men, often with alcohol problems (see figures 7.1–4 above). Thus this picture also challenges the notion that there is but *one* masculinity. If suicide is a masculine issue, then it is about a variety of masculinities.

A third way of making Finnish suicide meaningful originates in the perspectives of public health and psychiatry. Like heart disease, suicide has, since decades, been typically been more common in Finland than in other European countries. The incidence of suicide among middle-aged men rose rapidly from the early 1980s onward in the midst of an economic upswing (Lönnqvist 1988), even as public discussion increasingly depicted suicide as a threat to men in particular, who were seen as comprising a special population group now at risk (Lönnqvist 1988). From that time on, suicide was defined as a "major public health problem" and prevention projects were consequently initiated.[11] One of the most important of these is the National Suicide Prevention Program, led by a group of Finnish psychiatrists (Lönnqvist 1988; Lönnqvist et al. 1993). The project ended up categorizing depressive symptoms and depression as the main "risk factor" of suicide.

Prevention efforts, however, produced conflicting results. There was a slight decrease in suicide mortality in the 1990s, but the lowering liberation of the alcohol tax meanwhile resulted in a large number of deaths due to alcohol intoxication and poisoning (Mäki 2010). The project therefore recommended the use of psychopharmaca, especially antidepressant drugs, as the main preventive approach.[12] Antidepressant, notably serotonin antagonist use increased over the subsequent decade and is currently ten times more frequent than in the early 1990s (Klaukka et al. 2005; Lääkelaitos and KELA 2009). The prevention project has often claimed that the increased use of antidepressive medication has been effective. However, a careful analysis of the statistics points less to across-the-board efficacy than to growth in antidepressant use in the very group in which suicides are rarest: middle-aged women. Such gender-related difference in the use of medication reveal a socioeconomic difference in the use of anti-depressive medication and imply that women, typically in the more affluent classes, constitute the majority of users (Klaukka et al. 2005). A causal association between increased antidepressant use and a downturn in suicide rates has not been established in the Nordic data (Reseland et al. 2006). However, the public discourse of suicide has permanently changed to become psychiatrically influenced and depression-oriented.

ETHNOGRAPHY OF SUICIDE

Statistical materials on Finnish suicide raise questions about socially and culturally patterned (and male) violence. Criminologists have suggested cultural approaches to Finnish violence. I argue that an ethnographic approach can help to solve some of the problems while also contributing by raising new questions that will advance the understanding of suicide and related phenomena (see chapters 1 and 2 above). To understand what is hidden behind or revealed by the statistics, it is necessary to look at macro-social forces and their various impacts in different local settings. Then, however, the question arises as to how one carries out ethnographic study on suicide. Paradoxically, we cannot interview a person who has committed suicide; thus we cannot refer to firsthand narratives of suicide. However, anthropological research can focus instead on the cultural context where the suicide took place and explore the meanings local people assign to suicide or suicidal behavior (Staples and Widger 2012: 199). The anthropological point of view sees the suicidal act within a cultural logic, whereby the act loses its "irrationality" (in the psychiatric sense of an act committed by someone who is mentally ill and thus not a responsible person) and turns into a social phenomenon. Meanwhile, like María Cátedra (1992), I had the opportunity to analyze suicide letters in my own study (see also Shneidman 1979; Black and Lester 2002–3; Leenars 1988), in order to better understand the meaning of the suicidal act. In the following, I turn to suicidal men's own ways of describing the situation of a voluntary death.

Data on Suicide Notes

The men who wrote the notes were mainly middle-aged and mainly in their early forties. The majority were or had been married. Most of them belonged to a group within the lowest socioeconomic status and education level; the majority had a lower secondary-level education. About a fifth of them had experienced unemployment in the previous three months. The overall unemployment rate in Finland in 1987 was only 4 percent, because the late 1980s was economically a period of high conjuncture. Most often, the method of suicide was violent, such as the use of firearms or hanging.

The notes varied in their length and scope. Some of them were as long as letters and written to several audiences: the (present or earlier) wife or girlfriend, the parents, one or more friends. Some men wrote to their employers. The bulk of the addressees were women, most of them wives. Most of the notes were very short and formulaic, consisting of one or two sentences. The majority of the men who wrote a message were skilled or semiskilled manual laborers. In the late 1980s, electronic media were used infrequently or not at all.

I read all the letters, leaving out 39 notes that were incomprehensible, consisting of one or two isolated words that did not permit understanding (e.g., "fence"). Five broad themes emerge from my content analysis. Below I focus on the themes of social failure, evaluation of oneself, autonomy/independence, responsibility, and emotions such as rage, fear, sadness, and notably shame. In this chapter, through these themes my aim is to study how the writers understand and shape moral agency.

WHAT DID THE MEN WRITE?

Social Failure

The recurring theme of a deep sense of social failure features as a major discourse in the letters. The main reasons mentioned are the loss of a job or loved one, divorce, or unemployment. The risk of losing one's pride and honor frequently arises as a major cause for concern that some face with blame and anger directed outwards: "Greetings to the employer. Tell him to organize a bit better working conditions for the guy who follows me in this shit job. I feel I am a victim of extortion, I had to work too much. But go on following how things go on there."

However, another theme is more frequent: "I am disappointed with myself," a young man wrote after occupational misfortune, continuing: "I could not endure your gazes."[13] Voluntary death is considered an act that may relieve a painful situation or even rescue one from it. But several letters assign a high value to relationships and duties toward others, especially family members. Concerning unemployment, several men ponder the moral conclusions of their mistakes: "Everything is my fault, don't blame anybody." "You must pay for your own errors," another man writes. Suicide may be considered adequate payment and thus a proper action to save one's pride and protect oneself, and frequently to uphold family pride and avoid the social shame that lurks behind failure. Some men show decency regarding the addressee's situation: "Only Maija [the wife] knows the financial situation. It's all in order." But touching, everyday words are also used to take care of, and show care toward, those who are being left: "Give the little I have of underwear to Erkki if they fit and if he accepts them." Some writers delineate a testament in their letters: "Grandpa leaves the motorbike to you. Drive carefully. Take the school seriously and be a good man."

A self-reprimanding attitude and feelings of worthlessness against a background of social failure are major elements in the interpretations of loss in the letters. The discourse of the writer's own worthlessness runs through the majority of them. This same interpretation of social failure appears frequently in a recent anthology that depicts the Finnish working-class life. The collection is based on over eight hundred letters containing firsthand accounts of the experience of poverty (Isola et al. 2007). Unemployment, poverty, and divorce are interpreted as lack of personal value and ability among writers who are poor or long unemployed. In some letters, the sense of worthlessness upon social failure can be rather existential, as one man writes:

> But do you believe that there are lives which do not have any meaning? Like mine. This is why I have decided to end it on Christmas Eve. I leave a letter behind where I confirm in full power of my body and soul my last will and that you don't have anything to do with my death. Only my own feelings toward myself are important. I hate myself and that I write like this but someone must come to know what I aim at. I know that this is not fair for you. . . . If only I had trained and remained at home. I should not have started working at Firm X, not have gotten to know Jani and those . . .

"I am a shit," writes another, "it is better to die. Take my things to the dump." And "I am stupid, a real asshole, I am guilty of everything." Or "I am clumsy and an evildoer," as one man writes, going on to quote a popular rock verse from the late 1980s: "A crow flies over a field and does not cry at all."[14] Some notes have nuances of self-pity: "I was born to this life for no reason."

Themes of individuality and autonomy constitute a second discourse. A "good Finnish man" is portrayed as one who masters his life alone, without help from outside. Individuality includes solitary self-control as its necessary domain. Conclusions drawn from social failure can lead to suicide because, as we saw above, the cruel norm among men is the ethos of coping no matter what, or solitary self-control, or surviving, according to which one must be capable of not only mastering one's own life, but also—and crucially—always doing so alone. Meanwhile, the norm-breaker's destiny is to run aground onto society's margins, where men are exposed to experiences that can shape even more marginality. A potentially fatal dead end results. The accompanying emotion of shame is to be avoided at almost any cost. It is unbearably painful to experience one's own shame and even worse to express it to other people. The emotion of shame accompanies loss of dignity, defeat, transgression, or alienation. In the letters, sadness, grief, and the pain of not being accepted are transposed into shame, which somehow seems a cover emotion for everything else. Finnish studies, like that by the historian Juha Siltala (1994; also Lidman 2011) highlight the long duration of the Finnish man's risk of exposure to shame. It has been a core element of the process of education, especially in rural areas and working-class lives. Shame has proved effective in encouraging docility. However, in the long run, inculcation with shame runs the risk of destroying self-esteem and consequently precluding one's human value and right to exist. This process is well known to Finnish men, and it is scary. Some write of their fear: "I am scared of life. I do not know myself." Men who have violated the norm of solitary self-control would rather die than expose their shame. Some letters leave the impression that death by one's own hand is something of a duty, sacrifice, or "a service" to society and to humankind.[15]

The Tension between Autonomy and Dependence

Painful and ambiguous dependence on others constitutes a third discourse in the letters. Apart from the disturbing sense of losing control, over oneself and circumstances in the "game of life," some men write that they tend to regard their dependence on others as the most frightening aspect of the conditions in which they find themselves. Aging, illness, pain—and love—are threatening because they enforce the sense of dependence on others and thus expose the men to what they may regard as a feeling of personal weaknesses. Chronic illness or disability is referred to in this context. Older men who are sick and lonely emphasize their wish not to become a burden on others. Faced with the prospect of ending their life in the care of a hospital, they seem to conclude that they have no dignity left. "I don't want to wait for old age and impairment."

Love is *per definitionem* unpredictable and makes the lover dependent. Insofar as love, in this sense, is experienced as a lack of autonomy, this relationship of dependence is therefore considered the greatest threat to one's autonomy. This is painfully true when the loved one has left, as was the case in more than half of the letters. In the letters, this dependence on another combined with the loss of the loved woman, is met most often with rage. Some notes, however, are openly sorrowful or sad: "Hi Maija. I hoped this would not become a sad letter. I really mean that. But you will soon notice that I can't write in a happy way. People have their own principles, don't they?" The conclusions drawn from the situation are by preference drawn alone, in solitary written expressions, rather than in any open discussion with others.

Several letters describe women as deceivers, anyway. "Had I only been born blind," a man writes to his loved one,

> I would never have been able to see the facts. Had I only been born crippled, I would never have been able to touch you. Had I only been born as Casanova, I would have been able to catch one woman after another, and I could never have been able to love one particular woman. But no. Fortune knows no equality."

Another man writes to his wife in the midst of the process of divorce:

> You certainly had a great holiday. When you read this letter you will notice that someone is missing from the group, and that is me. . . . When you have read this you will certainly recognize where we are. . . . I can't endure pondering on this trying and trying in vain. Try to go on living with your own stakes.

A great many suicide letters are written to women that have left, for one reason or another. The reason for the break-up most frequently arouses self-pity or a desire for bitter revenge, the letter that opens this chapter being one of a few exceptions. One letter points out that its author could have directed his anger toward his loved one: "Should I have beaten you then? Several other men would have done so." However, is there any greater revenge than vengeance wrought from beyond the grave? "I made you a widow, darling," writes one man. Another promises, "I will come from hell to tease you"—yet after some lines also remarks, "and despite it all, I love you." Another man concentrates his last will as follows: "You can be sure I will haunt at your bedside." Or: "Let's haunt, dear. Veikko." Revenge by suicide gives the writers an idea of eternal control of the loved woman and her life.

In all the discourses, the theme of responsibility is present in the sense that the men draw their own conclusions of failure in life. However, love is an exception. When it comes to love, it is the women who are blamed. The painful dependence is attributed to women, as if they were somehow stronger and more capable of living, in addition to being deceivers "by nature": "I have been proud of you. You have everything that I don't. You are mentally strong—so was I at your age. But everything changes," one man writes, and adds: "You can go on living, dear. You just go." Another man writes: "Damn you forever. You stole my family," or even, "she has been whoring for two years now." "Alone I could not face the problems of life. When the difficulties started I was left alone."

Sometimes the men intend their suicide to be even more than a vengeful comment on their loved one's actions. Some men tend—metaphorically or literally—to write themselves into the lives of their women by implying that the suicide will always be present in her life, rendering them "together forever." As one man expressed himself before shooting himself in the bedroom he and his wife shared: "I shall write myself into your tapestry." Most do this less literally, but the tendency is present in several letters. The man means his death to be neither a rupture for others, nor the end of his own existence, but rather an eternal presence (in someone else's life).

Gradual loss of control, threats to one's autonomy, risk of exposure to a painful dependence—are all interpreted solely as a menace to one's honor and pride. Just beyond the pulverizing sense of losing face, the men anticipate shame[16]—a central theme in the letters. Accordingly, voluntary death is regarded as an act of bringing an end to the slow process of life without honor, equated with chaos and death. One man writes that "when we stop living, we also stop dying." Referring to a famous Finnish rock lyric by Juice Leskinen,[17] he uses the word "dying" to describe the feeling that his life is going to bits and pieces while he remains unable to control the process by any means. Here suicide can be considered a good death because it allegedly saves one's moral agency, that is, the value in one's own and others' eyes: at least one's personhood is left of life. But why is a good death defined like this?

The suicide letters open a window onto Finnish culture. Autonomy, independence, and surviving alone against overwhelming odds are at the core of cultural narratives within Finnish society especially among men. These themes embody a cultural form that provides the frame for shaping and affirming moral values over generations. The youngest men were only in their early twenties at the time of their death. Why is it unsatisfactory just to cope and survive? According to Kortteinen (1994: 50; see also Siltala 1994), the issue is much more than merely being content with the hard work one has done. An answer might be that the ethos of solitary self-control or surviving alone against overwhelming odds (*pärjääminen*) contains moral elements that are essential to these men's cultural identity: honor and pride. In life's uncertain situations, honor must be enacted and reenacted, while shame must be avoided at any cost. The never-ending process makes for a vicious circle. The demands of honor and pride are all too hard. If one does not face the challenge, someone more competent is always able to threaten one's sense of personal honor. In many other cultural contexts, just the usual coping for survival's sake would be reasonable and sufficient, but in the Finnish masculine "master discourse," honor is highly valued as a cultural practice and shame is to be avoided. In other words, the issue concerns men's way of maintaining a sense of personal control over their world and affirming their moral agency. The writers seem to see their own value as commensurate with their capacity for self-sufficiency.

Shame

How then, to draw conclusions from having failed? A common emphasis in the suicide notes, regardless of the discourse used, is that each person is alone responsible for his or her own life and misfortune, and misfortune is a sign of a bad or inferior person. It seems that the embodied cultural practices and "co-entanglement of narratives," as MacDonald and Naudin put it chapter 1, have led the men to believe that society demands that they compete, take risks, and take solitary control of all kinds of threats—in short, that they master "the tough guy's life." Men who lack the requisite abilities and qualities are breaking the norms that structure the suicide's ways of experiencing and interpreting society. This is probably one reason why shame is so central in the letters conceding defeat in the "game of life." The emotion of shame is described as perceiving oneself as a failure in the eyes of other men, loved ones, family members, or oneself. It is described convincingly as something powerful, a driving force toward death. It is believed that, having experienced various knocks and blows time after time, one has no right to live anymore: a loser's duty is to die. After describing himself as a loser, "a shit and asshole," a young man writes somewhat ironically that he wishes to have the following sentences on his gravestone: "He was born by accident in 1969, or in vain. Died: by his own hand as a service to Finland's folk and to the whole of humankind."

Suicide research has found shame to be one of the most significant emotions connected with suicide (Lester 1998). In studies carried out among people who have attempted suicide, shame is associated with or caused by the feeling of helplessness and the failure to live up to ideals, or to achieve important goals (e.g., Lansky 1991). Shame is a response to feedback from others suggesting incompetence or doubting competence in the face of expectations that one should be able to meet. As a cultural emotion, shame is enacted in both social interaction[18] and cultural scripts (Tomkins 1963; Sedgwick and Frank 1995). Anthropological research mostly considers shame and guilt to be moral emotions, and thus in the category of social emotions necessary to constrain the self from dangerous and asocial acts of impulse, lust, or violence (Rosaldo 1983). Michelle Rosaldo claims that guilt and shame are almost universally linked to violence and sex, just as they may concern the threat of circumstances or activity that undermines the ideal presentation of the self. All the studies find that shame is an emotion to be avoided, almost at any cost.

Compared with Japan, for example, where upholding honor and avoiding shame—that is, loss of face—are central in suicide, the Finnish situation exhibits both differences and similarities. What Finns and Japanese share in common are the cultural patterns of drawing conclusions of shame, and the possibilities for avoiding it, at any cost. In its traditional ritual form of hara-kiri or seppuku, the Japanese suicide process is collective and is based on the social and cultural judgment of important others (Benedict 1946; Kaneko et al. 2009). Also in Finnish suicide notes, the thought of a death sentence issued by society at large can be read implicitly between the lines. Yet even if this is so, the death itself is a solitary decision undertaken by the suicide himself, alone, according to an implicit, culturally sedimented command, without any concrete audience. The problem of shame in the Finnish context remains a dead end because the emotion is, in a way, locked within the ideal of an autonomous and independent man. This kind of person cannot accept help from others, because doing so challenges his independence and thereby exacerbates the pain of the assumed loss of face.

DISCUSSION

Letters left by several Finnish men describe a tremendous, solitary effort to maintain personal control over their lives. Their suicide notes frequently refer to the process of losing their grip on life, which they subsequently fail to control. Yet the suicide notes also portray another mode of acting, a final one in which the suicide displays his agency by *mastering* the world. Paradoxically, mastery is possible only after death, because this kind of success requires otherworldly power. In this sense too, suicide is considered a good and powerful death (see Kleinman 2007). According to Kleinman, what is moral needs to be understood as what is local. In the writer's life, voluntary death adds something to one's self and makes it more powerful. The threat to what matters most to us, as Kleinman puts it is under control. The possibilities for self-affirmation seem to extend beyond the act of suicide, because the written document survives for those who remain and remember. Suicide, as an act, is considered to redeem one's social and cultural self and to memorialize the rage aroused by shameful experiences.

Furthermore, it constitutes an important source of power (Siltala 1994). The suicide himself sees the act as projecting not the image of a shameful loser but the picture of a victorious man, though not necessarily to his loved ones or family members.

Reading the letters gives the impression of powerless rage and a fight to continue the mastery of the life that is slipping from one's grip and precipitating shame. In this respect, the men's means of fighting against shame is similar to what is described in suicide research more generally (see Lansky 1991). Each letter depicts a lonely man trapped behind a variety of social walls. Powerlessness is an important clue within the larger problematic. How often, indeed, do these writers, most of them unemployed working-class men, live their lives without access to social resources, meanwhile suffering continuous loss of such resources as work, health, and family? The fantastical image they portray of a Big Man accomplishing Big Acts is painfully known from popular cultural representations that are far from the men's reality. However, violence in the Finnish context is considered a vehicle for power.

Taking one's death into one's own hands is a way to possess power. Several men seem to take this *literally*. People who lack social power also more generally see violence as a proper method, a stance that in Finland holds true for all types of lethal violence (Kivivuori and Lehti 2012). A Durkheimian would blame anomie, meaning in this context that the regulation, or shelter, offered by the society is insufficient. This insufficiency allows personal requirements to exceed appropriate social limits and "throws open the door to disillusionment and consequently disappointment" (Durkheim 1952: 285). People in anomic situations feel that the (perhaps merely ordinary) life situation in which they live exceeds their capacity for mastery. Without a social shelter and an available, shared cultural interpretation system, people tend to blame themselves for this failure—or someone else close by, for Durkheim's notion of anomie concerns both suicide and homicide: "in the former case there will be only suicide; in the latter, suicide may be preceded by homicide or some other violent outburst" (285).

In addition to the general category of anomie, the altruistic suicide type is also present in the expressions in the letters. Sacrificing oneself for the honor of loved ones is an important theme. Besides the general typologies, a necessary task of ethnographic research is careful study of what the lack of access to social resources and consequent violence means for men on the social margins, and of how alternative modes of moral agency would be detected. What is needed in future research on suicide are careful ethnographic descriptions of cultural narratives and practices concerning how violence is created and re-created in social and historical processes, and how it is made meaningful in the web of micro-level social interactions and macro-level practices.[19]

However, and despite all the restrictions, the subjugated knowledge provided by these Finnish men demonstrates how moral agency is negotiated and enacted, and how it is not purely rational but embedded in a web of emotions, relationships, and virtues, as well as normative ideals of manhood. Suicide in the local Finnish context is intensively bound to violence and is largely determined by social factors like gender and socioeconomic position as well as age and area of residence. Violence, for its part, is associated with the heavy use of alcohol and hence alcohol-related deaths. Together, these elements form a pattern of marginality and social exclusion, a kind of social ground that nourishes violence. In the suicide letters, shame is present as a central emotion that mediates between social exclusion and violence, be it directed against the other or at oneself. The men's notes portray in a nutshell certain central cultural values and norms—interpreted for current purposes some literally—in terms of their origins in the formerly rural Finnish society. Some emphasize the positive aspects of their autonomy and condemn their dependence on others. Several men consider it their basic right to commit suicide, though the notes also depict suicide as the self-attributed duty of an autonomous man who judges himself a failure. Hence, some regard suicide, as the conclusion of one's life, as something to be admired. Aging, illness, pain, loneliness, and the prospect of dependence on others are all frightening possibilities because they are interpreted as weakness and as a threat to the ideal of autonomy and independence. Often the notes rage against the people (women) the suicides feel have deceived or deserted them, thereby revealing the degree of their sense that a loved one has threatened or destroyed their autonomy.

According to the letters, suicide can constitute an important cultural strategy for avoiding shame—"cultural" because suicide is ambiguously acknowledged as an honorable act in Finnish society and therefore affirms one's moral agency. (See also chapters 3 and 4 above.) Instead of being wholly rational or wholly autonomous, moral agency is embedded in cultural narratives and in nebulous webs of relationships in personal circumstances. Still, the notes convincingly depict the suicide as a morally competent actor, capable of evaluating and judging what a good life is about.

NOTES

I owe my warmest thanks to Ph.D. Netta Mäki for the figures and her kind work for refining the analysis of the time trends concerning suicide mortality.

1. All names have been changed.
2. These data consist of 389 suicide notes left behind by Finnish men and women who committed suicide in 1987, acquired through the National Suicide

Prevention Project's project "Suicide in Finland 1987," which collected data of all suicide cases during that year, including notes that were left behind. In 1987 a total of 1,397 people committed suicide: 1,077 men and 320 women. Of these suicides, 26 percent of the men and 33 percent of the women left a note. Altogether, my final analysis included 250 notes written by men.

3. Arendt (2003) further develops the question of intersubjectivity.
4. Responsibility is a key element in feminist relational ethics (see, e.g., Gilligan 1982; Diprose 1994).
5. For a comprehensive cross-cultural review, see Desjarlais et al. 1995; Wassermann and Wassermann 2009.
6. The Finnish verb *pärjätä* literally means more than to cope or to survive; it also connotes a comparison of oneself with others, being visible in others' eyes.
7. In these suicide letters, women apologized for their deed and expressed their forgiveness in multiple ways. In addition to love, they expressed fear and sadness but not moral emotions so prominent in men's letters. They also expressed their will to convince their audience of their love.
8. Pierre Bourdieu, notably 1990.
9. After centuries as a Swedish colony, Finland became an autonomous part of Russia from the early nineteenth century until it was awarded its independence in 1917. However, a Civil War erupted in 1918 and, additionally, Finland fought two wars against the Soviet Union (1939–40 and 1941–45).
10. School killings are a relatively new phenomenon in Finland, where a total of 18 people have died in three incidents since 2007. By comparison, 135 women were killed in domestic violence between 2005 and 2010 (Salmi et al. 2009).
11. The Suicide Prevention Program was launched alongside the World Health Organization's program "Health for All by 2000." By detecting various risks or exposing factors of suicide, the Finnish project aimed for a 20 percent reduction in the suicide rate by 1995 and thus to prevent "unnecessary deaths and to save 25 000 living years which are lost among the working-age population" (Lönnqvist et al. 1993: 2).
12. The project carried out a psychiatric post-mortem diagnostic categorization, based on a DSM IIIR, that demonstrates:
    93 percent mental health problem
    66 percent depression
    46 percent of women severe depression
    25 percent of men
    Conclusions for the prevention are:
    Depression is the major risk factor for suicide
    An effective care of depression in the Finnish population
    The goal—to decrease the depression rate by 20 percent in the population.
13. See also Oedipus blinding himself in chapter 3 of this volume.
14. This kind of representation of oneself as a loser is prominent in Finnish working-class novels by Kari Hotakainen, notably his *Juoksuhaudantie* (2002). The similarly very popular novels of Arto Salminen, such as *Kalavale* (2005) and *Paskateoria* (2001) concern the same theme.

15. See chapter 4 of this volume. According to Stoic ethics, even in extreme situations one's task as a rational being is still to choose the most virtuous act, even if it is suicide.
16. According to Sartre, shame is a "general feeling of being an object, that is, of *recognizing myself* in this degraded, fixed, and dependent being which I am for the other" (1956: 288, emphasis in the original text). This definition covers something important in the suicide letters.
17. Juice Leskinen, "Syksyn sävel," http://www.youtube.com/watch?v=LpDyN9E5BJk. The popularity of Leskinen, one of the most famous rock artists in Finland, was very much due to his ability to describe the deep feelings of despair, self-pity, and self-reprimand that are especially common among Finnish working-class men.
18. On shame as enacted and performed in social interaction, see notably Sedgwick 2003 and Heller 1985.
19. To understand voluntary death, we need to understand life in the specific cultural context. A detailed and comprehensive ethnography of violence on the social margins still remains to be done. Of course, the suicide notes, seen outside of their embeddedness in social and cultural interactions, portray only a layer of the problem area. As texts they include a special perspective and are written in a special genre, often reminiscent of a testament addressed to loved ones, family members, friends, enemies, and authorities.

REFERENCES

Abrahams, Roy. 1991. *A Place of Their Own: Family Farming in Eastern Finland.* Cambridge: Cambridge University Press

Achté, Kalle, and Juha Pentikäinen. 1989. *Kalevalan itsemurhista.* Helsinki: Yliopistopaino.

Arendt, Hannah. 2003. *Responsibility and Judgment*, ed. Jerome Kohn. New York: Schocken.

Benedict, Ruth. 1946. *Chrysanthemum and Sword.* Cleveland: Meridian Books.

Black, Stephen, and David Lester. 2002–3. "The Content of Suicide Notes: Does It Vary by Method of Suicide, Sex, or Age?" *Omega* 46 (3): 241–249.

Bourdieu, Pierre. 1990. *The Logic of Practice.* Cambridge: Polity Press.

Cantor, Christopher H. 2002. "Suicide in the Western World." In *The International Handbook of Suicide and Attempted Suicide*, eds. K. Hawton and K. van Heering. Chichester: John Wiley & Sons, pp. 9–28.

Cátedra, María. 1992. *This World, Other Worlds: Sickness, Suicide, Death and Afterlife among the Vaqueiros de Alzada of Spain.* Chicago: The University of Chicago Press.

Desjarlais, Robert, Leon Eisenberg, Byron Good, and Arthur Kleinman, eds. 1995. *World Mental Health: Problems and Priorities in Low-Income Countries.* New York and Oxford: Oxford University Press.

Diprose, Rosalyn. 1994. *The Bodies of Women: Ethics, Embodiment and Sexual Difference.* London: Routledge.

Durkheim, Emile. 1952. *Suicide: A Study in Sociology*, trans. John A. Spaulding and George Simpson. London: Routledge and Kegan Paul.

Eurostat. 2011. Death Due to Suicide, by Sex. http://epp.eurostat.ec.europa.eu/portal/page/portal/health/public_health/data_public_health/main_tables.

Farmer, Paul. 1988. "Sending Sickness: Sorcery, Politics, and Changing Concepts of AIDS in Rural Haiti." *Medical Anthropology Quarterly* 4 (1): 6–27.

Foucault, Michel. 2003. *Society Must Be Defended*, trans. David Macey. New York: Picador.

Granath, Sven, Johanna Hagstedt, Janne Kivivuori, Martti Lehti, Soenita Ganpat, Marieke Liem, and Paul Nieuwbeerta. 2011. *Homicide in Finland,the Netherlands and Sweden. A First Study on The European Homicide Monitor Data.* Research Report 2011:5. Stockholm: National Council for Crime Prevention.

Gilligan, Carol. 1982. *In a Different Voice.* Cambridge, MA: Harvard University Press.

Heller, Agnes. 1985. *The Power of Shame.* London: Routledge.

Honkasalo, Marja-Liisa. 2009. "Grips and Ties: Uncertainty, Suffering and Agency in the North Karelian Context." *Medical Anthropology Quarterly* 23 (1): 51–69.

Hotakainen, Kari. 2002. *Juoksuhaudantie.* Helsinki: WSOY.

Isola, Anna-Maria, Meri Larivaara, and Juha Mikkonen, eds. 2007. *Tiede, taide ja köyhä kansa. Arkipäivän kokemuksia köyhyydestä.* Helsinki: Avain.

The Kalevala: Epic Poem of Finland. 1888. Trans. John Martin Crawford, 2 vols. New York: J. B. John Alden.

Kaneko, Yoshihiro, Akiko Yamasaki, and Kiminori Arai. 2009. "The Shinto Rand Suicide in Japan." In *The Oxford Textbook of Suicidology*, ed. Danuta Wasserman and Camilla Wasserman. Oxford: Oxford University Press, pp. 37–47.

Kangas, Olli. 2000. "Distributive Justice and Social Policy: Some Reflections on Rawls and Income Distribution." *Social Policy and Administration* 34 (5): 510–528.

Kauppi, Anne. 2012. *Filicide, Intra-familial Child Homicides in Finland 1970–1994.* Publications of the University of Eastern Finlands. Dissertations in Health Sciences 118. Joensuu: Kopijyvä,

Kivivuori, Janne. 2001. "Patterns of Criminal Homicide in Finland 1960–1997." In *Homicide in Finland: Trends and Patterns in Historical and Comparative Perspective*, ed. Tapio Lappi-Seppälä. Helsinki: National Research Institute of Legal Policy.

Kivivuori, Janne, and Martti Lehti. 2006. "The Social Composition of Homicide in Finland, 1960–2000." *Acta Sociologica* 49 (1): 67–82.

——. 2012. "Social Correlates of Intimate Partner Homicide in Finland: Distinct or Shared With Other Homicide Types?" *Homicide Studies* 16: 60–77.

Klaukka, Timo, Juhana Idänpään-Heikkilä, and Pekka Neuvonen. 2005. "Keskustelu masennuslääkkeiden turvallisuudesta jatkuu." *Suomen Lääkärilehti* 39: 3874–3876.

Kleinman, Arthur. 1995. *Writing at the Margin.* Berkeley: University of California Press.

——. 2007. *What Really Matters: Living a Moral Life in the Midst of Uncertainty and Danger*. New York: Oxford University Press.

Kortteinen, Matti. 1994. *Kunnian kentät*. Helsinki: WSOY.

Lääkelaitos (National Agency for Medicines) and KELA (Social Insurance Institute). 2009. *Suomen Lääketilasto 2008* [Finnish Statistics on Medicines 2008]. http://www.kela.fi/in/internet/liite.nsf/NET/191109094828PN/$File/SLT percent202008.pdf?openElement.

Lansky, Michael. 1991. "Shame and the Problem of Suicide." *British Journal of Psychotherapy* 7 (3): 230–242.

Leenaars, Anton. 1988. *Suicide Notes*. New York: Human Sciences Press.

Lehti, Martti. 2009a. "Henkirikoskatsaus 2009." <http://www.optula.om.fi/Etusivu/Julkaisut/Kriminologisentutkimusyksikonjulkaisut/1284990217191>

——. 2009b. "Naisiin kohdistuva henkirikollisuus 2002–2007. Oikeuspoliittisentutkimuslaitoksen verkkokatsauksia 11/2009." http://www.optula.om.fi/1247667027206

——. 2011. "Henkirikoskatsaus 2010." http://www.optula.om.fi/Etusivu/Julkaisut/1290609746064.

Lehti, Martti, and Janne Kivivuori. 2005. "Alcohol-Related Violence as an Explanation for the Difference between Homicide Rates in Finland and the Other Nordic Countries." *Nordisk Alkohol och Narkotikatidskrift* 22: 7–24.

——. 2012. Homicide in Finland. In Marieke C. A. Liem & William Alex Pridemore (eds). *Handbook of European Homicide Research. Patterns, Explanations, and Country Studies*. Springer, New York, pp. 120–134.

Lester, David. 1998. "The Association of Shame and Guilt with Suicidality." *Journal of Social Psychology* 138 (4): 535–536.

Lidman, Satu. 2011. *Häpeä! Nöyryyttämisen ja häpeämisen jäljillä*. Jyväskylä: Atena kustannus.

Lönnqvist, Jouko. 1988. "National Suicide Prevention Project in Finland." *Psychiatrica Fennica* 19: 125–132.

Lönnqvist, Jouko, Hillevi Aro, and Mauri Marttunen, eds. 1993. *Itsemurhat Suomessa 1987 -projekti. Toteutus, aineisto ja tutkimustuloksia*. National Research and Development Centre for Welfare and Health, Research reports, no. 25.

Mahmood, Saba. 2005. *Politics of Piety: The Islamic Revival and the Feminist Subject*. Princeton, NJ: Princeton University Press.

Mäki, Netta, and Pekka Martikainen. 2007. "Socioeconomic Differences in Suicide Mortality by Sex in Finland in 1971–2000: A Register-Based Study of Trends, Levels, and Life Expectancy Differences." *Scandinavian Journal of Public Health* 35 (4): 387–395.

Mäki, Netta. 2010. *Not in All Walks of Life? Social Differences in Suicide Mortality* (Ph.D. diss., University of Helsinki).

Moreno, A. 2002. "Corruption and Democracy: A Cultural Assessment." *Comparative Sociology* 1: 495–507.

Nichter, Marc. 1981. "Idioms of Distress: Alternatives in the Expression of Psychosocial Distress: A Case Study from South India." *Culture, Medicine, and Psychiatry* 5: 379–408.

Nikunen, Minna. 2005. *Surman jälkeen itsemurha. Kulttuuriset luokituksen rikosuutisissa* [Murder-Suicide: Cultural Categorizations in the Crime News]. Tampere: Tampere University Press.

———. 2011. "Murder-Suicide in the News: Doing Routine and the Drama." *European Journal of Cultural Studies* 14 (1): 81–101.

Official Statistics of Finland. 2007. *Causes of Death 2006*. Helsinki: Statistics Finland. http://www.stat.fi/til/ksyyt/2006/index_en.html.

Piispa, Minna, Markku Heiskanen, Juha Kääriäinen, and Reino Siren. 2006. *Naisiin kohdistunut väkivalta 2005*. Oikeuspoliittisen tutkimuslaitoksen julkaisuja 225. Helsinki: HEUNI, Publication series No. 51.

Piispa, Minna, Jukka Taskinen, and Helena Ewalds. 2012. *Selvitys perhe- ja lapsensurmien taustoista vuosilta 2003–2012*. Helsinki: Terveyden ja hyvinvoinnin laitos, Sisäasianministeriö.

Radford, Jill, and Diana Russel, eds. 1992. *Femicide: The Politics of Woman Killing*. Buckingham: Open University Press.

Reseland, Svein, Isabelle Bray, and David Gunnell. 2006. "Relationship between Antidepressant Sales and Secular Trends in Suicide Rates in the Nordic Countries." *British Journal of Psychiatry* 188: 354–358.

Roberts, Fredric. 1989. "The Finnish Coffee Ceremony and the Notions of Self." *Arctic Anthropology* 26: 20–33.

Rosaldo, Michelle. 1983. "The Shame of the Headhunters and the Autonomy of the Self." *Ethos* 11 (3): 135–151.

Salmi, Venla, Martti Lehti, Reino Sirén, Janne Kivivuori, and Mikko Aaltonen. 2009. *Perheväkivalta Suomessa*. Optula: Verkkojulkaisu.

Salminen, Arto. 2001. *Paskateoria*. Helsinki: WSOY.

———. 2005. *Kalavale*. Helsinki: WSOY.

Sartre, Jean-Paul. 1956. *Being and Nothingness*, trans. Hazel E. Barnes. New York: Philosophical Library.

Savolainen, Jukka, Martti Lehti, and Janne Kivivuori. 2008. "Historical Origins of a Cross-National Puzzle: Homicide in Finland 1750 to 2000." *Homicide Studies* 12: 67–88.

Sedgwick, Eve. 2003. *Touching Feeling: Affect, Pedagogy, Performativity*. Durham, NC, and London: Duke University Press.

Sedgwick, Eve, and Adam Frank, eds. 1995. *Shame and Its Sisters: The Silvan Tomkins Reader*. Durham, NC: Duke University Press.

Shneidman, Edwin. 1979. "A Bibliography of Suicide Notes 1856–1979." *Suicide and Life-Threatening Behavior* 9: 57–59.

Siltala, Juha. 1994. *Miehen kunnia*. Helsinki: WSOY.

Simola, Hannu. 2005. "The Finnish Miracle of PISA: Historical and Sociological Remarks on Teaching and Teacher Education." *Comparative Education* 41 (4): 455–470.

Staples, James, and Tom Widger. 2012. "Situating Suicide as an Anthropological Problem: Ethnographic Approaches to Understanding Self-Harm and Self-Inflicted Death." *Culture, Medicine, and Psychiatry* 36 (2): 183–203.

Taylor, Charles. 1989. *Sources of Self: The Making of Modern Identity*. Cambridge: Harvard University Press.

Tomkins, Silvan. 1963. *Affect Imagery Consciousness*, vol. 2: *The Negative Affects.* New York: Springer.

Utriainen, Terhi, and Marja-Liisa Honkasalo. 1996. "Women Writing Their Death and Dying." *Semiotica* 109: 195–220.

Verkko, Veli. 1951. *Homicides and Sin in Finland and their Dependence on National Character.* Copenhagen: G.E.C. Gad Forlag.

Wasserman, Danuta, and Camilla Wasserman, eds. 2009. *Oxford Textbook of Suicidology*. Oxford: Oxford University Press.

Afterword

Arthur Kleinman

The introduction to this volume emphasizes a point of surpassing importance that the individual chapters further illustrate: namely, that suicide needs to be understood as human experience and practice. To do this we must liberate the subject from the category of pathology imposed on it by medical, psychological, and public health/social welfare institutions. As Georges Canguilhem stated over half a century ago, pathological models are often not a useful way to understand norms and normality (see the English translation from 2012). For psychiatrists, psychologists, and physicians in general, suicide is pathological. And herein, inadvertently, these professional fields serve a Foucauldian purpose of governance by the state via biopower, since most states are concerned with suicide not only to distinguish it from homicide, but also to control it and the populations/individuals that practice it. But de-pathologizing suicide does not mean that anthropologists and other interpretive humanists can study it without responsibility for responding to those in desperation and great need.

When I was trained in psychiatry at Harvard Medical School's Massachusetts General Hospital, I was taught that 90 percent of suicides are due to one or more mental disorders: depression, psychosis, alcohol abuse, and so on. But when I was studying mental health problems in Chinese communities, even when these disorders/risk factors were present, suicide seemed more aptly framed as a human condition, whereby it became a socially and personally available means to cope with a variety of human problems, surely including disease and substance abuse, but also gender, family, financial, and political troubles (see Kleinman 1986 and Desjarlais et al. 1985).

Paul Farmer famously uses the phrase "immodest claims of causality" (Farmer 2005) to critique culturalist and other reductionist accounts of complex, multisided biosocial phenomena, which he also interprets as in need of resocializing approaches. Those approaches locate the roots, processes, and consequential effects of these biosocial phenomena in specific historical and political economic contexts that are requisites for knowledge that can make a human difference in how we remedy, prevent, or otherwise respond to such sources of pain and suffering.

Similarly, our responsibility as researchers and scholars with respect to suicide is to understand it in human contexts that can enable sense to be made, and, when necessary, can also launch interventions that respond to the problems that suicide articulates so fatally and finally, including, as Charles Macdonald and Jean Naudin point out in this book, suicide's "statistical stability and its individual unpredictability." Thus, these authors insist that in addition to the overdetermined cultural, historical, and psychological origins, an inherited predisposition must be examined, and by doing so these authors animate the biosocial paradigm. They do this from the seemingly distant explanatory model of phenomenological psychology/psychiatry via the concept of "melancholy type," *Typus Melancholicus*, created by that model. That is to say, biological inheritance and the inherited contexts of social life co-create a type of self. But wisely, these authors recognize that other suicides in the southern Philippines, where their findings were derived, require different yet equally biosocial explanations that also illustrate "co-entanglements of (hi)stories." These co-entanglements are stories and histories from all sides—genetic, familial, cultural, relational, socioeconomic, political—that may not (will not) offer a single or simple causal connection. Yet they do show the complex interactions that are true to the immense and confused diversity of life that forms the source of suicidal ideas, practices, and consequences.

María Cátedra's meditation on suicide among the Vaquieros of northwestern Spain highlights moral suicides in the family that result from the influence of the inheritance system or the actual inheritance of suicidal actions, again returning to Macdonald and Naudin's co-construction language. Here biology and fate are two linked faces of the same set of constraints.

Miira Tuominen returns us to one of the iconic examples of deaths in European society, Socrates' death in Plato's *Phaedo*, to survey a variety of ancient Greek accounts of suicide, including ones attributed to shame and guilt. Yet Socrates' discussion on suicide in the *Phaedo*, Tuominen argues, also juxtaposes the feeling of living imprisoned to the idea that the gods, who are our caregivers, watch over us, including our decisions to die. Looking at the ancient Greek situation, the reader also feels trapped by the alternatives. Hence the author makes the powerful contention that the problem of whether Socrates' death was a suicide is undecidable because of the layering and stitching together of social, cultural and psychological causes. Hence too, whether a given suicide is caused by one specific thing or many interacting things is often undecidable. This is more than a philosophically interesting point; it calls into question the designation of all self-killings as suicides (see also Goldsmith, Pellmar, Kleinman, and Bunney 2002). Thus, whereas the psychiatric perspective is prone to the hubris of medicalization, which enables claims of definitive knowledge, the philosophical perspective usefully debunks such certainty, implying that, as in other fields, our claims far outstrip the evidence and its interpretive validity. Indeed, most of us in this field find our own work lodged between radical indeterminacy and absolute surety. And that tension is conducive to an oblique vision that brings the most human of insights to bear on what Albert Camus once called the truly foundational philosophical question of lived experience.

This question comes to the fore in the chapter on Epictetus, Seneca, and other Stoics, who viewed death as ethically "indifferent," neither good or bad, but outside of one's control and less significant than striving for one's peace of mind. Philosophy was meant to be therapeutic and lead to happiness, so suicide, if it secured one's life or that of others from tragedy, was not regarded as pathological or even undesirable (though it was usually not recommended). It could be a rational choice in response to suffering, especially if it did not injure others. Reflection on one's situation and that of close others, says the author Malin Grahn, was the way to make this choice. What sounds narrowly Roman is in fact not that far from the popular contemporary view held by rural Chinese, especially young women, that should their situation become unbearable, suicide is an available, if not ideal, coping strategy. The main difference would seem to be the ancient focus on individual choice, versus the contemporary view that what we once considered choices are often better modeled as practices that are part of local moral worlds where there may not be an actual choice, but rather a combination of habit, practices, and actions.

Because Christian doctrine held that suicide was wrong, medieval scholars who took the Bible as the source of their faith argued against suicide on various grounds. Autonomy and freedom created a domain of human experience where national rights held authority, and self-preservation was one of those rights. For Aquinas, suicide was either the unlawful destruction of God's property or failure to observe God's power over mind and body. Humans had freedom to do otherwise, but the divine goodness of self-preservation would lead away from suicide. Casuistry provided subtle arguments against suicide as a desirable or defendable outcome. Here the twenty-first-century reader feels that the legal wrangling and philosophical sleight of hand to keep the faithful from suicide makes the entire cultural historical enterprise seem not so much dated and irrelevant as in need of a somewhat sardonic Foucault-style argument that asks what the state gains from these religious inhibitions and sophistry. Why does the state need the prohibition against suicide to be always morally normative and naturally normal? The political implications of suicide, perhaps, challenge the absolute power of kings and God. Talal Asad's critique (1997) of medieval law and morality would seem to support this conclusion. The larger point is the deep interconnection between body, moral experience, religious practice, and political processes.

The case of the female suicide bomber would appear to bring an entirely different perspective to bear on the politics and morality of suicide. First is the question of whether this is yet another face of suicide, or rather an aspect of warfare and "military" killing. Then there is the particular contested meaning of suicide for questions of terrorism and being a female "martyr" in Islam. And finally, there is the media's presentation of individual stories of female suicide bombers, which tends to depict them as traumatized young women whose different personal backgrounds supposedly made them ripe for terrorist acts that resolved their ambiguous emotional and moral conditions. This author's return to Durkheimian altruistic suicide as a possible explanation is a challenging and fraught way to provoke discussion of this type of murder-suicide. Can murder be altruistic in the way we understand certain suicides to be—say, that of a seriously ill aged parent who seeks to spare the family bankruptcy caused by medical bills? I personally doubt this, even when the suicide bomber explicitly claims altruism on behalf of some political or religious cause. Not just her suicide, but her act of murdering and mutilating others must be seen in light of the victims' claims as well as her own. Hence, from my perspective, female suicide-bombers are not first and foremost suicides. They are by definition killers, whose own death is not the primary motivation or intention but a consequence of killing others. Indeed, certain of these women appear compelled to kill themselves not by a desire to die but in order to do what they most want to do: destroy the lives of people they are against and act for the military purpose of the causes they serve.

Ohnuki-Tierney's study (2006) of the diaries of World War II-era Japanese kamikaze pilots reveals that many did not want to die at all, but acted against feelings of self-preservation to be loyal to their military leaders and co-combatants. In Chinese history, the great heroes in a Han army would stand in front of their fellow soldiers, facing the enemy, and kill themselves as an act of great bravery meant to scare the enemy (see Lee and Kleinman 2003). Again, even from the standpoint of altruism it is hard to consider this kind of self-killing the same as most of the suicides dealt with in this volume. And yet it clearly is suicide. The same can be said of the enduringly famous suicide of Qu Yuan, the Chinese official who, hundreds of years ago, killed himself as a way of politically criticizing and morally rebuking the king he had served. This surely was a suicide, but its commission on behalf of moral and political processes seems out of keeping with the ordinary self-killings of the vast majority of suicides. So it too needs to be seen as a special case. Lumping these kinds of suicides with those in which political issues are absent creates a class of such different kinds that little is gained in understanding suicide per se. It is better, in my view, to examine the great number of ordinary self-killings on their own terms and see these other types as atypical, and requiring a different kind of understanding. But I can understand readers' objecting to this point and making the case for very different kinds of suicide that together represent what suicide is.

Marja-Liisa Honkasalo returns our attention to the much broader class of everyday suicide, so to speak. She asks how moral agency is "enacted at the social edge of human life" and answers this crucial question by examining the death letters of men who have committed suicide. Their context is Finnish society in the late 1980s with its heavy emphasis on male autonomy, independence, and other individualistic values that she regards as inherited from Finland's rural past. Honkasalo takes these suicides to be moral evaluations of their authors' lives in their cultural context. That context, she insists, emphasizes, at least for men who were socialized in earlier decades, "coping no matter what or solitary self-control." Given a reasonably well-off society with relatively little poverty, income inequality, or corruption and a substantial welfare system, along with high levels of trust and stability, the Finnish paradox of high rates of murder and suicide, especially among men, cries out for interpretation and intervention. The usual response has been to blame depression or high rates of alcohol abuse as the source of violence to others and self. The medicalization of suicide as the result of depressive disorder has significantly increased the use of anti-depressant drugs, and the suicide rate has decreased, but there is no evidence that the former caused the latter.

The recurring themes in these suicide notes—social failure, worthlessness, self-blame, painful dependence on others (especially women who have left), revenge, rage, shame—are the gist of this ethnographer's interpretation of Finnish men's suicide. Among the marginal and socially excluded, suicide becomes a moral act of mastering these troubles by affirming the suffering individual's agency through a self-willed death that provides a kind of victory in and over life. This argues for a culturally constituted ultimate coping strategy resembling to some extent what Wu Fei (2010) describes in a vastly different context for young rural Chinese women.

I return to the question of the implications of this knowledge. Is it sufficient to claim a deep understanding of society and subjectivity, or is it ethically required that this knowledge fuel intervention programs that act to prevent suicide? In the current phase of medical anthropology, it seems the answer is the latter. What does anthropological—and historical, literary, philosophical, psychological, and other—knowledge contribute to clinical and public health programs? Quite a lot, when these forms of "evidence" are used to complement biomedical and public health interventions with anthropologically guided intervention programs. What kind of programs would those be for, say, suicide in Finland? The answer is crucial to health but also to anthropology as a field of knowledge generation and transmission.

One could envision programs for reducing suicide among marginal Finnish working-class males that make use of the powerful insights gleaned from such men's suicide notes, but these programs clearly would also need to attend to impulsivity, access to lethal means, alcohol abuse, and untreated psychiatric disorder. To what extent are the anthropologist and the humanist who study suicide—that is, the kinds of scholars who contributed to this insightful volume—responsible for implementing intervention programs? Today, I believe the answer is that they bear some of this responsibility. And yet all too often, the kinds of evidence and wisdom contained in this book are still excluded from medical and public health programs. To the extent that this is so, physicians and public health experts must be faulted. And to my mind, this shared fault is true of psychiatry in particular because this field, which fifty years ago sought to integrate findings from all the relevant fields—biological, psychological, anthropological, historical, ethical—has narrowed precipitously to include only biological factors and biological interventions that have not succeeded in preventing death from suicide. Psychiatry should be indicted for this fundamental failure. But anthropology should not be exonerated from this judgment until it itself clarifies to what extent it has tried to overcome the barriers put up by psychiatry and public health. I believe the upshot of that enquiry would also be damning. Only a biosocial approach that draws on all the relevant disciplines and "evidence" can adequately support intervention programs that are up to the task of reducing suicide deaths and providing persons with appropriate alternatives.[1]

Thus, this volume is an invitation to resocialize suicide research and prevention programs with the kinds of social science and humanitarian knowledge that can foster social and psychological interventions that work together with biological ones. The next question is how to transfer this knowledge to other fields so that it is appropriately used. I believe that the decades to come will see more and more efforts to do just this, and that the moral responsibility for contributing to intervention programs will be more widely acknowledged among social science and humanities scholars. When that happens, contributions such as those in this book will of necessity include a section on the uses and limits of the knowledge developed on subjects such as suicide, which so deeply affect people's lives.

Suicide, like health and social problems more generally, cannot be left to medicine and public health alone but must be examined in the broadest and deepest context of human experience. As I write, the Commonwealth of Massachusetts in the United States is voting on a proposal to give those at the end of life some greater control over how they die by enabling physician-assisted death. Known as assisted suicide or euthanasia or simply death with dignity, it is a policy response to a groundswell of concern among elderly Americans and their families, who want greater control over their final days so that they, not their medical professionals, can make some of the key decisions at end of life. Framed as assisted suicide, this becomes yet another face of the many-sided story of suicide in our times, which is changing so rapidly that it is hard to predict where we will be a decade from now. The issues examined in this book will therefore remain unsettled for a long time yet. They are, after all, central to what it means to be a human being in a particular local moral world with a particular subjectivity and particular ways of thinking about and practicing our shared, yet still culturally particular, humanity.

NOTES

1. For a wider discussion of this issue in the field of global health see Farmer, Kim, Kleinman, and Basilico (in press).

REFERENCES

Asad, Talal. 1997. "On Torture, or Cruel, Inhuman and Degrading Treatment." In *Social Suffering*, ed. Arthur Kleinman, Veena Das, and Margaret Lock. Berkeley: University of California Press, pp. 285–308.

Canguilhem, Georges. 2012. *Writings on Medicine*, trans. Stefanos Geroulanos and Todd Meyers. New York: Fordham University Press.

Desjarlais, Robert et al. 1985. *World Mental Health*. New York: Oxford University Press.

Farmer, Paul. 2005. *Pathologies of Power: Health, Human Rights, and the New War on the Poor.* Berkeley: University of California Press.

Farmer, Paul, Jim Kim, Arthur Kleinman, and Matthew Basilico. *Case Studies in Global Health: A Textbook.* Berkeley and Los Angeles: University of California Press (in press).

Fei, Wu. 2010. *Suicide and Justice: A Chinese Perspective.* London: Routledge.

Goldsmith, S. K., T. C. Pellmar, A. M. Kleinman, and W. E. Bunney, eds. 2002. *Reducing Suicide: A National Imperative.* Washington, DC: The National Academies Press.

Kleinman, Arthur. 1986. *Social Origins of Distress and Disease: Neurasthenia, Depression and Pain in Modern China.* New Haven, CT: Yale University Press.

Lee, Sing, and Arthur Kleinman. 2003. "Suicide as Resistance in Chinese Society." In *Chinese Society: Change, Conflict and Resistance*, ed. E. J. Perry and M. Selden. New York: Routledge (2000), pp. 221–240; revised and updated in 2nd edition (2003), pp. 289–311.

Ohnuki-Tierney, Emiko. 2006. *Kamikaze Diaries: Reflections of Japanese Student Soldiers.* Chicago: The University of Chicago Press.

Contributors

María Cátedra is professor in anthropology at the Universidad Complutense de Madrid. Since defending her Ph.D. thesis, on the cosmology of death of Vaquiero people in Asturias, at the University of Pennsylvania in 1984, she has worked as a visiting professor at the University of Chicago in 1992, among other posts. In addition to her book *This World, Other Worlds: Sickness, Suicide, Death, and the Afterlife among the Vaqueiros de Alzada of Spain* (University of Chicago Press 1992), she has published a vast array of books and articles on death and, recently, on the historical aspects of urban anthropology.

Susanne Dahlgren has been working as an Academy of Finland research fellow at the Helsinki Collegium for Advanced Studies. She studied anthropology at the University of Edinburgh, London School of Economics and Political Science, and University of Helsinki. Her book *Contesting Realities: The Public Sphere and Morality in Southern Yemen* was published in 2010 by Syracuse University Press. She has written numerous articles on notions of Islam, law, morality, sexuality, and urban space. Currently she teaches anthropology at the Department of World Cultures at the University of Helsinki.

Malin Grahn defended her doctoral thesis on Stoic philosophers' views on gender and sexuality in 2013 at the University of Helsinki, and she has also been a member of the Centre of Excellence in Psychology, Morality and Politics in the History of Philosophy (2008–13). She has published articles and book reviews on themes related to gender and sexuality as well as equality, freedom of conscience, and therapeutic philosophy.

Marja-Liisa Honkasalo (MD, Ph.D.) is professor of culture and health at the University of Turku, Finland. She has worked as an Academy of Finland research fellow at the University of Helsinki, at the Helsinki Collegium for

Advanced Study, and as Professor in Medical Anthropology at the University of Linköping, Sweden, and has also been a visiting scholar at Harvard University and at La Sapienza, Rome. She has done fieldwork mainly in Finland and in West Africa. She has published monographs, edited volumes, and numerous articles on illness, death, and more recently on technology of the body in post-welfare context.

Arthur Kleinman is the Esther and Sidney Rabb Professor of medical anthropology and cross-cultural psychiatry at Harvard University. He has been the chair of the Harvard Department of Anthropology and currently serves as the Director of the Harvard University Asia Center. Kleinman's extensive research concerns, for example, Chinese society, depression, somatization, schizophrenia, suicide, and other forms of violence. He has also written on the intersection of public health, anthropology, and international issues as well as social suffering, on cross-cultural psychiatry, and on the experience of pain and disability. Kleinman founded the journal *Culture, Medicine, and Psychiatry*. His most influential work is *Patients and healers in the context of culture* (1980), a groundbreaking work of medical anthropology, followed by *Social origins of distress and disease: depression, neurasthenia, and pain in modern China* (1986) and *The Illness Narratives: suffering, healing, and the human condition* (1988). Currently, he is a consultant to the WHO committee of the Nations for Mental Health Action Program.

Charles J.-H. Macdonald is a senior research fellow emeritus (Directeur de Recherche Emérite) at the French National Center for Scientific Research (CNRS) and is also affiliated to the University of Aix-Marseille II (Université de la Méditerranée). He has a Ph.D. degree and a Doctorat d'Etat from the University of Sorbonne. Most recently, he has worked as a visiting professor at the University of Princeton and as a visiting senior research fellow at the University of Singapore. Macdonald has conducted extensive fieldwork in the Philippines (mostly in Palawan island) and South Central Vietnam among the Raglai. In recent years, he has published several books and numerous articles on suicide, Christianization in Asia, naming practices, and anthropological theory. His previous publications concern, among other topics, Palawan and Raglai ethnography, mythology, social structure, religion and rituals, and kinship.

Virpi Mäkinen is currently an acting professor of systematic theology at the University of Helsinki. She has also acted as a deputy director of the Centre of Excellence in Philosophical Psychology, Morality and Politics. A permanent senior lecturer in theological and social ethics at Helsinki, she has been named both a collegium fellow and Academy Research Fellow at the Helsinki Collegium for Advanced Studies. Among her main publications are *Property Rights in the Late Medieval Discussion on Franciscan Poverty* (Peeters 2001), *Transformations in Late Medieval and Early-Modern Rights Discourse* (co-edited with Petter Korkman, Springer 2005), *Lutheran Reformation and the Law* (ed., Brill 2006), and numerous scholarly articles.

Jean Naudin is professor of psychiatry at Marseilles Medical School, where he started his career in 1984. He has also worked in Nagoya Medical School, Japan (1988–89) and as a private practitioner in Marseilles (1989–2002), among other posts. His most important publications include "The Minimal Self in Psychopathology: Re-examining the Self Disorders in the Schizophrenia Spectrum" (*Consciousness and Cognition* 2007, co-written with M. Cermolacce and J. Parnas), "Schizophrenia: Two-faced Meaning of Vulnerability" (*American Journal of Medical Genetics* 2002, with J. M. Azorin), and "Forging the Links between Phenomenology, Cognitive Neuroscience, and Psychopathology: The Emergence of a New Discipline" (*Current Opinion in Psychiatry* 1998, with A. Mishara and J. Parnas).

Since defending her Ph.D. thesis "Ancient Philosophers on Principles of Knowledge and Argumentation" (University of Helsinki 2001), **Miira Tuominen** has published two monographs–*Apprehension and Argument: Ancient Theories of Starting Points for Knowledge* (Springer 2007) and *Ancient Commentators on Plato and Aristotle* (Acumen and University of California Press 2009)–and numerous articles. She has worked at two centers of excellence in Finland, at the Centre for Advanced Study of the Norwegian Academy of Science and Letters, and at the Helsinki Collegium for Advanced Studies. She is on leave as University Lecturer in Philosophy at the University of Jyväskylä and currently works as an Academy of Finland research fellow.

Index

www.ingramcontent.com/pod-product-compliance
Ingram Content Group UK Ltd.
Pitfield, Milton Keynes, MK11 3LW, UK
UKHW021838100926
8556IPUK00004B/409

9 781782 382348